Reorganising the
National Health Service

ASPECTS OF SOCIAL POLICY

General Editor: J. P. Martin

Professor of Sociology and Social Administration
University of Southampton

Penal Policy in a Modern Welfare State
A. E. BOTTOMS

The Social Context of Health Care
P. BREARLEY, J. GIBBONS, A. MILES, E. TOPLISS, G. WOODS

Social Policy: A Survey of Recent Developments
edited by MICHAEL H. COOPER

The Poverty Business
JOAN M. HIGGINS

Understanding Social Policy
MICHAEL HILL

Capitalism and Social Welfare
ROGER LAWSON

The Child's Generation
JEAN PACKMAN

The Organization of Soviet Medical Care
MICHAEL RYAN

Provision for the Disabled
EDA TOPLISS

Alternative Strategies for Coping with Crime
edited by NORMAN TUTT

Efficiency in the Social Services
ALAN WILLIAMS and ROBERT ANDERSON

R. G. S. BROWN

Reorganising the National Health Service

A Case Study in Administrative Change

BASIL BLACKWELL · Oxford
MARTIN ROBERTSON · Oxford

First published in 1979 by Basil Blackwell & Mott Ltd.,
Oxford and Martin Robertson & Co. Ltd., Oxford

ISBN 0-631-18130-X

Filmset by Vantage Photosetting, Southampton
Printed and bound by Richard Clay Ltd., Bungay, Suffolk

Contents

III — ANALYSIS

Preface

The decade 1965–75 saw several major reviews of British administrative institutions. At the level of central government, the innovations included new forms of government machinery, a new top structure for the civil service, and the decision, fortified by decimal currency, centigrade weather reports and metric bricks, to join the European Economic Community. Various devices for steering the economy were created, dismantled and reestablished by successive governments. The constitutional framework of the United Kingdom, the parliamentary and legal systems and the fabric of industrial relations all came under critical scrutiny, if not actual reform. Further down the line, there was a major overhaul of local government, first in London and then in the rest of the United Kingdom, and new structures were created for the administration of the personal social services and of the national health service. Hardly any established institution escaped without challenge. There is a good general account of the period in the late Frank Stacey's *British Government 1966–1975: Years of Reform* (Oxford University Press, 1975).

Comparing this with earlier periods of administrative upheaval in the years following the first and second world wars, one is struck by the atmosphere of dissatisfaction, sometimes approaching iconoclastic panic. Whereas in the late 1940s, for example, it was necessary to forge new instruments like the national health service in order to meet new social commitments, there often seemed in the 1960s to be an espousal of institutional change for its own sake, inspired by a belief that any alternative to existing arrangements must be for the better. This is not to deny that there were deep underlying problems, notably in the failure of the British economy. In the health service, as we shall see, there were in fact good reasons for doubting the ability of a structure devised in the 1940s to accommodate the technological and environmental pressures of the 1970s. But throughout the later period there was a pronounced tendency to assume that the faults lay in our institutions rather than in ourselves. In *The Treasury Under the Tories 1951–64* (Penguin Books, 1964) Samuel Brittan had already noted that 'Politicians can never free themselves of the hope that better information, or improved administrative machinery, can prevent the policy dilemmas which they so much dislike from emerging'. A year later, in *The Art of Judgement* (Chapman and Hall, London, 1965), Sir Geoffrey Vickers commented on the pressures on government not to let sleeping dogs lie 'in cultures which, like those of Western societies today, find the confession of impotence intolerable'. Both warnings came from writers who were themselves convinced of the need for institutional overhaul, so long as it was properly thought out. Perhaps the true irony is that so many changes had their roots in the 1960s, when it was possible to describe Britain as a stable consensual society whose outstanding problems were technological and administrative. By the time they were implemented, the consensus had been severely strained by political and economic tensions to which administrative solutions could at best be palliative.

It is not surprising that some of the administrative reorganisations that were instigated in this climate failed to yield the advantages claimed for them. The cycle of change often seemed to go through three phases. In the first, discontent with the performance of existing institutions grew to such a pitch that reorganisation became politically inevitable. The second was characterised by a frantic attempt to reconstruct administrative machinery, without any cessation of ongoing services, while fighting off the predatory groups who saw opportunities for themselves in any upheaval. The third phase was one of disillusionment and recrimination when it was discovered that the underlying problems were still there, while the new system appeared to be less effective than the old one, or more expensive, or both. Alternatively, there was relief and self-congratulation that, after all, things were going on much as before.

What tended to be missing was any systematic attempt to evaluate the gains and losses resulting from a reorganisation and to compare the net balance of advantage, if any, with the immediate costs of implementing the change in the short term. It is highly probable that an administrative change of any importance is accompanied by a transitional period of diminished efficiency due to uncertainty, anxiety and the diversion of effort. If the change is well-conceived, and the new system is allowed to run for some time without further disturbance, this should be compensated in the long run by improvements resulting from the reorganisation. Large-scale administrative change is obviously very costly. There are great difficulties in attempting any kind of measurement, not least the difficulty of isolating the direct effects of an administrative reorganisation from contemporaneous changes in personnel, technology and environment. But until something of this sort is attempted, it is impossible to reach sensible decisions about the overall desirability of similar exercises in the future.

The reorganisation of the national health service in April 1974 seemed to offer an excellent opportunity to study the process of administrative change. Its primary object was to create a capacity for more comprehensive planning and rational decision-making about priorities and the use of resources at all levels in the administrative system. The chosen instrument was a new structure which would bring together three previously separate administrative systems, usually serving different geographical areas, under a unified structure which was aligned at key points with the new structure of local authorities providing related services. The implementation of the new structure was associated with a number of other changes, reflecting currently fashionable ideas about management and consumerism and the need to review the role which health professions played in the management of the service. The resultant package entailed four major changes. Existing authorities had to be wound up and new ones established with wider functions and, usually, oversight of a larger geographical area. Officers had to be appointed and trained to fill completely new roles. Professional advisory machinery had to be restructured to fit in with the new authorities and a new management structure. Operational services had to be re-grouped within the new boundaries and, ultimately, in accordance with new concepts of functional interdependence. All this had to be done without disturbing the day-to-day operations of a vital twenty-four-hours-a-day service which was already operating under considerable pressure, and without incurring significant additional costs: the explanatory memorandum to the National Health Service Reorganisation Bill allowed £17 million (less than three-quarters of one per cent of the total annual budget) over three years for the transitional costs of the change and contained a clear indication that new developments resulting from the reorganisation in the longer term should represent alternative uses of resources rather than additions to total expenditure.

A study of the transition from the old to the new structure in a particular part of the country seemed likely to throw light on the amount and kinds of work involved in the reorganisation and to suggest some general lessons. In addition, those who were present at the operating table might be expected to have a unique opportunity to study the anatomy and physiology of the national health care system. The dynamics of a politico-administrative system are more exposed at a time of change than during periods of normal working. The health service is complicated by the interplay of many different forces, professional, managerial and political. Any insight that could be obtained from studying these forces at work during a relatively fluid period, when old patterns were being broken up and new ones established, seemed likely to be fruitful. On this basis the Nuffield Provincial Hospitals Trust, always interested in research which might contribute to the understanding and improvement of the administration of health care, was invited to support a study of health service reorganisation in the new county of Humberside. The grant enabled a team to be appointed for three years, covering eighteen months before and eighteen months after the formal implementation of the new structure. The study was later extended to September 1975, and subsequent developments were followed up to the end of 1977.

The core of this book is a descriptive case-study of the establishment and early work of the Humberside Area Health Authority. Running commentaries on events up to mid-1975 were produced at the time: R. G. S. Brown, S. C. Haywood and S. Griffin, *Preparation for Change: Waiting for Guidance; The Shadow and the Substance; New Bottles: Old Wine?* (Institute for Health Studies, University of Hull, 1973–5). What is reproduced here is greatly condensed from the original and modified in the light of comments and subsequent developments.

The case-study is preceded by introductory chapters describing the nature and objectives of the reorganisation. The last three chapters in the book attempt to draw general lessons, both about administrative change and about the national health service.

Acknowledgements

The case-material in chapters 5 to 8 is based on research carried out by Stuart Haywood and Stephen Griffin between 1972 and 1975. The present book appears under one name only, since the author has been responsible for selecting, editing and interpreting the material collected under his general direction. He wishes, however, warmly to acknowledge the contribution of his former colleagues in preparing interim reports, which were published in joint names, during the main reorganisation period.

The research involved several hundred people in Humberside, including officers and members of the Area Health Authority, Family Practitioner Committee, Community Health Councils and professional advisory committees. They tolerated our inquiries and presence with courtesy, good humour and patience. The occasional protest only underlined the readiness with which large numbers of members and officers completed questionnaires and submitted to interview. To all of them the research team is most grateful.

We are also grateful to the many people who took the trouble to comment on the interim reports or provided opportunities to discuss them at seminars, conferences and training courses. Two of these occasions were provided by the Nuffield Provincial Hospitals Trust, whose generous financial support made the fieldwork possible. After 1975, further monitoring and analysis was facilitated by a grant from the Social Science Research Council.

Mrs Georgie Conboy coped with the typescript with her usual skill and good humour.

*In memory of Frank Stacey and his
contribution to the study and practice
of health service administration.*

Ronald Gordon Sclater Brown

Ron Brown died on 28th June 1978 at the early age of 49. He left a legacy of published material which will be a constant reminder of his valuable contribution to public administration. In two spells of academic life he produced as much in seventeen years as most aim to produce in a full lifetime. His energy was prodigious. In his twelve years at Hull University he undertook major research into the recruitment of male nurses, the distribution of general practitioners, the reorganisation of the NHS, the information needs of managers in the reorganised service and the operation of its decentralised administration, and helped to get off the ground enquiries into the recruitment of para-medical personnel and the impact of Members of Parliament on the NHS. He also pioneered and ran the Institute for Health Studies, wrote 5 books, countless articles and many reports and took more than his fair share of responsibilities on national committees. The record speaks for itself, and it is one of which his family can be proud.

His last major work, *Reorganising the National Health Service,* was produced for the practitioner and the academic. While he wrote to influence policy makers, he demonstrated in all his publications a capacity to bridge the gap between the interests of the doer and the thinker, with forceful analyses of central issues in public administration. He was also able to spare the general reader much of the jargon of the social scientist without any loss of academic rigour or clarity of argument. The combination of a lucid style, strong opinions, relevance and intelligent analysis remains a rare mixture and Ron Brown's premature death has made it rarer.

Stuart Haywood
September, 1978

I
THE 1974
REORGANISATION

CHAPTER 1

The NHS before 1974

This chapter and the two following provide the background for the case-study in Part II. The present chapter describes how the national health service was structured between its creation in 1948 and its reorganisation in 1974. It also touches on some of the attempts made to modify weaknesses that appeared in that period. The next chapter will describe the objectives of the 1974 reorganisation and relate them to the main provisions of the NHS Reorganisation Act, 1973. Chapter 3 outlines the machinery through which the transition was effected from the old structure to the new. While the facilities provided by the national health service are available throughout the United Kingdom, there is separate legislation for Scotland and Northern Ireland, and there are significant differences in the administrative structures in these countries. For simplicity, therefore, the descriptions apply only to England and Wales and, in the latter part of the period, to England alone. (The Welsh health service has been separately administered since 1969.)

Since 1948, the objective of the NHS has been to make services available to meet all the individual health needs of the population, whether in hospital, a doctor's surgery or their own homes, mainly at no cost to themselves. Those who do not wish to use the NHS can turn to the private sector. There is a flourishing private market in dentistry, spectacle frames, and pharmaceuticals over the chemist's counter. But, partly because of its cost, the private hospital sector is not large and the demand for general practitioner services outside the NHS is virtually non-existent.

Within the state sector, the NHS does not include environmental health, which is concerned with sanitation and hygiene—notably the purity of food, air and water—although it does cover health education and the prevention of ill-health. Nor is the NHS responsible for occupational health services at and in connection with an individual's place of work. Until 1974,

3

when it was merged with the main service, there was a separate health service for schoolchildren, based on regular medical and dental examinations and their follow-up. But the great bulk of health care has been provided by the NHS, which employs most of the doctors, nurses, and members of other health professions in Britain.

The NHS employs about a million people, whole-time or part-time (about four per cent of the working population). Its cost has grown to absorb nearly seven per cent of the gross domestic product and over one-tenth of government expenditure. Central government responsibility for the service rests in England with the Secretary of State for Social Services and, under him, the Department of Health and Social Security (DHSS)—until 1968, the Minister of Health and Ministry of Health respectively, with responsibilities extending to Wales as well as England. From 1948 to 1974, local administration was entrusted to three different types of machinery.[1]

HOSPITAL AUTHORITIES

Prior to 1948, hospitals had been controlled either by voluntary boards of governors or by local government authorities. Under the National Health Service Act, 1946, most of the former and all of the latter were nationalised and taken over by the Minister of Health. The objective was to improve the distribution of hospital and specialist facilities and to provide a secure basis of finance from the national exchequer. Assurances were given that the Minister did not intend to interfere in day-to-day administration. Three kinds of agent authorities were set up to run the hospital service on the Minister's behalf.

(a) *Regional Hospital Boards.* England was divided into thirteen (later fourteen) hospital regions. Wales at that time was treated as an additional region. Each provincial region was based on a medical school, as a centre of medical excellence and innovation. The London medical schools were divided among four 'Metropolitan' regions. Although the regions were defined geographically, they bore little relationship to other regional structures of government and often cut across local government boundaries. For each region, the Minister appointed a regional hospital board (RHB) which consisted largely of people nominated by local authorities, medical associations, medical schools and other bodies with an interest in hospital matters including, initially, members of the former hospital boards and committees. Members were part-time and unpaid. Initially, about a quarter were doctors; but this was later reduced to about a fifth.

The main functions of the RHBs were to satisfy themselves about the arrangements for local hospital management and to provide services which offered significant economies of scale. Among these were blood-collecting, mass-radiography screening for tuberculosis, architectural services for major new developments, in-service training and the appointment of specialist medical staff. Latterly, they became more involved in the detailed supervision of local hospital management. To carry out these functions, the RHBs appointed their own staff who were headed (often in an uneasy partnership) by a secretary and a senior administrative medical officer.

(b) *Hospital Management Committees.* The great majority of hospitals were grouped under some 400 local hospital management committees (HMCs). The groups were based on buildings rather than on populations served. Some 'groups' consisted of a single mental hospital serving a city many miles away. Others covered all general hospitals in a medium-sized town and some of these also included small mental hospitals. In the conurbations, however, some groups consisted only of specialised hospitals. The result was a tangled web of responsibilities and catchment areas. By 1974, many of the original groups had been amalgamated into larger units with wider responsibilities.

The members of hospital management committees were appointed by RHBs and their composition was very similar, although more locally-based. Like the RHBs, HMCs appointed their own staff, apart from senior medical and dental staff, who were appointed by RHBs and might work in more than one hospital group. Their principal officer was a group secretary. There were also secretaries and matrons at individual hospitals.

(c) *Boards of Governors.* Although the regions were based on medical schools, the teaching hospitals themselves were kept outside the RHB/HMC structure. This was part of the bargain which Aneurin Bevan, Minister of Health at the time, struck with the powerful medical Royal Colleges as part of his efforts to persuade the profession as a whole to come into the proposed new health service. The teaching hospitals in the provincial centres, as well as some of the smaller London teaching hospitals, were grouped under Boards of Governors (BGs) whose composition gave direct representation to senior medical staff and to the parent university. The larger London teaching hospitals had their own BGs. All thirty-six BGs had direct access to the Minister and did not hesitate to exploit this privilege. Although there was overlapping membership, the independence of BGs made it difficult for RHBs to make comprehensive arrangements for patients in their regions. When, therefore, new teaching hospitals were designated to cope with the expansion of medical education in the 1960s, they were not placed under BGs but under special University HMCs. These came under the general supervision of RHBs although they retained some special privileges.

EXECUTIVE COUNCILS

The services which in 1974 were collectively designated as 'family practitioner' services appear in the 1946 Act as general medical, dental, pharmaceutical and supplementary ophthalmic services. Since 1912, a growing proportion of the population had been members of insurance schemes covering the services of a general practitioner, who was paid a capitation fee for each patient on his 'list', and the cost of any drugs he prescribed. If there was enough money left in the fund, it could be used to pay for dental treatment and spectacles on an 'item of service' basis. Local insurance committees were set up to administer this scheme, while the local practitioners who contracted to give services organised themselves in local professional committees to regulate their affairs and protect their interests. The local medical committees were virtually sub-committees of the General Medical Services Committee of the British Medical Association.

When these arrangements were overtaken by the NHS, there seemed no obvious reason to change them, apart from extending their scope and coverage to the whole population. Indeed, any other arrangement would have been difficult to sell to the general practitioners. Accordingly, executive councils (ECs) were set up to keep lists of patients and pay the fees (negotiated nationally with the Ministry) of contracting practitioners. The ECs also kept the availability of services under general review and concerned themselves with such matters as branch surgeries and the chemists' night rota for essential drugs. But in general these matters were left to be regulated by the professions themselves, through statutory local medical, dental, pharmaceutical and ophthalmic committees. Each of these local professional committees was directly represented on the EC: of the total membership of thirty, fifteen were appointed from the professional committees, eight by the relevant local authority and seven by the Minister of Health. Unlike the hospital authorities, each EC elected its own chairman. In general, the 134 ECs matched the local health authorities (see below) although there were some combinations and special arrangements had to be made for Inner London.

LOCAL HEALTH AUTHORITIES

Since the nineteenth century a natural vehicle for statutory health services had been local government. Local authorities acquired responsibilities for the prevention and treatment of infectious disease, including tuberculosis, nursing and midwifery services for mothers and young children, and the care of the mentally ill and mentally handicapped. When the Poor Law was broken up in 1930 they gained the power to provide general hospitals. In 1948, these were nationalised along with the mental, maternity and isolation hospitals that had appeared over time under various statutes. But the local authorities retained a rag-bag of functions relating to health education and the prevention and treatment of ill-health in the community. The most important of these were health visiting, home nursing and home help. They also became responsible for health centres and for ambulances.

The 1946 Act consolidated and strengthened these local authority functions and tidied up their administration by placing responsibility on the major county and county borough authorities, assisted by their Medical Officers of Health. Each authority was compelled to set up a health committee (which could be combined with a welfare committee) to administer its NHS functions.

Local health authorities (LHAs) differed from ECs and hospital authorities in being independent bodies and not merely agents of the Minister. Health committees consisted largely of elected councillors. While, therefore, they had to act within the statutory framework of powers and duties determined by central government, they had considerable freedom in interpreting their responsibilities. The cost of their services fell primarily upon the local rates. It was not therefore surprising that there was considerable variation in levels of expenditure and standards of service (although this should not be taken to imply that the public enjoyed uniformly excellent hospital and family-practitioner services from bodies which were more directly under the Minister's control). An advantage was that they were able, if they wished, to integrate their health functions with other services under their control, notably welfare services for the elderly and handicapped persons and (in a county borough) special housing facilities.

The original total of 145 LHAs in England and Wales was increased after 1958, when an amending Act provided for the delegation of both health and welfare functions from county to county district level, so long as the district had a minimum population of 60,000 and wished to assume responsibility. Where this was done, it strengthened the housing link, since county district authorities were also responsible for housing. The London boroughs, also, became health authorities following the break-up of London County Council in 1965, although the Greater London Council became responsible for ambulances.

PAPERING THE CRACKS

This tripartite structure came under criticism from its inception. There were obvious clumsinesses. For example, responsibility for elderly long-stay patients was now divided between hospital and local welfare authorities—often in the same building, since the 'hospital' part of old Poor Law institutions, where such patients were often housed, had been taken over by the Minister, while the 'welfare' end stayed with local authorities. Meantime, the local health authority was providing nursing and home help for elderly people in their own homes. The separation of hospital from community services also fragmented provision for mental illness, childbirth and tuberculosis (which was a major problem at the time). It also seemed wrong that local authorities were responsible for providing health centres when they had no responsibility for the family practitioners who would use them, or for supplying ambulances to take patients to and from hospital.

More fundamental was the organisational wedge which was driven between general practice and hospital medicine, accentuating a traditional division between the two branches of the profession in Britain.[2] For the normal patient, hospital treatment should only be one element in the management of an illness which starts and ends under the care of his general practitioner. But if this is to work, there has to be good communication and mutual respect between hospital specialist and GP. The structure did not encourage this.

Moreover, hospital and community services were increasingly seen to be interdependent. If community services are inadequate, patients who could have been looked after in their own homes may have to be admitted to hospital. Conversely, a policy of early discharge to make more efficient use of hospital beds may place great strains on the community services: a nursing mother who is discharged forty-eight hours after delivery instead of fourteen days does not cease to need help in the other twelve days.

The first authoritative review of the tripartite structure was made by the Guillebaud Committee in 1956.[3] The committee recognised these difficulties but felt that it was too early for another upheaval. Nor was it attracted by the alternatives. Hospital authorities could not take over local health authority services without severing them from other community services to which they were closely related. Local authorities, as they then were, were in no shape either geographically or financially to assume responsibility for hospital services. (Twelve years later, the Redcliffe-Maud Commission on local government reform was to argue that the larger and stronger local authorities which it proposed would be quite able to run the NHS.[4]) So long as responsibility for hospital and community care was divided, there seemed no advantage in merging family practitioner services with either. Instead, the Guillebaud Committee made a number of specific suggestions to improve liaison and coordination.

This theme was taken up by a series of commissions and committees in relation to mental illness,[5] maternity[6] and the future of general practice.[7] For example, the Cranbrook Committee on maternity services found it alarming that an expectant mother could receive ante-natal advice from her GP, from a local authority midwife and from a hospital ante-natal clinic, that there seemed to be no rational basis for admitting some to hospital for the confinement while others were delivered at home, and that there were similar uncertainties about responsibility for post-natal care. The committee suggested that the case for hospital confinement should be considered against a scale of priorities, and that there should be closer links between hospital and domiciliary midwives. (The partial implementation of these ideas helped the health authorities to cope with the rising birthrate in the early 1960s, but was overtaken by the recommendation of a later committee that all births should be in hospital[8] and by the rapid decline in the birthrate after 1964.) Even the Seebohm Committee, while arguing for further separation between health and social services, recognised that they would have to work closely together until, if ever, unification became possible.[9]

The isolation of the general practitioner was to some extent mitigated by encouragement to do sessional work in local authority clinics and in hospitals and by the requirement that medical graduates should undertake a year in hospitals before receiving full registration from the General Medical Council. (By coincidence, these were areas where there was a shortage of supporting staff.) A new pay-structure, which was implemented in 1966, included allowances which encouraged GPs to work in groups, to attend postgraduate education courses and to employ adequate supporting staff. This was followed by a drive to build health centres, at a time when many GPs were experiencing difficulty in finding suitable practice premises. In 1968, an amending Act made it legally possible for local authority nursing and other staff to work from a GP surgery; progressive Medical Officers of Health took the opportunity to attach health visitors and others, thus helping to develop the concept of a primary care team.[10]

In the meantime, there were some imaginative initiatives in cooperation between hospital and local authorities, especially in the provision of services for the mentally ill.[11] But these tended to depend on the enthusiasm of a charismatic personality. Too often, such initiatives were lacking, or were stifled by the sheer difficulty of establishing contacts within the tangled network of responsibilities: an early study found many Medical Officers of Health unable to identify which hospital authorities provided services for patients in their districts. By the early 1960s, medical opinion was veering towards some form of integration of health services under area health boards.[12] In 1968, the Minister of Health suggested that 'the organisation of medical and related services in the community and in the hospitals, has now progressed almost as far as is possible within the present divided administrative structure'.[13]

THE ROLE OF THE CENTRE

On paper, the 1946 Act gave great power to the Minister of Health. He controlled the purse-strings of the hospital service, appointed the members of regional hospital boards, and had almost unlimited powers to issue directions to a hospital authority, set up inquiries into its performance and if necessary put it into suspense. He had similar powers in relation to executive councils. These did not extend to individual GPs and other contractor–practitioners; but there was machinery, for example, to steer doctors away from over-doctored areas[14] and to discipline practitioners who failed to honour their contracts.[15] Even the local authorities were subject to control: the Act stipulated that they had to prepare schemes showing how they intended to exercise their powers under the Act, and that any amendment which the Minister cared to make to such a scheme would then become binding on the authority; the Minister was given power to set up inquiries and to take over the duties of a local authority which he held to be in default.

Such powers are used, of course, only when a Minister decides to use them—in other words, when he feels that the political or administrative need to wield the big stick outweighs the political and administrative cost that will be incurred. The more drastic powers are about as usable in practice as nuclear weapons. None can be used as an instrument of day-to-day control. In the NHS, the power of direction has been used very sparingly—mainly to compel hospital authorities to keep within conditions of service agreed by national negotiating machinery.[16] 'Awkward' RHB members have been quietly dropped and HMCs have been reconstituted, rather less quietly, after criticisms of their performance, usually in the management of long-stay institutions, by committees of inquiry. But it is hard to find an example in connection with executive councils or local authorities. Even in the hospital service, a senior Ministry of Health official told a parliamentary committee in 1957, 'the Minister seeks always to act by moral suasion'.[17]

For at least the first half of the 1948–74 period we are considering, Ministers of Health had neither the will nor the means to intervene in the work of health authorities. Apart from rows over the introduction of charges in 1951 and 1952, there was little political controversy over the NHS and it failed to attract much public or parliamentary interest. The exchange with the House of Commons Estimates Committee mentioned above was occasioned by disclosures about the extravagant contracting habits of a teaching hospital board of governors. Apart from matters of that sort, parliamentary interest has centred on the rising cost of the service and on routine constituency and pressure-group complaints. From time to time the Ministry issued good advice, often emanating from a review by the Central Health Services Council, and invited health authorities to 'bear in mind' this and that (whatever that might mean). But there was seldom any follow-up, and no sense that the velvet glove clothed a mailed fist. Consequently the advice was frequently, and safely, ignored.[18]

In an authoritative study of relationships between central and local government, published in 1966, Griffith commented that the Ministry of Health was conspicuous among government departments in its laissez-faire approach to local health authorities.[19] An equally authoritative analysis of the hospital service by the Acton Society Trust had already criticised the Ministry of Health for its lack of leadership and for the poor quality of management throughout the service.[20]

In truth, the central department had little choice but to rely on 'moral suasion'. In comparison with any industry of comparable size, its headquarters staff was very small and was, moreover, preoccupied with routine and parliamentary business, with little scope for policy-making and review. Apart from a few medical staff with roving commissions, the Ministry was organised in divisions matching the various branches of the service, whose main business was to react to requests coming up from the health authorities and to deal with advice from advisory committees and complaints from MPs. There was no equivalent to the inspectorates of schools or constabulary. Regional officers paid pastoral visits to local authorities to jolly them along, and regional medical officers visited GPs whose prescribing costs were significantly above average for their area; but there were no teeth in any of this. The central information and research services were particularly weak: until 1956 the Ministry had no statistician, no economists and no research staff or management experts apart from a small group of work study officers. Consequently the information reaching the Ministry from the field was of poor quality and little used.

To a large extent, this lack of central capacity was a hangover from two of the operative assumptions of the 1940s. One was that the field authorities and the clinicians they employed should be left alone to do their job and that the main function of the central department was to supply them with money. (This meant, incidentally, that RHBs were not originally regarded as supervisory over HMCs. The Ministry initially dealt with HMCs direct and as a result was swamped with detail.) The other assumption was that the cost of the NHS would gradually decline as the existing 'pool of sickness' was gradually mopped up by new services. There can seldom have been a more egregious error. But it helps to explain why a strong controlling headquarters organisation was felt to be unnecessary as well as undesirable.

One result of this approach was that inherited imbalances in the quality of services tended to remain if not actually increase.[21] The initial budgets of hospital authorities were based on estimates by the outgoing administration of what was needed to maintain ongoing services; inevitably some of these were inflated. But the real inherited costs also reflected differences between well- and under-provided regions and hospital groups. In subsequent years, these budgets were treated as a base-line which was adjusted for inflation, actual spending (thus profiting the authorities which were astute enough to overspend), and the cost of new developments (which were more likely to be put forward by authorities with the capacity to implement them and the imagination to conceive them). The result was that services which were already well-developed tended to increase their lead over those that were initially under-provided. Specifically: hospital costs tended to rise more rapidly than costs in the other sectors (partly, it is true, as a result of technological innovation); teaching hospitals tended to do better than non-teaching; prosperous regions developed faster than poor ones; glamorous and expensive services for acute patients expanded at the expense of 'Cinderella' services for the chronic sick and elderly, mentally ill and mentally handicapped. These trends, in fact, persisted into the early 1970s.

The early 1960s, however, saw the beginnings of a change, partly inspired by the reports of the Guillebaud Committee and the Acton Society Trust reports already cited.[22] The Ministry strengthened its statistics and intelligence services and became a major sponsor of research. New information services made it possible to monitor hospital costs and bed-usage in some detail. Economic advisers were appointed and the Ministry developed its own operational research teams. Advice and guidance material began to flow to hospital authorities. A ten-year plan for balanced hospital development was published in 1962,[23] and local authorities were encouraged to plan their community health and welfare services for a similar period.[24] Laissez-faire was slowly being replaced by the language of priorities and value for money. But this more analytic approach was not yet associated with any fundamental change in relationships with the field authorities.

The stimulus for that was political. In 1967 a book was published alleging that there was serious mismanagement and neglect in hospitals for long-stay patients.[25] The initial reaction was official disbelief. But the publicity given to the original complaints encouraged others, which eventually became a torrent. Independent inquiries had to be set up and have indeed become commonplace. The earlier ones had the most impact, and made it very clear that some hospital authorities were failing to exercise any effective supervision over the services under their control and that, in spite of substantial increase in hospital expenditure, conditions in some long-stay hospitals remained appalling. In the face of this, Ministers began to take a closer interest in what was being done in their name.

The most ineffective HMCs were reconstituted or merged with better ones. There were still no directives, but it was made very clear to hospital authorities what was expected of them. Minimum standards of care were laid down, and authorities had to report on the extent to which they had been achieved. A professional inspection team was established to visit long-stay hospitals and to report direct to Ministers on what they found.[26] Their annual reports (which did not name individual hospitals) were made public. Later, when further inquiries revealed that hospital authorities were paying insufficient attention to complaints, a complaints commissioner was appointed with a duty to report to Parliament.[27] All this tended to tighten up the machinery of central control and to set the scene for the 1974 reorganisation.

HOSPITAL MANAGEMENT

Within the hospital service, also, there was a gradual tightening up of the managerial structure. Initially, the place of regional hospital boards had not been seen as one of great importance. In 1948 most of the experienced hospital administrators sought posts with hospital management committees and with boards of governors rather than with RHBs, which looked like weak planning and coordinating bodies. The Ministry of Health soon found that it was easier to work with fourteen RHBs than with 388 HMCs. But the interposition of RHBs between HMCs and the central department caused great resentment. This worried the Guillebaud Committee, who advised that 'Regional Hospital Boards should be told, and Hospital Management Committees should accept, that the Regional Boards are responsible for exercising a general oversight and supervision over the administration of the hospital service in their Regions'.[28] Part of the difficulty was that HMCs were made up of local people, who felt that they had some claim to understand local needs (at least two-fifths were local councillors or doctors), whereas the RHB, appointed by the Minister, was seen as remote and insensitive. Years later, Crossman described RHBs as self-appointed satraps who had to be reappointed on their own self-estimation since a Minister had no means of checking their credentials.[29] By that time the RHBs had become very important in the implementation of the hospital building programme that was instituted in the early 1960s, which gave them direct leverage over HMCs through control of building schemes and the development money that went with them. Partly for this reason, RHB posts had become much more attractive to administrators of ability.

But the most important development was in administrative training. Following some critical remarks by the Guillebaud Committee about the general quality of hospital administrators, the Ministry of Health started in 1956 to recruit small numbers of graduates and able in-service candidates for a training scheme which would equip young administrators to work in any part of the service. A cadre of well-qualified administrators was slowly built up, ready to fill many of the top posts in 1974. In 1963, another committee recommended that national and regional staff committees should be set up to supervise administrative staff recruitment and development; this would include better management training and 'planned movement' to enable selected trainees to obtain experience in a variety of health authorities.[30] These arrangements left officers with the need to find a post with one of several hundred independent employing authorities, many of whom naturally preferred a local candidate, after completing their initial training. A national scheme of assessors was eventually introduced to assist appointment panels for senior posts. While authorities adopted these schemes with varying degrees of enthusiasm, some of the elements of a national career structure had therefore been introduced for hospital administrators by the late 1960s.

There were also developments in nursing administration. Prior to 1948, the hospital matron had been a powerful figure, especially in voluntary and teaching hospitals. In multi-hospital groups, however, she then found herself at a level below the administrative group secretary. There followed a difficult period when traditional housekeeping functions of the matron were gradually being taken over by specialists in catering, laundry, domestic service management, sterile supplies and so forth; these were accountable to the administrator. Recommendations from the Ministry of Health that a senior matron should attend HMC meetings to present a nursing point of view fell largely on deaf ears.

By the mid-1960s, however, it had been realised that there were major problems of recruitment, turnover and deployment within nursing and that, in the tight labour market of that time, failure to solve these problems could impede the development of the hospital service. A committee recommended a more sophisticated managerial structure to make the most effective use of the large nursing labour force. Above the level of ward sister, instead of matrons and assistant or deputy matrons with rather ill-defined duties, there should be a hierarchy of nursing officers, culminating in a chief nursing officer for each hospital group.[31] Since the current stereotype portrayed the nurse as handmaiden to the doctor, the idea of a separate nursing hierarchy was regarded with some misgivings, both by the doctors (who still complain that the best nurses have been sucked up into administration) and by the nurses themselves. The Ministry decided to proceed with caution, introducing the new system in a few selected groups whose experience would be carefully evaluated. But before this had been completed, nurses' pay was referred to the National Board for Prices and Incomes, whose investigations confirmed that the main problem was effective deployment and whose report recommended that the 'Salmon' structure should be introduced universally as soon as possible.[32] Nevertheless, it was 1975 before the new structure was introduced in some hospitals. By that time management training courses for some thousands of hospital nurses had been sponsored by a national nursing staff advisory committee and the position of nursing management had been transformed by reorganisation.

In the meantime, the position of local authority nursing staff had been reviewed by yet another committee, which recommended that these nurses also should have their own managerial structure, culminating in a Director of Nursing Services for each local authority.[33] Like the new hospital arrangements, this not only enhanced career prospects for local authority nurses but promised them some independence from medical domination.

Rather similar arrangements were made, following a succession of reports, for the internal management of other health professions, like pharmacy, engineering and scientific services. Those for hospital doctors deserve a section to themselves.

HOSPITAL DOCTORS

It may be tedious to refer yet again to conditions prior to 1948. But the past does shape the present, and it is worth remembering that doctors who are retiring in 1978 were already in their thirties when the NHS was established; their experience has had an important influence on medical folk-memories. Prior to 1948, then, there were two patterns of medical organisation. In the voluntary hospitals, specialist surgeons and physicians held honorary appointments, which meant that they treated poor patients free of charge, drawing their income from private patients referred by general practitioners who were impressed by the status conferred by a hospital appointment. Within the hospitals, the board of governors was in no position to exercise management control, and the doctors were generally left to regulate their own affairs. By contrast, medical staff in local authority hospitals were usually salaried, and came under the general direction of a powerful medical superintendent, whose slavonic title reflected his bureaucratic authority. Local authority work had low prestige, because of the kind of patients treated; in England (but not in Scotland) supervision by the medical superintendent was regarded as an infringement on clinical autonomy and on the doctor's primary responsibility to his patient.

On the institution of the national health service, therefore, the Minister was under great pressure to extend the voluntary hospital system to all senior hospital doctors, while at the same time providing them with the security of a salary. This was accepted, as part of the price of securing their cooperation, and medical superintendents gradually disappeared — more slowly in mental than in general hospitals.

But this left a vacuum of responsibility and communication. If every doctor was autonomous, how could hospital authorities secure his cooperation in the effective management of health resources (which, remember, was not seen as a major problem in 1948)? The first attempt to deal with this was in the report of the 1954 Bradbeer Committee.[34] In almost every hospital or group of hospitals, there was a medical staff committee which met in private to determine its own affairs. The Bradbeer committee recommended that this should be formalised as a medical advisory committee (MAC) to give collective advice to the HMC. The chairman of the MAC would often be a medical member of the HMC. In at least the major hospitals, he would join the hospital secretary and the matron to form a tripartite management team, thus taking on some of the functions of a medical superintendent without any implication that other doctors were subordinate to him.

This worked, after a fashion, although it was noted that most of the interchanges with MACs tended to be initiated from the management side rather than by the doctors, and that when the MAC became part of the official machinery, the doctors nearly always set up a parallel medical staff committee which continued to meet in private.[35] But the MAC system proved too blunt an instrument to reflect the varied interests of consultants as their numbers grew. New specialties were proliferating and additional appointments made in established ones. An influential committee (whose report became known as 'Cogwheel' because of the cover design) recommended a two-tier structure. The medical staff in the main specialties, or groups of specialties, should meet as 'divisions'. One or two representatives from each division would then form a medical executive committee (MEC) which would take an overall view of medical policy.[36] Great hopes were placed on this structure as a forum for discussing the management of clinical resources, waiting lists and admission and discharge policies. It had become obvious that better use could be made of hospital facilities by adopting more efficient clinical procedures such as day-treatment and shorter length of stay to reduce unnecessary bed-days. Since these matters depended on individual clinical decisions, it was felt that improvements were most likely to follow from discussion among the doctors concerned.

In practice, the structure was slow to get off the ground.[37] Many doctors were not greatly interested in management. Meetings were often badly attended and dominated by the articulate few. There was great reluctance to discuss each other's work, and the divisions often confined their agendas to small but useful items like the allocation of theatre time and the closure of wards for painting. Some of the wider issues could not, in any event, be discussed effectively without statistical expertise, which was often not available. The MEC perhaps functioned most effectively as a medical pressure group when there was something important to discuss, and as a pool from which doctors could be appointed to working parties to consider, for example, proposals for a new hospital.

However, the Cogwheel structure offered a model for medical participation which would be built upon in the 1974 reorganisation. Although it was primarily a hospital concept, it is relevant that both the old-style medical advisory committees and the newer MECs usually found a place for a Medical Officer of Health and occasionally for a general practitioner. Conversely, hospital consultants were sometimes represented on local medical committees.

CONSUMER MOVEMENTS

Another feature of this period was the growth of pressure groups concerned with particular areas of health care. We have had, for example, AEGIS (Aid for the Elderly in Government Institutions) and AIMS (Association for the Improvement of Maternity Services). More stable groups include MIND (the National Association for Mental Health) and Age Concern (formerly the National Old People's Welfare Council), as well as the all-purpose Patients' Association, which was originally formed to protect the rights of patients in teaching hospitals and research institutes.[38]

The influence and geographical coverage of these voluntary organisations was patchy and uneven. In general they were more effective at national than at local level. But their emergence should be related to a wider movement in society and to a realisation that the public might on occasion have to defend itself or its weaker members against the apparently monolithic apparatus of state services. SHELTER and the Child Poverty Action Group are good examples of similar movements in other social services. Another manifestation was a growing interest in the political organisation of local communities. The Royal Commission on Local Government, while recommending that the main local government services should be administered by larger and more powerful bodies, also thought that 'local councils' should have the duty of representing the wishes of their inhabitants on any matter that affected the local community, and the right to be consulted by the main authority on such matters.[39] In the event, local government reorganisation did not take the form recommended by the Commission. But the local council idea survived in the form of community councils and even smaller neighbourhood councils.

SUMMARY

By the late 1960s, the climate was right for a fresh look at the organisational structure of the NHS. Twenty years earlier, the main problems had been (a) to find a secure basis for hospital planning and finance and (b) to make medical care freely available throughout the country by improving the distribution of facilities and removing financial barriers to treatment. In these terms, the tripartite structure was not a bad answer to the problems of the day. It made good deal of sense to organise the hospitals on a regional and national basis while leaving the general practitioner, often practising single-handed from a front-room or lock-up surgery, as an independent contractor, and leaving the community services under local authority control where they could be linked with other services of the local authority. But the structure began to look less attractive when the emphasis changed from simply making services available to providing them in the most effective and efficient way. The administrative divisions cut into the essential unity of medical care, and geographical anomalies compounded the problem of coordinating services which were interdependent. There was a widely-felt need for integration.

The pressures for efficiency and effectiveness, especially in the expensive hospital sector, led to increased centralisation and to more emphasis on management. Inevitably, this tended to erode the autonomy originally granted to hospital management committees and strengthened the position of the regional boards. New management structures were established for most of the health professions and new collegiate structures created to involve doctors in management. On the other hand, there was an anti-managerial movement to protect the interests of consumers and local communities.

How this was to be reflected in the new structure will be discussed in the next chapter.

NOTES

1 For a fuller account of the original NHS structure, see H. Eckstein, *The English National Health Service*, Harvard University Press, 1964.
2 R. Stevens, *Medical Practice in Modern Britain*, Yale University Press, 1966, is the

best historical account up to the date of writing. See also G. Forsyth, *Doctors and State Medicine*, Pitman Medical, London, 2nd ed., 1973.

3   *Report of the Committee of Enquiry into the Cost of the National Health Service* (Guillebaud), HMSO, Cmnd. 9663, 1956. The committee was originally set up in response to concern about the rising cost of the service, but its report covered a much wider range of issues.

4   *Report of the Royal Commission on Local Government in England 1966–69* (Redcliffe-Maud), HMSO, Cmnd. 4040, 1969, paras 359–67.

5   *Report of the Royal Commission on the Law relating to Mental Illness and Mental Deficiency*, HMSO, Cmnd. 169, 1957.

6   Ministry of Health, *Report of the Maternity Services Committee* (Cranbrook), HMSO, 1959.

7   Central Health Services Council, *The Field of Work of the Family Doctor* (Annis Gillie), HMSO, 1963.

8   Central Health Services Council, *Domiciliary Midwifery and Maternity Bed Needs* (Peel), HMSO, 1970.

9   *Report of the Committee on Local Authority and Allied Personal Social Services* (Seebohm), HMSO, Cmnd. 3703, 1968.

10 Central Health Services Council, *The Organisation of Group Practice* (Harvard Davies), HMSO, 1971. See also *Report of the Royal Commission on Medical Education*, HMSO, Cmnd. 3569, 1968, ch. 2.

11 H. L. Freeman and W. A. J. Farndale (eds), *Trends in the Mental Health Service*, Pergamon Press, Oxford, 1963.

12 Medical Services Review Committee, *A Review of the Medical Services in Great Britain* (Porritt Report), Social Assay, London, 1962.

13 Ministry of Health, *The Administrative Structure of Medical and Related Services in England and Wales*, HMSO, 1968, foreword.

14 J. R. Butler *et al.*, *Family Doctors and Public Policy*, Routledge, London, 1973.

15 R. Klein, *Complaints against Doctors*, Charles Knight, London, 1973.

16 Acton Society Trust, *Hospitals and the State*, vol. 5, 'The Central Control of the Service', Acton Society Trust, London, 1958.

17 *Ibid.*

18 R. Stewart and J. Sleeman, *Continuously Under Review*, Bell, London, 1967, show how little attention was paid to exhortations about hospital out-patient waiting times. R. G. S. Brown, 'The Course of a Circular', *Hospital*, London, June 1962, shows how Ministry of Health advice about food waste was treated in a number of management committees.

19 J. A. G. Griffith, *Central Departments and Local Authorities*, Allen and Unwin, London, 1966.

20 Acton Society Trust, *Hospitals and the State*, vol. 6, 'Creative Leadership in a State Service', Acton Society Trust, London, 1959.

21 M. H. Cooper, *Rationing Health Care*, Croom Helm, London, 1975, ch. 7.

22 See notes 3 and 16 above.

23 Ministry of Health, *A Hospital Plan for England and Wales*, HMSO, Cmnd. 1604, 1962 (revised 1966).

24 Ministry of Health, *The Development of Community Care*, HMSO, Cmnd. 1973, 1963 (revised 1964, 1965).

25 B. Robb, *Sans Everything*, Nelson, London, 1967.

26 The Hospital Advisory Service was set up in 1969, initially to visit and report upon hospitals for the mentally handicapped and mentally ill. In 1972, hospital services for the geriatric and chronic sick were aided. After the 1974 reorganisation, the HAS became the Health Advisory Service, with a duty to monitor all the inter-related health and personal social services for children, the mentally ill and the elderly.

A separate Development Group was established to supervise services for the mentally handicapped. The Department of Health and Social Security published the first annual report from the HAS in 1971.

27 A Parliamentary Commissioner for Administration was appointed in 1967 to investigate complaints against government departments. In the following year, the Minister of Health made tentative suggestions that a similar commissioner should be appointed to investigate complaints against NHS authorities. The doctors objected strongly and it was not until 1972, after the Whittingham hospital scandal, that his successor announced that provision for a Health Service Commissioner would be included in the Reorganisation Bill, but that he would not be able to investigate matters involving clinical judgement. The first Commissioner (who also holds the office of Parliamentary Commissioner) was a former permanent secretary of the Department of Health and Social Security. He publishes annual, quarterly and special reports, which are considered by the Select Committee on the Parliamentary Commissioner for Administration. In 1977 the Select Committee recommended that clinical matters should be included within his jurisdiction.

28 *Op. cit.* (note 3), para. 212.

29 R.H.S. Crossman, *A Politician's View of Health Service Planning* (Maurice Bloch lecture), University of Glasgow, 1972.

30 Ministry of Health, *Report of the Committee of Inquiry into the Recruitment, Training and Promotion of Administrative and Clerical Staff in the Hospital Service* (Lycett Green), HMSO, 1963.

31 Ministry of Health, *Report of the Committee on Senior Nursing Staff Structure* (Salmon), HMSO, 1966.

32 National Board for Prices and Incomes, *Report No. 60* ('Pay of Nurses and Midwives in the National Health Service'), HMSO, Cmnd. 3585, 1968.

33 DHSS, *Report of a Working Party on Management Structure in the Local Authority Nursing Services* (Mayston), DHSS, 1969.

34 Central Health Services Council, *Report of the Committee on the Internal Administration of Hospitals* (Bradbeer), HMSO, 1954.

35 R. G. S. Brown, 'Medical Committees', *Hospital*, London, Jan. 1962.

36 Ministry of Health, *First Report of the Joint Working Party on the Organisation of Medical Work in Hospitals*, HMSO, 1967. The second 'Cogwheel' report, which reviewed progress and difficulties, was published by DHSS in 1972 and the third, which recommended that the Cogwheel structure should be retained after reorganisation, in 1974.

37 G. McLachlan (ed.), *In Low Gear?*, Oxford University Press for Nuffield Provincial Hospitals Trust, London, 1971.

38 C. J. Ham, 'Power, Patients and Pluralism', in K. Barnard and M. Lee (eds) *Conflicts in the National Health Service*, Croom Helm, London, 1977.

39 *Op. cit.* (note 4), para. 408.

Chapter 2

The Nature and Purpose of Reorganisation

The 1974 reorganisation was intended to remove the operational difficulties that seemed to be associated with the tripartite 1948 structure. Basically, the local health authority services were nationalised and brought under the same management as hospital services, while the administration of family practitioner services was aligned with the new authorities. But a number of other elements were included in the reorganisation package. Some merely consolidated trends that were already emerging, particularly in the management of hospital services. Others, like the planning cycle and the arrangements for consumer representation, were new.

The chapter begins by reciting the statutory changes that followed from the National Health Service Reorganisation Act, 1973.[1] This is followed by a discussion of the new management arrangements. The chapter ends by looking at the broader objectives of the reorganisation.

SCOPE OF THE NHS

The scope of the NHS remained broadly unchanged. However, the school health service, previously an educational responsibility, became part of the NHS. Environmental health remained outside, as did welfare provision for the elderly and handicapped. In respect of social aspects of medical care, an important change had already occurred. Following the report of the Seebohm Committee,[2] it had been decided that from 1971 the main social-work services of local authorities, which had previously been scattered among health, welfare and child care departments, should be merged in new professionally-managed social service departments. These departments acquired any services which were more social than medical in character. Thus, home helps, hostels and day centres which were not

22

medically supervised had gone into social services, whereas health education, health visiting and home nursing remained with the local authority health departments until they were nationalised three years later. On the same principle, medical and psychiatric social workers, who had been employed by hospital authorities for specialised work, were then transferred to local authority social service departments, somewhat against their will. The local authorities are also responsible for such aspects of the care of mothers and young children, the prevention of illness and the care of persons suffering from illness as the Secretary of State does not consider 'appropriate' as part of the health service. But family planning is part of the NHS.

REGIONAL AND AREA HEALTH AUTHORITIES

The Act abolished local health authorities, regional hospital boards, hospital management committees and nearly all boards of governors. The Secretary of State was required to divide England into regions and appoint regional health authorities (RHAs). The fourteen regions are broadly similar to those of the old regional hospital boards. Minor changes were made to align them with new local authority boundaries: thus the Yorkshire region acquired south Humberside (previously in Lincolnshire) from the Sheffield-based Trent region, and the Northern region gained from North-West that part of north Lancashire which went into Cumbria.

The basis of membership is also much as before. RHAs are appointed by the Secretary of State, after consulting various bodies listed in a schedule to the Act, and include at least two doctors, a nurse and a member nominated by the relevant medical school(s). When the membership was reviewed in 1976, the opportunity was taken to increase the proportion nominated by local government to one-third of the total and to include trade-union nominees. The Secretary of State appoints the chairman who (unlike his RHB predecessor) receives a part-time salary.

There are two main differences between RHAs and regional hospital boards. The RHAs are responsible for supervising all health services, not just hospitals, in their regions. And they were made responsible for undergraduate teaching hospitals: only a few postgraduate teaching hospitals in London remained directly responsible to the Secretary of State under their own boards of governors.

The regions were subdivided into areas for which area health authorities (AHAs) are responsible, as agents, to the RHA. The principle was that health areas should match, as nearly as possible, the areas served by local social services authorities (viz. the shire counties, the London boroughs, and districts within the six metropolitan counties). The intention was to facilitate coordination: the Act requires health and local authorities to consult each other and to provide each other with necessary services. In practice, some local authority areas in London and Merseyside had to be combined for health purposes. Moreover, the territory of some AHAs had to be modified to accommodate hospital catchment zones. There are ninety AHAs compared with 106 social service authorities.

Originally, AHAs varied from fifteen to twenty-eight members. The chairman is appointed by the Secretary of State and is paid a part-time salary. The Act stipulated that at least four members should be nominated by the matching local authority and the remainder appointed by the RHA after consultation; these had to include at least one member nominated by the regional university medical school. There are always two doctors and a nurse. In 1976 the authorities were enlarged to allow further local authority appointments up to one-third of the total membership apart from the chairman; these were intended to provide links with housing and environmental health and therefore, in shire counties, are nominated by the district councils which provide these services. Two places on each authority were at the same time allocated to staff nominees. At the time of writing, AHAs vary in size from nineteen to thirty-four.

The changes in the original RHA and AHA membership were made after a Labour government had taken over in 1974 from the Conservatives, who constructed and implemented the Reorganisation Act. They reflect continuing controversies, which can be traced in various documents about the NHS structure, about the nature of these bodies. The Act itself embodies principles set out in a Conservative White Paper in 1972.[3] But this had been preceded by a consultative document in 1971 and by two Labour government Green Papers in 1968[4] and 1970.[5] The 1968 Green Paper was written at a time when the official view was that most local services in England should be administered in forty to fifty units. It raised the possibility that an integrated NHS could be administered by local authorities if they were reorganised on that model. As an alternative, it suggested that there should be an equivalent number of 'area health boards' which should be small and consist of about fifteen members appointed on the basis of their managerial experience. The boards could report direct to Ministers and there would be no need for a regional tier, although it was recognised that for some purposes the individual boards would be too small and would have to form consortia.

These proposals were not well received. Moreover, the shape of local government turned out rather different from what had been envisaged, mainly as a result of splitting the conurbations into districts. The second (1970) Green Paper ruled out the local government option and established the notion of about ninety area health authorities, with enlarged membership. Out of a total of twenty to twenty-five, one-third might be elected by the medical, dental and nursing professions, one-third appointed by the relevant local authority and the remainder, including the chairman, appointed by the Secretary of State. In addition, it was proposed that there should be about 200 district committees, with coopted members of the local community and NHS staff, but without a budget, to supervise the running of services at that level. (Hospital planning was then geared to a target pattern of about 200 district general hospitals serving populations of around a quarter of a million.) It would also be necessary to retain a regional tier; but the Green Paper suggested that regional hospital board responsibilities for major building schemes could be carried out by regional offices of the Department of Health and Social Security, while the RHBs themselves could be replaced by 'regional health councils' on which each area authority would be represented. The councils would have mainly advisory duties relating to the planning of hospital and specialist services.

This looked like the perfect political compromise, with something for everyone.[6] If the Labour government had not lost the 1970 election, this structure would have been implemented in 1974. But the incoming Secretary of State had other ideas. The consultative document of 1971, which provided an accurate foretaste of the White Paper in the following year, reverted to the managerial tone of 1968; at the launching press conference, Sir Keith Joseph said that his document leaned towards management where the 1970 Green Paper had leaned towards participation. Area authorities would consist of about fifteen members, appointed on the criterion of management ability. Elected staff representation was not acceptable: other arrangements would be made both for professional advice and to protect the interests of the local community. (Nevertheless, and somewhat incongruously, the document established the two-doctors-and-a-nurse formula and accepted that some members of each area authority would be nominated by the local authority; a gap was already emerging between rhetoric and reality, which did not save the rhetoric from attack.) On the basis of ninety areas, there would have to be a strong regional tier, with executive and supervisory functions rather than advisory ones; in particular, areas should receive their budgets from the regional authority and not directly from the Secretary of State.

Although the proposals in the consultative document were largely put into effect in April 1974, they were much attacked both by the Labour opposition and by trade unions and professional associations. The British Medical Association criticised the 'obsession with management' and passed resolutions demanding one-third medical membership and the right of each authority to elect its own chairman. Mr Crossman claimed that the task of health service boards and committees was not to manage but to represent people and to control the officials who were the real managers. His successor in the 1974 Labour government (Mrs Barbara Castle) was unhappy about the structure she inherited and issued a paper which, while accepting the need to avoid another major upheaval, went some way to restoring the earlier concept.[7] Local government representation on the health authorities was increased and consultations were started with a view to having directly elected representatives of doctors, nurses and other NHS staff on each authority.

Evidence submitted to the Royal Commission on the National Health Service in 1976–7 was almost unanimous that the compromise structure was unsatisfactory. But suggestions for improvement varied from those of the Confederation of Health Service Employees, who proposed that area health authorities should be elected (half by the staff and half by the general public), to those of the Royal College of Surgeons, who proposed that they should be replaced by bodies resembling the old hospital management committees.

In the meantime, the Government has held to the doctrine that, whatever their origins, health authority members are collectively accountable to the Secretary of State (through the RHA in the case of AHAs) and do not represent particular constituencies. This looks like political schizophrenia.

FAMILY PRACTITIONER COMMITTEES

When the Medical Services Review Committee first proposed area health boards in 1962, it was envisaged that they would have separate committees for each of the three sectors.[8] But the 1968 Green Paper suggested that the tripartite structure should not be perpetuated within a unified administration: any committee structure at health board level should cover all parts of the service, while its headquarters organisation should be based on functional requirements — staffing, finance, logistics and planning — and not on existing divisions of the service. This was unacceptable to the British Medical Association. The next Green Paper suggested that in each area the family practitioner services (which include chemists, opticians and dentists as well as general practitioners) should be administered by a special statutory committee, similar to the Executive Councils described in the last chapter and, like them, separately financed from the exchequer. The area health authority would thus be responsible for coordinating the family practitioners with other services and for providing supporting services and health centres but would not have GPs under its direct control.

This concession closed that part of the discussion. Provision for separate Family Practitioner Committees was made in the Reorganisation Act. Although FPCs are formally committees of the area health authority, the authority is obliged to delegate to them the functions of regulating family practitioner services and meeting reimbursement claims from the practitioners. Each FPC consists of thirty members, of whom exactly half are appointed by the professionals themselves — eight by the doctors, three by the dentists and two each by the chemists and opticians. Of the remainder, four are appointed by the local authority and eleven by the area health authority (of whom only one need be a member of the AHA itself). Each FPC appoints its own chairman.

The new arrangements for general practitioner services are therefore very similar to those which were established in 1948 and indeed under Lloyd George's National Health Insurance Act of 1911. The desire of the FPCs to maintain their separate identity is shown by their reluctance to join the National Association of Health Authorities which was formed by regional and area health authorities after reorganisation. Instead, they formed a Society of Family Practitioner Committees which has acted independently in such matters as submitting evidence to the Royal Commission on the NHS.

PROFESSIONAL ADVISORY COMMITTEES

The British Medical Association had always argued for strong medical advisory machinery. This was accepted in 1971, partly to compensate for the loss of elected professional membership of health authorities. The Reorganisation Act provided for statutory professional committees, with the duty to advise and the right to be consulted, at area and regional levels.

The relevant section does not refer only to doctors. It places a duty on the Secretary of State to recognise committees which are sufficiently representative of doctors, nurses, dentists, pharmacists, opticians and other unspecified categories of staff in each region and area. These committees then become official professional advisory committees to the regional and area authorities.

The details were negotiated separately with each profession. Those for doctors were agreed with the BMA. Each area medical committee (AMC) has to consist of equal numbers (to be decided locally) of general practitioners and hospital specialists. There has to be some representation of junior doctors, and here again trainee GPs and junior hospital doctors have to be equal in number. Finally, some places have to be allocated to doctors in community medicine—a category which includes medical administrators as well as those working in, say, school health services; if the area medical officer is not elected, he should be an *ex officio* member. Each AMC elects its own chairman; but if the chairman is a hospital specialist, the deputy chairman should be a general practitioner, and vice versa. Regional medical committees are confederate structures. The chairman of each area medical committee is automatically a member and, again, a second representative is required to balance out his special interest. Additional members can be coopted to represent special interests that do not emerge from this process.

For doctors, therefore, an advisory system was constructed in such a way that it could not be dominated either by hospital interests (which was the main worry) or by general practitioners. Parallel attempts were made to construct balanced committees for dentists, opticians, pharmacists and nurses. Special machinery was needed to overcome the problem that nursing covers a vast range of skills, some of which are represented by the Royal Colleges of Nursing and Midwives, while others more appropriately fall within the sphere of conventional trade unions like the Confederation of Health Service Employees (COHSE), the National Union of Public Employees (NUPE) and the National and Local Government Officers Association (NALGO); there is considerable tension between the professional associations and the unions. A national steering committee, on which all these bodies were represented, was established to consider nominations for every nursing advisory committee and share out the places.

The most obvious group which was left out of these arrangements was the paramedical staff, covering a great variety of fairly small professions like radiography, chiropody, speech therapy, physiotherapy, medical laboratory technicians and many others. These categories are too numerous to be represented separately, but are notoriously reluctant to accept any system of collective representation.

COMMUNITY HEALTH COUNCILS

The abortive 1970 Green Paper had contained a reference to community-based district committees with supervisory duties. The 1971 document envisaged a much sharper division between management and community representation. The area health authorities, as we have seen, were not then conceived as representative bodies. Another forum was needed to represent the communities they served. It was therefore proposed to set up a community health council (CHC) for each district.

There was considerable ambiguity about what the CHCs would do, and which of several 'communities' they were intended to represent (users of the NHS; vulnerable groups needing special protection; the local population at large—which might be 'anti-health' on such matters as the location of centres for the mentally handicapped?). Their relationship to the health authorities was also unclear. In the House of Commons, Mrs Shirley Williams described them as 'the strangest bunch of administrative eunuchs any department had yet foisted on the House, a seraglio of useless and emasculated bodies'.[9]

After a good deal of debate and amendment, the Reorganisation Act provided that CHCs should be independent of area health authorities and that there should be no overlapping membership. Half the membership of each CHC is appointed by the relevant local authorities, one-third by voluntary organisations and the remainder by the regional health authority from trade-union and other sources to secure a balanced membership. The RHA meets administrative costs. Total membership is left for local arrangement and varies from eighteen to thirty-six. Each CHC appoints its own chairman.

There are 207 CHCs in England, two more than the number of health districts: special arrangements had to be made to represent isolated sub-districts in south-east Cumbria and the Isles of Scilly (as well as in parts of Wales).

Regulations gave CHCs the right to call for information, to visit hospitals and institutions, to make representations to the area authority on the consumer's behalf, and to be consulted about development plans. Later, CHCs were given a leading role in decisions about the closure or change of use of hospitals: if the CHC agreed, the AHA could normally go ahead with the closure; if not, the whole question was referred to higher levels. Each CHC has to prepare an annual report, and has a statutory annual meeting with the AHA.

In 1974 Mrs Castle suggested that CHCs should nominate two of their members to sit on the AHA. This looked likely to cause further confusion, however, and in the following year a CHC representative was enabled to attend and speak at AHA meetings, but without a vote. In 1977 the next Secretary of State (Mr David Ennals) invited family practitioner committees to extend similar privileges; but this aroused intense opposition from some FPCs and was not pressed.

MANAGEMENT TEAMS

The Reorganisation Act did not lay down internal management arrangements for the new authorities; the Secretary of State deals with such matters administratively, although he has the power to make directions. The management structures were the outcome of discussion and compromise by a large study group, whose method of operation will be discussed in the next chapter.

It had been assumed in some quarters that a unified health service, in which there would be a heavy emphasis on the management of resources and value for money, would need a strong executive structure.[10] The main uncertainty was whether the chief executive would be a doctor, like the Medical Officer of Health, or a general administrator, like the hospital group secretary. What in fact emerged was a system of management by multi-professional teams, each member of which was separately accountable to the parent authority. It is interesting to trace the erosion of the original chief executive concept. The 1968 Green Paper envisaged a directorate of departmental heads, including a medical director of planning and operations, which would carry collective responsibility; but it was suggested that a chief administrative officer would preside over the team.[11] By 1970, functions like personnel and supply warranted departments but not directors. The emphasis was now on a planning team, in which the chief administrative medical officer would play a major role, although the chief nursing, administrative and finance officers (in that order) would also be core members. Administration had become a residual function, although the chief administrator was still the coordinator of non-medical services.[12] By the end of 1974 the management study group had recommended that management should be entrusted to a consensus management team at each level of administration. The smaller teams would have four members—an administrator, treasurer, medical officer and nursing officer. At the operational (district) level these four professions would be joined by two clinicians, one a GP and the other a hospital specialist, chosen by their peers. In the regional authorities, the basic four would be joined by a regional works officer because of the importance of his function at that level. In each case, a veto by any member would prevent the team from reaching a decision.[13]

The team concept was fashionable in the management literature of the time. Its application to the NHS seems to have arisen partly from the reluctance of medical members of the study group to accept any form of chief executive, either medical or non-medical, and partly from the need to build bridges between management and clinicians. It was thought that the second objective could best be accomplished by involving clinicians, through their chosen representatives, in major decisions. Once admitted to the team, there was the problem that clinical representatives might find themselves outvoted, and certainly outweighed, by permanent officials who carried personal responsibility for considerable staff and other resources. Hence the concept of the veto, or 'consensus management'. The study group seems to have expected that the administrator would normally be appointed team chairman. In fact, most authorities failed to nominate a chairman and their management teams generally avoided the problem by taking the chair in rotation or, in some cases, by having no chairman at all. No single officer, therefore, can be held responsible for matters which require team decision because they involve more than one profession. If the team fails to agree on any matter, the authority itself has to step in.

The doctrine of *pares inter pares* had an odd side-effect on the English structure. (On this, as on some other matters, the Scots and the Northern Irish managed to steer a less complex course.) If all members of the district teams are equal, what about the relationship of district to area officers? The team could hardly operate as a consensus of equals if its four permanent members had to look over their shoulders at hierarchical superiors. In pursuance of this logic, the district officers and teams were made directly accountable to the area health authority, and not through the area team of officers. A four-district AHA thus has five officer teams and twenty permanent team members (as well as the area works, dental and pharmaceutical officers, who although not part of the area team are not subordinate to any team member) separately accountable to it. In such circumstances, a district administrator is subject to far less supervision by his authority than, say, a group secretary was to his hospital management committee. The area officers cannot instruct their district counterparts: they can only 'monitor' their performance, try to sort things out informally, and report to the AHA if they are unsuccessful. The officers of the RHA have a similar monitoring role in relation to the performance of AHAs and their officers. The relationships are shown in fig. 1.

It is worth stressing that this whole system was novel to most of those who would have to operate it. The RHBs had grown accustomed to a system of joint hierarchies, in which they looked to their senior administrative medical officer for control of medical staffing and advice on service development, and to their secretary for everything else, although it was recognised that the treasurer and chief architect had their specialist fields. Most HMCs, however, had never known medical administration and looked in all respects to their group secretary (again admitting the special role of the treasurer) just as local health authorities did to their Medical Officer of Health. On translation to the new service, both these groups lost some of their personal authority to the multi-professional teams. Treasurers had not quite gained their autonomy by 1974; for most of them, team membership brought a wider challenge and perhaps a small increase in status. For nurses, the change represented a tremendous jump. Less than ten years earlier, the most senior nurses at operational level had usually been in charge of an individual hospital or a category of community nursing staff. The process of creating a managerial hierarchy under chief nursing officers was not complete by 1974. Now nurses were given the opportunity to take part in planning and administering services on a very large scale and on equal terms with administrators and medical officers with years of experience and tradition behind them. For clinical members of the management teams, cooption into management was a logical development from the representative system that had been developed in, at least, the larger hospital groups; but the 'Cogwheel' structure had not been introduced everywhere and involvement in health service management at this level was entirely new to general practitioners who had not been members of hospital management committees.

MEDICAL REPRESENTATION

The structure of advisory machinery at area and regional level has been discussed in an earlier section. There is a 'balanced' area medical committee (AMC), from which representatives go forward to the regional medical

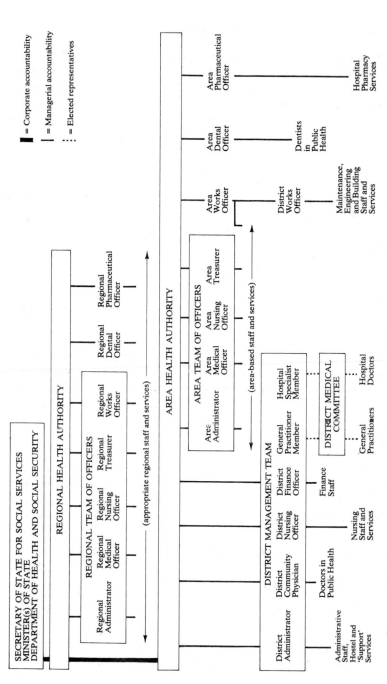

Fig. 1 NHS Management Structure. Formal accountability in a multi-district area (only one district shown)

committee. Also at area level, general practitioners have a local medical committee (LMC) which feeds into the family practitioner committee and supplies some of its members. But medical members of the health authorities do not necessarily emerge from these committees. They are appointed in their personal capacities and it would probably be very difficult for the chairman of an area medical committee to function in the independent way expected of an AHA member.

At district level, however, the clinical members of management teams are expected to be both spokesmen and representatives. They are a bridge between management and their clinical colleagues. In a single-district area, the chairman and deputy chairman of the AMC are automatically members of the area management team(subject to the universal rule that one must be a GP and the other a hospital specialist). In a multi-district area, it is necessary to have machinery from which representatives can emerge. District medical committees were therefore created on the same basis as, but separately from, the statutory AMC. The chairman and deputy chairman of this district committee became the clinical members of the district management team.

In total, the machinery for medical representation is very complex, especially if national machinery is taken into account (see fig. 2). The local (FPC) medical committees are plugged into the BMA's General Medical Services Committee and the main health professions are represented on the Central Health Services Council, which advises the Secretary of State, and its standing committees.

The responsibility for helping it to work rests with the area medical officer and his district counterpart, the district community physician. Their involvement in the medical committee structures can be traced in the diagram. These medical administrators are not in charge of medical work in hospitals and GP surgeries. They are responsible for service planning and for advising their teams and the area health authority on medical aspects of policy and management. Such executive duties as they have are partly of the old 'medical officer' type, including the supply of advice and services to local authorities. But they also include responsibility for medical staffing and research and information about the health needs of the community. Their job is largely a new one created by the new structure and its emphasis on comprehensive planning. The generic title of 'specialists in community medicine' is in some ways misleading because it gives too little indication of their administrative roles. But it does suggest that their territory is different from that of doctors who treat individual patients. As administrators, they

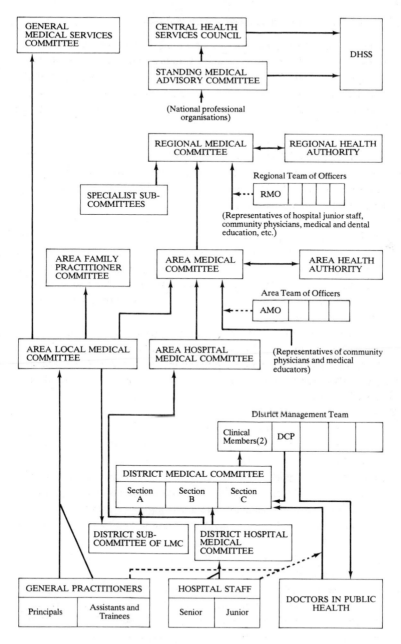

Fig. 2   Medical Representative Machinery

are not medical superintendents under a new name; their influence over clinical colleagues depends on negotiation and persuasion. The appointment of medical administrators at every level of management was not thought to diminish the need for representative channels of communication with doctors in clinical practice.

PLANNING

The last administrative innovation that needs to be mentioned here is the planning cycle. Planning capacity was regarded as an important feature of the new structure, which would enable rational decisions to be taken about the best use of resources in the face of changing needs, including improvement in the neglected sectors of care and a fairer distribution of resources to different parts of the country. It was hoped that the new structure would itself facilitate planning: the new authorities were responsible for meeting the health needs of their areas across the board, and would be assisted by the new breed of medical administrators. But it was also felt necessary to introduce a new planning process.

The concept of planning can be broken down into several components. One is the extension of time-horizons, so that this year's developments can be linked to a grander plan to be achieved over perhaps a decade. Another is prioritisation—deciding, against a background of limited resources, which cherished schemes may have to be sacrificed in order to pay for others. A third aspect is the determination of goal-hierarchies, which means being clear about the broad overall strategic objectives under which specific objectives can be subsumed and by which they can be assessed (*Why* do we want a new hospital? What will it contribute to the general state of health? Will it absorb resources that would make a larger contribution if they were used in a different way? and so on). There had been plans of a sort in the old NHS, mostly in the form of ten-year forward looks. But there had been little attempt at prioritisation between sectors, and very patchy success in relating particular developments to broad strategies. In the hospital service, 'planning' really meant the physical design and construction of new buildings.

The new planning cycle attempted to exploit both the hierarchical structure of the NHS and the wealth of information and ideas that was expected to flow through the consultative and advisory machinery.[14] The Department of Health and Social Security would issue guidelines about strategic objectives and priorities within the resources likely to be available.

To enable it to do so effectively, the Department was itself reorganised into multi-professional service development groups, coordinated by a central planning unit; the task of the groups was to review the needs for both health and personal social services of client groups like the mentally ill and the elderly. (It was pointed out later that this left general hospital services without a sponsor.[15]) Regional health authorities would relate these guidelines to their own situation and issue more specific guidelines to the area authorities. These in turn would prepare guide material for their own management teams. Some of it would be based on exercises in joint planning with the local authority.

The teams would then review the needs of their districts and identify deficiencies which would form the basis of their own district plans. Contributions would come from the heads of services represented on the management team itself, from doctors through their representatives, from community health councils and from any *ad hoc* planning teams set up to look at specific services. The community health council would be shown the final plan, and its comments forwarded with the plan itself to the AHA. With the assistance of their own team of officers, the AHA would check that the plans were consistent with the guidelines and also test them in a widespread programme of consultation with the matching local authority, the area professional advisory committees, the family practitioner committee and any groups of staff who had not been involved at district level. (Clearly, all this is much simpler in a single-district area.) When finally satisfied, the AHA would forward the plans to the RHA, which would go through a similar process and forward a consolidated regional plan to the DHSS. In so far as the plans were agreed, they would become firm commitments and it was hoped that monitoring progress towards their implementation would become the main instrument of control between one level of authority and the next.

This is a rather breathless summary of a very complex process. In fact, the DHSS was unable to produce its first set of consolidated guidelines until 1976, over two years after the reorganisation. Part of the reason was the uncertainty of the economic situation, and hence the difficulty of setting out realistic assumptions about the resources likely to be available. In the event, they could be stated for only four years ahead instead of the intended ten. Moreover, Ministers had decided that it was unrealistic to subsume concrete proposals for the year ahead under a strategic planning process. Accordingly, it was decided to distinguish between long-term strategic planning, which would be a relatively infrequent exercise (perhaps every third year), and operational planning of concrete service developments, which would be annual but only cover three years ahead. Operational plans for the areas could be approved by the RHA.

The first strategic plans reached the DHSS early in 1977. Their quality was generally poor, even allowing for the novelty of the exercise. But this is anticipating the assessment in chapter 8.

In the meantime, a rather blunter instrument had been adopted to even out regional inequalities through central control of the budget. In his last year of office as Secretary of State, Richard Crossman had decided to help the poorer hospital regions to catch up by allocating them a proportionately greater share of the money available for new development each year. For a number of reasons, too technical to explore here, this had little effect. In 1975, a working party was established to look at the whole question of resource allocation in relation to the new structure, which for the first time enabled total resource-use to be compared with the populations served by each health authority. The working party came up with a formula, based partly on the age-structure of the population served and partly on indicators of its state of health, from which the 'ideal' distribution of the national health budget could be calculated.[16] Some regions were enjoying considerably more than this target allocation and others considerably less; differences between areas were even greater. On advice from the working party, the Secretary of State 'froze' the allocations of the richer regions from April 1976.

AIMS OF THE REORGANISATION

These details of the 1974 structure (revealed in its full glory in fig. 3) and of its planning processes, are absorbing for the participants. But they are interesting to the outsider only in relation to their purpose. It might therefore restore a sense of perspective to spend a few paragraphs on the intentions behind the reorganisation and the vehicles chosen for their realisation.

The broad aims can, indeed, be stated fairly simply. They appear almost identically in the two Green Papers and in the 1972 White Paper, differences being either in political rhetoric or in the details of implementation. To underline the continuity, the aims listed below are taken from the Labour government's Green Paper of 1970,[17] while the substantive changes are, of course, derived from the Conservative government's White Paper two years later.

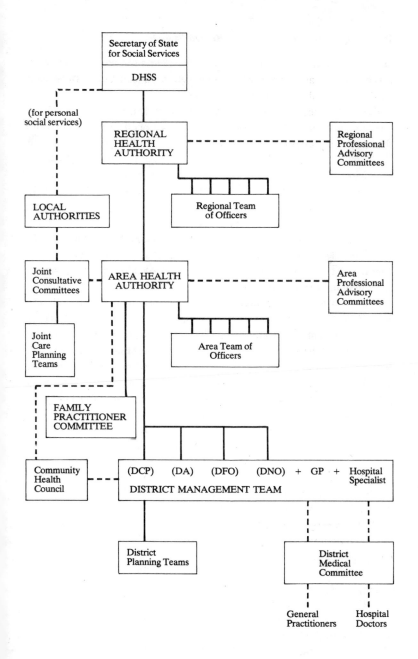

Fig. 3 *NHS Structure after Reorganisation*

(a) To unite the National Health Service. Not only must the different branches be controlled by the same authority but the separate services must be integrated at local level.

The machinery employed here was the nationalisation of local authority services and the appointment of health authorities and management teams with responsibility for meeting health needs across the board. But this sits oddly with the decision, already made in 1970, to maintain separate machinery for general practitioner services. The involvement of general practitioners as numerically equal partners on committees and on district management teams does, however, give them a voice in overall health service planning.

(b) To establish close links between the National Health Service and the public health and social services provided by local government.

The division of responsibility for health and social care weakened the concept of unification. In 1956 the Guillebaud Committee had pointed out that the separation of hospital from welfare services for the elderly was even then a major weakness. This split survived the 1974 reorganisation and was increased by putting all social support services, including home helps, on the local authority side of the line, while community nursing staff went to the health authorities. To ease the problem (and perhaps pave the way for eventual amalgamation), the boundaries of health areas were matched with those of local authorities, statutory committees were established for joint consultation, and certain NHS officers were given the specific duty to liaise with and advise the local authorities.

(c) To place the maximum responsibility for administering the National Health Service, consistent with national plans and priorities, on area health authorities in which there must be strong local and professional participation, and to involve each community in the running of the services of its district.

While the Reorganisation Act places responsibility firmly on the Secretary of State, who retains overriding powers of control, administrative policy is to delegate as much as possible to regional, area and, indeed, district level; difficulties have, of course, emerged in practice. The composition of area and regional authorities has changed and will, no doubt, change again. But each specification has included the allocation of a proportion of seats to doctors, nurses and local government nominees. Doctors are represented also by statutory advisory committees and through their chosen representatives on district management teams. All management teams include the relevant head of nursing services. At district level, different sorts of 'community' are represented on the community health council. It is arguable whether the CHC is 'involved . . . in the running of the services'. It can certainly offer advice and criticism, and has the means of ventilating them through the local press. Moreover, the planning process is intended to give CHCs, as well as the matching local authorities and advisory committees representing the main health professions, an opportunity to comment on development plans before they are finalised.

(d) To provide effective central control over the money spent on the service and to ensure that the maximum value is obtained for it.

Supporting paragraphs in the Green Paper made it clear that there were three different issues involved here. There was the general managerial point that some authorities had not been very efficient in the past and that the Secretary of State, being himself responsible to Parliament, intended to keep a closer watch on their performance.[18] The second point was the need for central determination of norms and priorities to ensure that the Cinderella services were no longer neglected.[19] The third was the need for action to even out differences in standards between regions.[20] The last has been pursued by adopting a formula for resource allocation very similar to the one outlined in the Green Paper. Otherwise, as we have seen, the planning system has been presented as the principal instrument of central control and the main basis monitoring performance. In practice, however, planning is not yet well enough developed to carry this weight: specific controls over administrative costs, financial management and other matters abound; and there are interventions of a different sort when industrial action, or some scandal, arouses political interest.

THE TASK

Starting from the point in 1971 when it was definitely decided to proceed with reorganisation along the lines outlined in the consultative document, there were many things to be done. The most important were:

1   The preparation and passage through Parliament of a Reorganisation Bill.

2   The determination of exact boundaries for the regions, areas and districts.

3   The appointment of members to the regional and area health authorities, family practitioner committees and community health councils.

4   Decisions about the division of functions between the DHSS, RHAs and AHAs.

5   Decisions about the management structure at regions, areas and districts.

6   The appointment of officers to the new posts.

7   The transfer of existing staff to the new authorities.

8   The transfer of property and liabilities from the old authorities to the new ones.

9   Finding officers for the new authorities.

10   The collection of information about the services which would come under the control of the new authorities and district teams.

11   Arrangements for liaison between health and local government authorities.

12   The preparation of guidance for members of the new bodies.

13   The preparation of senior staff for their new responsibilities.

14   Arrangements to restructure professional machinery to align with the new geography, and to give effect to undertakings about professional involvement in management.

15   Maintaining the continuity of services during the transitional period.

16   The introduction of the new planning process.

The list could be extended into details like the physical transfer of Executive Council records to match the areas served by the new family practitioner committees. But most of the important changes can be subsumed under one or other of these sixteen headings. The case-study in Part II is concerned with the way these problems were overcome in one multi-district area which was radically different in shape from what had preceded it. But first it is necessary to say something about the national machinery for change.

NOTES

1   The *National Health Service Reorganisation Act, 1973*, redefined the duties of the Secretary of State to cover the transfer of community services from local authorities, as well as transitional aspects of the reorganisation. The permanent changes were incorporated into the *National Health Service Act, 1977*, which consolidated legislation relating to the service. Both Acts refer to Wales (under the Secretary of State for Wales) as well as England. Detailed provisions for regions, areas, etc., were made in orders and regulations under the Acts.

2   *Report of the Committee on Local Authority and Allied Personal Social Services* (Seebohm), HMSO, Cmnd. 3703, 1968.

3   *National Health Service Reorganisation: England*, HMSO, Cmnd. 5055, 1972.

4 Ministry of Health, *The Administrative Structure of the Medical and Related Services in England and Wales*, HMSO, 1968.

5 DHSS, *The Future Structure of the National Health Service*, HMSO, 1970.

6 The ideas in the second Green Paper (note 5) were developed by Richard Crossman during the period covered by the third volume of his *Diaries of a Cabinet Minister* (Hamish Hamilton and Cape, London, 1977). The *Diaries*, which are well-indexed, contain fascinating glimpses of their gestation as Crossman tried to reconcile the needs of the NHS with his own dislike of regional authorities and appointed (as distinct from elected) bodies.

7 DHSS, *Democracy in the National Health Service: Membership of Health Authorities*, HMSO, 1974.

8 Medical Services Review Committee, *A Review of the Medical Services in Great Britain* (Porritt), Social Assay, London, 1962.

9 *House of Commons Debates*, 1 July 1971.

10 King Edward's Hospital Fund for London, *The Shape of Hospital Management in 1980?*, King's Fund, 1967. But compare the emphasis on multi-disciplinary teams in the paper by M. Naylor and A. Willcocks in G. McLachlan (ed.), *Challenges for Change*, Oxford University Press for Nuffield Provincial Hospitals Trust, London, 1971. Naylor was an experienced health administrator who subsequently became a member of the management study group.

11 *Op. cit.* (note 4), paras 65–8.

12 *Op. cit.* (note 5), paras 70–4.

13 DHSS *Management Arrangements in the Reorganised National Health Service*, HMSO, 1972, paras 1.22–1.27 and 2.39–2.96. The only departure from these proposals has been in a number of districts or single-district areas serving two centres of population, which have four clinical members (two from each centre).

14 *Ibid.*, paras 3.3–3.14. See also *Guide to NHS Planning*, DHSS, 1975, which introduced the difference between strategic and operational planning.

15 *Regional Chairmen's Enquiry into the Working of the DHSS in Relation to Regional Health Authorities*, DHSS, 1976.

16 DHSS, *Sharing Resources for Health in England*, HMSO, 1976. See also ch. 8, note 11, below.

17 *Op. cit.* (note 5), para. 6.

18 *Ibid.*, para. 60.

19 *Ibid.*, para. 1(ii).

20 *Ibid.*, para. 79.

CHAPTER 3

The Machinery of Change

For some of the changes, the ground had been well prepared in the debates on successive sets of proposals. Even before the first Green Paper, for example, the Welsh branch of the British Medical Association had started to consider the possible shape of integrated health areas. The Nuffield Provincial Hospitals Trust commissioned papers on various aspects of the change.[1] There was no end of speculation, proposals and counter-proposals in the journals of the health professions. But official action started in earnest in 1971 when working parties were appointed to study detailed arrangements for management in the new structure and for collaboration between the NHS and local government. Most of the matters listed at the end of the last chapter had been settled by, or soon after, reorganisation day on 1 April 1974. But some took much longer, and a few questions were still unresolved three years later.

By that time, as already noted, some of the original ideas had been modified by the Labour government which took office in 1974. These arose partly from ideological differences, but more often as a result of financial and economic problems. In May 1976 a Royal Commission was set up

> to consider in the interests both of the patients and of those who work in the National Health Service the best use and management of the financial and manpower resources of the National Health Service.

One of the Commission's sub-committees was concerned with management and finance; others covered manpower, the quality of service and services to patients. It seems probable that the Commission will recommend further changes. But these are beyond the scope of this book.

THE REORGANISATION ACT

In England and Wales, the NHS reorganisation depended on changes in the structure of local government. The Reorganisation Bill could not therefore be presented to Parliament until the Local Government Act, 1972, had been passed. Most Bills start their course in the House of Commons, but this one was taken first in the Lords to help to balance the timetable of the two Houses. The Bill was presented in November 1972, only three months after the White Paper. The principal debate in the Lords was in December and in the Commons in February 1973. Thereafter, progress was delayed because the Houses did not agree on certain amendments: the Bill was in fact considered twice by the Commons and three times by the Lords. Eventually it received Royal Assent on 5 July 1973. By a nice touch, this was exactly twenty-five years after the original National Health Service Act came into effect in 1948. (In fact, this date had little practical significance, since the Act did not come into effect until 1 April 1974 and administrative preparations had already been under way for some time; but some formal steps like the appointment of members to the new authorities could not be taken without statutory cover.)

It is interesting to compare the Act with the original Bill. There were manny amendments, mostly of a minor drafting character. But some were quite significant. For example, the Bill provided for community health councils to be appointed by area health authorities; this caused much discussion, and amendments were passed which transferred the responsibility to the regional authority, specified the sources from which members were to be drawn, and ruled out overlapping membership of a CHC and a health authority. Other changes clearly reflect pressure from various interest groups. Trade unions, nurses, dentists and opticians were included among the groups that had to be consulted about health authority membership. It was made almost impossible for a health authority to involve itself in the administration of family practitioner services. The provisions about professional advisory committees were tightened up by placing a duty on health authorities to consult them and transferring the duty to recognise them from the authorities to the Secretary of State. The power of the Health Service Commissioner to investigate complaints was slightly increased. Numerous obligations to consult staff associations (e.g. about transfer schemes) were introduced, and an entirely new section was included to allow officers over fifty to retire early on generous terms under conditions to be prescribed by the Secretary of State. Finally, a section dealing with family planning was amended so that charges for the supply of contraceptives, if levied at all, would be in line with those for medical prescriptions.

This clause, of course, had nothing to do with reorganisation and had been tacked on to the Bill as a matter of convenience. But it aroused controversy between the Opposition, which wanted the supply to be free (as it in fact became after the change of government in 1974), and those who were opposed to the whole idea of family planning within the NHS. Differences between the Lords and the Commons on this issue were the main cause of delays in the passage of the Bill. The debates also gave the Opposition the chance to state their view that the proposed new structure was excessively managerial, over-centralised and undemocratic. It would take another book to elucidate the meanings attached to these terms and relate them to what the opposing parties in fact did while in office: the last chapter has tried to show how narrow the gap was, even on the focal question of the composition of health authorities.

THE MANAGEMENT STUDY

Accusations of managerialism could more fairly be laid against the group which advised on management arrangements within the new authorities (the 'Grey Book').[2] Some such review was probably inevitable; a similar working party had been set up to advise on management arrangements in the reorganised local authorities.[3] But its precise form seems to have been influenced by advice from the businessmen recruited by the 1970 Conservative government to introduce the principles of management efficiency into the public sector.

The study group proper consisted mainly of civil servants, plus a medical officer of health, a senior nurse, administrators from different parts of the health service and a business manager. The group was assisted by the management consultancy firm of McKinsey and Co., which carried out many commissions in the public sector during the managerialist vogue of the late 1960s, and by a team from Brunel University. The study group worked under the general direction of a much more political steering committee. This consisted of twelve civil servants (including two medical officers, a dental officer and a nursing officer) and twenty-two non-departmental members (including seven doctors, five health administrators, four nurses, two management experts, a dentist, and a pharmacist).

The study group was 'required to take account of the present arrangements for the administration of the individual parts of the NHS and of current developments in the organisation of the work of the medical nursing and other relevant professions' as well as of Government decisions already taken about the NHS structure and of other relevant studies. It was influenced from three other sources:

(a) The Health Services Organisation Research Unit at Brunel. This unit practised a technique called 'social analysis',[4] which entailed the clarification of role-structures through discussion with those who participated in them. Studies in a number of hospitals had suggested that the relationship between, say, a group secretary and a chief nursing officer was not hierarchical but involved 'monitoring' and 'coordinating' relationships. (Proponents of another school of analysis would say that they reflected a 'negotiated order' where the realities of power contradicted a formal structure which was itself ambiguous.[5]) The concepts of consensus management, monitoring relationships between one level of officials and another, and the fuzziness of the administrator's role in the present NHS structure all owe much to the concepts generated by this team and adopted with some enthusiasm by professional interest groups who were anxious to thwart an accountability system which might threaten their own autonomy.

(b) The McKinsey team had a philosophy of streamlining management structures, while at the same time strengthening the role of top management, by simultaneously restricting their interventions to key issues and increasing their capacity to deal with them. For example, the structure they recommended for the administration of city services in Hull involved a reduction in the number of committees and an increase in the number of policy-making officials—a recipe which was roundly denounced as undemocratic and abandoned after a change in political leadership.[6]

Their main contributions to the NHS structure seem to have lain in the planning system (which in essence involves the concentration of control on a few key strategic indicators) and the restricted policy role accorded to authority members, on the 'board of directors' analogy. As well as advising on the management role and structure of regional and area health authorities, McKinseys were involved in restructuring the DHSS.

(c) The third influence was the steering committee, whose members were understandably less concerned with rational structures than with the implications of reorganisation for the status and autonomy of their own professions. For example, the 'leap to status' which the new structure entailed for nurses can be explained only in terms of alliances between nursing and medical representatives on the steering committee. It is significant that, after consultation with the professions concerned, the Secretary of State felt able to accept nearly all the recommendations of the management study.

Nevertheless, the study group went about its business in a reasonably systematic way. At an early stage, it formulated a set of 'tentative hypotheses', which were tried out in seven of the proposed new areas with widely varying characteristics. The lessons from these trials were fed into the group's final recommendations. By and large, these have been adopted.[7] Their practical implications have been explained in chapter 2.

THE COLLABORATION WORKING PARTY

In the summer of 1971, at the same time as the management study group, a working party was set up to examine the arrangements for collaboration between the new health authorities and local government. This was a very large working party: its forty-seven members included eighteen civil servants (four medical), eighteen representatives of local government (including five medical officers and a chief nursing officer) and eleven of the NHS (of whom six were doctors). The working party remained in being during and after the passage of the Reorganisation Bill, and produced three reports[8] as well as spawning a fresh working party on collaboration in the field of social work.[9] Most of the work was done in six sub-committees and four specialist groups with an additional coordinating committee. But the full working party did not accept all the sub-committee recommendations.

The working party reports are interesting not just because of what they recommend but because of what they reveal about clashes of interest between different groups. (On this point the management report was silent, containing only one short paragraph which recognised that not every member was in agreement with every recommendation.) It is clear that the local government members were determined to resist any central government interference in their affairs, while the NHS members (particularly the doctors) were worried that collaboration would be one-sided unless the health authorities had some leverage. For example, the doctors argued unsuccessfully that health authorities should pay for any social work support that they needed, and should in return be reimbursed with the cost of medical and nursing services which they provided for the local authorities. The local government people, quite rightly, saw this as an attempt to influence the selection of priorities within local authority departments. The final decision on that issue was that each authority should carry the costs of any services which it was bound to provide for another by statute, but that additional services should be subject to reimbursement.

The recommendations of the working party (which were all endorsed by the Secretary of State) do in fact look rather one-sided. It was agreed, for example, that overlapping membership was a good thing; but whereas local authority representation on area health authorities was to be statutory, a statutory provision for the cooption of health authority representatives to the relevant local authority committees was held to be inappropriate. Similarly, the Secretary of State was recommended to use his powers of direction over a health authority that failed to provide a local authority with the services it needed; but this was thought unnecessary in the reverse case. In short, the local government representatives played a good hand. But it should be remembered that area health authorities and their local authority counterparts are not equal partners. The health authorities are agents of the Secretary of State in a way that the local authorities are not. In a sense, the real negotiating partners were the Secretary of State, as head of the NHS, and the local authorities as responsible providers of related services.

The main recommendations, which were announced early and incorporated in the NHS Reorganisation Bill, were that health and local authorities should have a duty to collaborate, through statutory joint consultative committees, and that they should have the duty to provide each other with professional medical, nursing and social work services. It was agreed that in general one consultative committee, with appropriate officer support, would be sufficient except in the shire counties, where housing and environmental health were administered at a different level from social services and education; here it was thought that one committee would be needed for consultation between the area health authority and the county council and another for consultation with the district councils. More complicated arrangements were made for London, where one health area was to cover several London boroughs and would impinge on the work of the Greater London Council and the Inner London Education Authority.

As well as these major questions, the working party dealt with two other types of problem. First, the NHS reorganisation upset a number of existing arrangements within local authorities, such as the role of medical officers in examining children suffering from handicaps which required special educational treatment; the working party had to consider how such arrangements would be maintained in the new structure. Second, there was a need to identify fields in which collaboration would be beneficial. The specialist groups put a good deal of work into the second question, and made a

number of detailed suggestions about the advantages of pooling information, transport, accommodation and catering services. Altogether, over
eighty recommendations were made. The working party on social work
went into a similar amount of detail, suggesting for example that each joint
consultative committee should have a social work sub-committee and that
the attachment of social workers to groups of general practitioners should
be a high priority. But once the main questions had been settled, the
exercise ceased to command much interest and it is likely that the more
detailed suggestions (which the Secretary of State merely commended in
general terms) were not given a great deal of attention at a time when there
were many other things to do.

JOINT LIAISON COMMITTEES

To prepare the way for the appointed day, the expiring authorities in each
of the new areas were invited to nominate two officers each to joint liaison
committees. The machinery was very simple. A regional officer of the
Department of Health and Social Security called the nominees together at a
meeting where he explained the purpose of the committee and invited
nominations for the chairman and secretary. He then left the chair,
although continuing to offer assistance. The subsequent work of the
committee depended very much on the initiatives of its chairman and
secretary.

The task of the JLCs was, first, to collect information about the existing
services that were to be merged (the 'area profile'), second, to prepare staff
for the change and, third, to give preliminary consideration to matters
which would have to be decided by the new authorities in due course,
including headquarter premises, the districts (if any) into which the area
should be divided, and arrangements for the actual changeover. These
broad tasks were considerably refined and modified by the DHSS as time
went on. In addition to the area committees, JLCs were appointed for each
region; these normally consisted of two or three representatives from each
area JLC within the region plus two from the regional hospital board.

The JLCs differed considerably in vigour. Some set up a complex pattern
of working parties and produced voluminous reports detailing how the new
integrated service should work. Many issued newsletters. Others failed to
produce a satisfactory area profile. The complexity of the task facing them
also varied a good deal. At one extreme, the Isle of Wight retained its status
as a separate county; the main problem was how to bring under the

successor authority the staff and resources then administered by a single hospital management committee, the county health authority and the executive council. At first, the JLC would have consisted only of six people. Somewhat more complicated was the Newcastle area JLC (originally ten members), which had to deal with services run by two local authorities (Newcastle and Northumberland) and the matching executive councils, as well as the Newcastle University Hospital Management Committee. Near the other extreme was Humberside (originally thirty-eight members), which had to make some sense of a pattern of services run by eight hospital management committees, six local authorities and five executive councils.

The JLCs were in a position to exercise a good deal of influence on the new authorities, which would not have time to do much homework before the appointed day. But legally they were networks without power or status: the DHSS had to warn them on several occasions against preempting decisions which properly belonged to the new authority. Similar networks were established to prepare for the reorganisation of local government, also in April 1974; but in general, the local government officer committees worked under the umbrella of councillor committees whose members were in a better position to commit their successors. The possibility of setting up member committees in the NHS was raised but not pursued. Technically, of course, the JLC members merely represented their own authorities and could have reported back for instructions. In practice, this probably did not happen much, if at all. The operative instructions came from the DHSS. Except on the question of district boundaries, whose political importance was not recognised at the time, it is, however, fair to comment that the matters handled by the JLC machinery were generally of a technical or managerial nature which would in any case have been left to officers.

These important preparatory tasks, therefore, were undertaken by a largely self-appointed group of senior officers in each area and region. They had power to coopt others, both to working parties and to the main JLC. The Newcastle JLC, for example, enlarged itself by coopting two hospital consultants, two general practitioners and the two principal nursing officers—one hospital and the other local authority. Later, the DHSS instructed all JLCs to coopt members from these categories if they had not already done so. Most participants in the JLC machinery were eligible for an addition to their salary to compensate for the additional work involved. Furthermore, a small amount of money was made available to the most relevant expiring authority to cover incidental costs. This had to come out of the £17 million which was allowed for the reorganisation—other items being the cost of the NHS Staff Commission (see later), senior staff training, and maintaining the old and new authorities for a period in parallel.

SHADOW APPOINTMENTS

Well before the Reorganisation Bill reached the statute book in July 1973, consultations had been set in train with interested bodies about possible members of regional and area health authorities. But nothing could be done formally about making appointments to bodies that did not officially exist. Moreover, the local authorities could not take up their quota of AHA places until elections for the reconstituted councils had been held in April 1973 and the new bodies had met in shadow form.

Immediately after the Royal Assent, the Secretary of State made Orders defining the boundaries of the regions and areas and the size of the relevant authorities. The appointment of RHA chairmen was announced soon after. They had to be consulted about the selection of AHA chairmen as well as the allocation of other seats on the regional authorities. In turn, the views of area chairmen were taken into account before the RHA finally decided whom to appoint to the AHA places under its control. Local authorities and universities with medical schools also had to make their nominations. Most of this was accomplished with great speed, thanks to the preparatory work already done, and the new authorities were generally able to meet in shadow form in September or October. At that time there were still many gaps, either because bodies had not made their nominations—it was obviously difficult for medical schools to find members for half a dozen or more area authorities during the long vacation—or in some cases because there was a doubt about eligibility. Members of management teams were ineligible for appointment as authority members. This raised a difficulty in the case of nurses, since the obvious nurse member was often an equally obvious candidate for a senior nursing post in the new structure. Although in some cases the difficulty was resolved by appointing a nurse from another area, or by making an interim appointment, the nursing vacancy was often held in abeyance until area and district nursing officers had been appointed.

The shadow authorities inherited the material prepared by the joint liaison committees and had to settle down to prepare themselves for the takeover. At this stage they had no staff, although the JLCs arranged for some clerical support and somewhere for them to meet. The DHSS supplied a formidable list of things to be done during the six-month shadow period. Prominent among them was the appointment of officers. In this they were both aided and constrained by the work of the Staff Commission. The Commission exercised tight control over the arrangements for filling the most senior posts, and its advice had to be followed in making appointments to intermediate ones. Below that, of course, came the great majority of NHS staff who would simply be transferred from the old authorities to the new ones without any change or break in their duties or conditions of service.

The first round of appointments at area and regional levels was in the autumn of 1973. Progressively, 'shadow' chief officers were able to take over the burden of preparation from the JLCs and from the authority members.

NHS STAFF COMMISSION[10]

The 1970 Green Paper had pointed out that reorganisation would involve considerable redeployment of staff.

> This must be effected as smoothly as possible, with full consideration of the interests and circumstances of staff who may be called upon to move. A national staff commission or similar machinery will need to be established at an early stage in consultation with representatives of the staff to undertake this work.[11]

The change of government did not affect that commitment. Provision was made in the Reorganisation Act for the appointment of a National Health Service Staff Commission to keep under review the arrangements for recruiting and transferring staff to the new bodies and to advise the Secretary of State on any steps required to safeguard their interests. Although the Commission could not be established until the Act had become law, which was far too late to be any use, the Secretary of State promised in November 1971 to set it up, in shadow form, as an advisory committee. The committee started work early in 1972.

By that time the National Staff Committee for hospital administrative and clerical staff and the National Nursing Staff Committee had gained experience in assessing manpower needs and in assisting health authorities with their selection and promotion procedures. The new committee built on that experience and the secretary of the National Staff Committee became its secretary. The committee itself consisted of five members under the chairmanship of Sir Richard Hayward (an experienced negotiator on the staff side of the civil service Whitley Council). NHS staff organisations were not directly represented on it, although one of the members, a former HMC chairman, was a prominent trade unionist. Two members—a former town clerk and a manager from ICI—had no direct link with the service. The remaining member had experience of all three branches of the service.

The first year was spent largely in identifying problems, in consultation with health authorities and organisations representing staff interests. One of the first to be tackled was that of redundant senior officers. Since the number of separate authorities was being reduced there would also be fewer top posts. When the London boroughs were reorganised in 1965, chief officers were allowed to retain their status in the new authorities, so that Camden, for example, had groups of three 'associate chief officers' for a time.[12] Both the NHS advisory committee and its counterpart in local government agreed that it would be more efficient to allow officers who were not needed in the new structure to retire early. Provision for this was accordingly made in the Reorganisation Bill (which already contained guarantees that no transferred officer would be worse off as a result of the reorganisation and that compensation would be paid to any who became redundant).

The next task of the committee was to ensure that posts were filled on a basis which was seen as fair both by the staff themselves and by their new employing authorities. The initial field of competition for each post was restricted to officers already working in services which would be affected by the reorganisation; some posts were open to all NHS officers in England and Wales (excluding the London postgraduate hospitals, which were not being reorganised), some to those in England only, while less senior posts were open only to officers employed within the region or area. To avoid the chaotic situation in social services departments a few years earlier, when aspiring directors of the new departments played musical chairs with the appointing authorities, the committee decided to control the first round of 'all-England' appointments itself. National advertisements invited eligible officers to apply for up to ten posts, of which five could be at region and five at area level. A panel of assessors then went through the applications and took up references, rejecting candidates whom they considered unsuitable and drawing up short-lists for each post from the remainder. The panel fixed specific dates for interviews, to commence as soon as the new authorities were in a position to nominate selection committees, on a programme which enabled candidates to be considered for each post for which they were short-listed. The panel also appointed an assessor to advise each selection committee. By the end of May 1974, the panels had processed over 17,000 applications for 766 posts. After the interviews, selection committees placed candidates in an order of preference; but the final allocation was made by the committee itself (now a statutory Commission) after taking account of the candidates' own preferences as between different posts. This could not be done, of course, until the full round of interviews had been completed.

Less senior posts were filled on an intra-area or intra-regional basis by regional appointments units employing similar methods. Their work was assisted by field officers whom the advisory committee had appointed to groups of regions to deal with queries from staff and employing authorities. The Commission also issued circulars and an information bulletin which was intended to keep all NHS staff informed about its work.

The influence of the staff committee/Commission extended far beyond the actual selection procedure. As early as December 1972, on its advice, the DHSS instructed hospital authorities and advised local health authorities not to fill any senior posts which fell vacant after that month without consulting the joint liaison committee and obtaining DHSS permission. Until it was wound up in July 1975, the Commission was still operating restrictions on authorities that wished to advertise posts which could not be filled from within the service; this was made so difficult that there was virtually a ban on outside recruitment to senior posts from the beginning of 1973 to the end of 1974.

One group of posts, however, was withdrawn from the control of the Commission. As Secretary of State, Mrs Barbara Castle was determined that community health councils should have a free choice in the appointment of their secretaries. Accordingly, the Commission was informed that no restrictions should be placed on the field of recruitment.

COMMUNITY HEALTH COUNCILS

The new regional health authorities were asked in January 1974 to set up community health councils in each health district. It will be recalled that CHC members were to be drawn from three sources: nominees of local authorities; nominees of voluntary organisations; and nominees of the RHA. The size of each CHC was left to be determined locally, as were the arrangements for allocating places within the quota for each category. Even the local authority side of this was not always straightforward, since health districts did not necessarily bear much relationship to local government boundaries, and several local authorities might therefore have to agree on a formula for distributing seats. The voluntary organisations, however, presented the main difficulty, since their numbers, strength and involvement in the NHS varied from district to district.

The RHAs approached the problem in different ways. Lists of voluntary organisations were obtained from the most relevant local authority. It was then necessary to decide which organisations should be invited to make nominations, and how the places should be allocated. In some regions, the 'approved' organisations were invited to a meeting where a formula for allocation could be thrashed out. Sometimes the local council of social service was invited to arrange elections. In other cases, the RHA simply seems to have decided on its own formula and asked the favoured organisations to nominate representatives. A study of the initial appointments found that the composition of CHCs varied widely from region to region, although they did tend to reflect regional characteristics.[13]

The intention was to have CHCs functioning by April 1974. This turned out to be impossible. One region did not complete its CHC structure until June 1975. But most CHCs were in being by the autumn of 1974. Until secretaries and supporting staff could be appointed, they were assisted in most cases by officers from the relevant district headquarters.

The Secretary of State appointed two advisers (Lady Marre and Councillor Ken Collis) to observe and advise on the work of CHCs in their early stages. Among their recommendations was that a national association of CHCs should be established, as provided for in an amendment to the Reorganisation Bill, if the CHCs themselves wanted one. Until this could be ascertained, the King's Fund Centre in London (itself a voluntary organisation devoted to health matters), financed a steering committee and a newsletter. A national association of CHCs was finally instituted in July 1977.

TRAINING

There was a massive investment in training in the years 1972–4. Nationally, the DHSS made arrangements with half a dozen universities to provide two- to four-week courses for senior officers and clinicians who were likely to be involved in the process of reorganisation. These were 'multidisciplinary': membership was controlled so that officers and staff from different professions and different branches of the NHS could meet and discuss common problems. The course syllabus varied, but generally included sessions on problems facing the NHS, the contribution that reorganisation was expected to make to their solution, and some introduction to management theories that were likely to be relevant in implementing the change. Over 1500 senior officers attended these courses. The Department also sponsored short seminars, usually residential, to give clinicians a chance to learn and discuss the changes that were in the offing. Later, introductory seminars were arranged for members of health authorities, community health councils, and CHC secretaries. These official arrangements were often supplemented by local initiative. Joint liaison committees were responsible for training within their areas and districts. This was a period of great uncertainty about new roles and relationships and those who were most closely involved sought opportunities to meet and talk things out.

In addition to formal training courses, new information channels were opened to keep staff informed. The DHSS issued *NHS Reorganisation News*. The Staff Commission issued its own circulars and bulletin. So did many of the joint liaison committees. Official DHSS circulars were also widely read.

These were all broad-brush arrangements. One group of staff had very specific training needs. After 1974, there would no longer be a place for the local authority medical officer of health (although arrangements had to be made to carry out some of the functions of that office). There would, however, be a need for medical administrators at every level in the reorganised NHS and it seemed inevitable that most would be found among displaced officers. A working party on medical administrators reported in 1972.[14] It coined the phrase 'specialists in community medicine' to describe those doctors who would be concerned with assessing the need for health services, evaluating the effectiveness of existing services, planning the best use of health resources and promoting the functional integration of health care. Although at least one reviewer saw the report as an attempt to find a job for displaced medical officers of health, it was noted that the skills and knowledge needed for the two jobs were substantially different.[15] A series of short conversion courses was mounted. These were intended to hold the fort until new entrants began to emerge from the more leisurely training arrangements worked out by the Faculty of Community Medicine of the Royal College of Physicians, which was founded only in 1972.[16]

DEPARTMENT OF HEALTH AND SOCIAL SECURITY

The late Frank Stacey tells us that in 1967 Mr Kenneth Robinson decided to set up a small high-powered planning team which remained in continuous existence until the Bill was passed in 1973 and gave all its time to planning the reorganisation.[17] This may explain the thread of continuity in style and even in content running through the series of Green and White Papers: apart from political differences on the composition of health authorities (and a good deal of rhetoric), each document can be seen largely as a development of the one before it, filling in the detail and incorporating the latest round of concessions to interest groups. As the reorganisation grew closer, of course, other sections of the Department gave increasing attention to aspects that concerned them, such as the personnel divisions' involvement in training and with the Staff Commission. In 1972 the Department was itself reorganised, with the assistance of McKinsey and Co, in order to deal more effectively with policy-making and with the supervision of regional health authorities.[18] (Although this was never fully implemented, the 1976 review team of RHA chairmen were emphatic that the result was an excess of civil servants producing unrealistic policy ideas.[19] In 1977 another, largely civil service, team was set up to review the management structure of the Department.)

The leading role of the Department, even on matters of detail, is illustrated by the series of health reorganisation circulars which began in June 1972 and ran to December 1974 (see Appendix A). Until the end of March 1974 the circulars were addressed to the expiring authorities, with copies to joint liaison committees. From September 1973 they were also directed at the new shadow authorities. Early in 1974, however, the reorganisation series began to be superseded by an interim series of permanent circulars: only four reorganisation circulars were issued after the appointed day. There was some initial confusion about the proper way of communicating with the new authorities and their many-headed teams; the various channels were not consolidated until the beginning of 1976.

In all, the DHSS issued eighty-seven reorganisation circulars. They fell into three main types. One was mainly informative. Thus, a circular announcing the passage of the NHS Reorganisation Act contained a restatement of its objectives and of the practical consequences that would follow. Similarly, a circular about the composition and appointment of the new authorities included several paragraphs about the qualities their members would be required to have and about the kind of role they would be expected to carry out. None of this was new to readers of the White Paper and the 'Grey Book'; but it was no doubt convenient to have the material set out in a form which could be given to authority members as they were appointed. More specific circulars in this group contained background information which was intended to guide or prepare the way for action. For example, the joint liaison committees (which initially had been given very broad terms of reference) were advised in December 1972 to defer consideration of certain issues until the DHSS had formulated advice. Another listed the tasks that would have to be completed by the end of March 1974. Another explained the lines on which the DHSS was exploring and testing concepts of the new planning and monitoring system.

A second category of circulars contained instructions, couched in various terms, e.g. to adopt certain population assumptions in preparing an area profile, to submit proposals for new management structures by a given date, to appoint selection committees in conformity with the Staff Commission's timetable, to establish staff consultative committees, to set up family practitioner committees and joint consultative committees, and a host besides. Some of this 'guidance' consisted of no more than gentle prodding. But some of it went into great detail. For example, in setting up a selection committee for the appointment of an area dental officer, authorities were required to appoint a committee of five, of whom the majority had to be dentists (one from the teaching hospital, one from hospital and one from contractor practice) and one of the others was to be nominated by the local authority.

The third group contained authorisations, for example to fill out parts of the management structure without waiting for full consideration of a management scheme.

It was noticeable that the circulars tended to become more detailed and more directive as the appointed day approached. Part of the reason, of course, is that the DHSS came under increasing pressure to restrict the freedom of area health authorities both to avoid extravagance in matters like administrative staffing and, from the staff associations, to protect the interests of their members.

Another feature of the series was the high proportion of background circulars which dealt with community services. Certainly, difficulties were likely to arise in this sector, which was being taken under national control for the first time. But the quantity of information went far beyond immediate requirements of this sort. The absence of similar briefing material about hospital services (e.g. policy on the welfare of children in hospital or the management of out-patient departments) suggests either that the authorities were considered to be in a better position to cope with hospital problems or (more likely) that the DHSS policy divisions were more active and more exhortation-minded on the community side.

SUMMARY AND COMMENT

The activities listed in this chapter are, of course, only the tip of the iceberg. Behind the various working parties and circulars—and even behind the passage of the Reorganisation Bill—were successive layers of consultation within and between professional groups and between them and central government. But even the machinery described here involved an immense amount of time and effort, concentrated into a limited amount of time.

With very few exceptions this had to come from people who already had full-time jobs. The activists in the joint liaison committees were carrying a double workload, punctuated by absences on training courses, until they secured posts in the new structure. Others then had to act up to keep the old authorities functioning after their seniors had left. The most crushing load of all was probably due to the procedures adopted by the Staff Commission, since assessors had to be found, mainly among existing senior staff, to sit in on many hundreds of interview panels.

It is difficult to see how public representatives could have contributed effectively to this process apart from the amendments made by MPs to the Reorganisation Bill. But it is in some ways remarkable that there was so little public involvement in shaping the details of a structure which was by now the subject of considerable political controversy. With civil servants from the DHSS holding the ring and offering guidance, the management arrangements grew out of compromises among professional interest groups, pressures exerted through the Staff Commission and local interpretations by senior officials on the joint liaison committees. Even the composition of the various working parties gave interested parties considerable scope for exerting influence, which was not mediated through political channels.

It is also notable that, under the British system of government, so much preparatory work could and indeed had to be done in advance of legislative approval.

How it worked out in one of the new health areas we shall see in Part II.

Page:

NOTES

1 G. McLachlan (ed.), *Challenges for Change*, Oxford University Press for Nuffield Provincial Hospitals Trust, London, 1971.
2 DHSS, *Management Arrangements in the Reorganised National Health Service*, HMSO, 1972.
3 Department of the Environment, *The New Local Authorities: Management and Structure* (Bains), HMSO, 1972.
4 R. W. Rowbottom, *Social Analysis*, Heinemann, London, 1977.
5 R. M. Cyert and J. G. March, *A Behavioral Theory of the Firm*, Prentice-Hall, Englewood Cliffs, New Jersey, 1963.
6 For examples, see R. Greenwood and J. D. Stewart, 'Corporate Planning and Management Organisation', *Local Government Studies*, Oct. 1972.
7 *Health Service Reorganisation Circular HRC (73)3*, DHSS, 1973.
8 DHSS, *Reports from the Working Party on Collaboration between the NHS and Local Government on its Activities:* (a) *to the End of 1972*, HMSO, 1973; (b) *from January to July 1973*, HMSO, 1973; (c) *from July 1973 to April 1974*, HMSO, 1974.
9 DHSS, *Social Work for the Health Service*, HMSO, 1974.
10 For a full account of the work of this body, see DHSS, *National Health Service Staff Commission Report (1972–5)*, HMSO, 1975.
11 DHSS, *The Future Structure of the National Health Service*, HMSO, 1970, para. 100.
12 E. Wistrich, *Local Government Reorganisation: the First Years of Camden*, London Borough of Camden, 1972.
13 R. Klein and J. Lewis, 'Community Health Councils: the Early Days', *Health and Social Services Journal*, London, 7 Dec. 1974, pp. 2824–5; also *The Politics of Community Representation; a Study of Community Health Councils*, Centre for Studies in Social Policy, London, 1976.
14 DHSS, *Report of the Working Party on Medical Administrators* (Hunter), HMSO, 1972.
15 M. Jeffreys, review in *Journal of Social Policy*, London, Jan. 1973, pp. 86–7.
16 R. M. Acheson, 'Basic and Continuing Education of Community Physicians', *Health Trends*, DHSS, 1975, pp. 53–7.
17 F. Stacey, *British Government 1965 1975: Years of Reform*, Oxford University Press, 1975, ch. 10.
18 *The DHSS in Relation to the Health and Personal Services*, review team report, DHSS, 1972. See also *Management Arrangements in the Reorganised NHS, op. cit.* (note 2), Appendix 2.
19 See ch. 2, note 15, above.

II
THE CASE-STUDY

CHAPTER 4

The Research Project

The four succeeding chapters are concerned with the actual process of implementing the changes associated with the 1974 reorganisation of the NHS. Most of the material is drawn from a field study in Humberside, one of the new health areas. The present chapter explains the aims of the study, the topics chosen for special examination, and the methods employed.

AIMS OF THE PROJECT

There were three main objectives for the research. The first was to clarify the mechanics of change: we wanted to observe, chart and analyse exactly what was involved in a major reorganisation and to study how far current theories about the implementation of change seemed relevant and helpful. The second objective was to illuminate the dynamics of national health service management by studying political and inter-professional roles and relationships as they affected the implementation of the new structure and adjustment to it. Third, we hoped to make some contribution to ongoing discussion about the merits of reorganisation, at least by identifying the costs and consequences of change in the selected area.

The last objective was clearly the most difficult to operationalise. Some consequences might take a long time to appear, and what seemed a cost to one group of participants might well be seen as a benefit by others. However, the project ran from September 1972 to September 1975, eighteen months before the official date of the change and a corresponding period after it. A three-year observation period seemed to offer a reasonable prospect of covering the main activities and attitude-changes associated with the reorganisation, including some of its unforeseen consequences and, at worst, a partial adjustment to new roles and patterns of working.

The research was not designed to test the assumption that administrative reorganisation would have a beneficial effect on the delivery of health care at the bedside and in the community. Such effects are notoriously difficult to measure and were in any case unlikely to become apparent within the time-span of the project. Although the quality of care delivered to the patient is of the first importance, and its improvement offered the ultimate justification for the whole exercise, our concern was with administrative structures, processes and personnel. In them, however, are to be found the enabling conditions from which improved and more rational patterns of patient care should eventually develop.

Reorganisation was intended to procure certain changes in the direction and operational priorities of the NHS, while safeguarding such principles as clinical autonomy and independent contractor status for general practitioners. Behind each structural change (ignoring later modifications for the moment) it is possible to detect a hypothesis. For instance:

(a) The careful separation of management, entrusted to regional and area authorities and their teams of officers, from consumer representation through community health councils, would avoid the sort of role-confusion that had bedevilled hospital management committees (and perhaps also local authority committees) and facilitate both better management and more effective representation.

(b) The overall responsibility of area health authorities for the quality of primary care services would ensure a more coherent approach to the organisation of these services without encroaching on the independent status of general practitioners, which was to be safeguarded by the autonomy of the family practitioner committees.

(c) The development of 'monitoring' techniques would permit maximum delegation downwards from one level of management to another without endangering the accountability upwards demanded by the overall responsibility of the Secretary of State.

(d) The statutory requirement to appoint joint consultative committees, and to make health and local government services (e.g. social workers) mutually available to meet the reasonable requirements of the parallel authority, was sufficient guarantee of effective collaboration in overlapping services.

(e) The inclusion of a district community physician in each management team would lead to a more critical assessment of the relevance of services to the needs of the population served.

(f) 'Consensus management' by teams of officers would integrate different viewpoints and satisfy the requirements of administrative coordination without overburdening the appointed authorities.

(g) The strengthening of professional advisory machinery, and the inclusion of elected clinicians in each district management team, would (1) provide authorities with a reliable measure of clinical opinion, (2) encourage clinicians to take a more synoptic view of clinical priorities and their relationship to the management of resources.

(h) The careful balancing of general practitioners and hospital medical staff throughout the advisory and management team system would further promote the development of a balanced and integrated clinical viewpoint.

(i) The planning system, and the associated consultative processes, would compel authorities to produce coherent strategies which were robust as well as sensitive to local needs and national priorities.

These issues will be taken up in the concluding chapters, and they are latent in the entire case-study. But, for reasons that will be explained shortly, it was not practicable to devise precise research instruments by which the hypotheses could be tested systematically.

AREAS FOR STUDY

It was clearly impossible to keep fully in touch with developments affecting some 13,000 staff, in a great variety of professional groups and in the employment of eighteen different authorities. We had to choose a limited number of issues, compact enough for a team of two full-time research workers to handle, which together would give a fairly representative picture of the change processes and their outcome.

After a number of exploratory discussions with senior officers in the existing health service eight topics were picked out. Four of these were general and four rather specific. The general ones were:

(a) *The new authority*. The role of the new seventeen-member area health authority was crucial to the new structure. It was the lowest level of authority (although not of management) and, in accordance with the new managerial philosophy, was expected to carry out a different role from any of the authorities it replaced, neither becoming involved in details of management nor reflecting consumer interests but setting policy guidelines for officers to follow, attending to the broad principles of good organisation, and reviewing performance. In relation to the services it controlled and to the bodies it replaced, the area authority was relatively small. It was clearly important to try and find out how members were selected for this new managerial role, who they were, what sort of experience they brought to their task, and how they set about it. We also studied, but in less depth, the roles of the family practitioner committee and community health councils.

(b) *The creation of a top management structure.* An area team of chief medical, nursing, administrative and finance officers had to be appointed to provide staff assistance for the area authority and to control services (e.g. personnel work, ambulances and the provision of services for local authorities) for which responsibility was located at area level. Outside the area team, important posts included those of chief ambulance officer, area personnel officer and administrator to the family practitioner committee. At district level also, permanent medical, nursing, administrative and finance officers had to be appointed and made accountable to the area authority both individually and, as members of the district teams, collectively for the management of services in their district.

Teamwork is hardly new in the health service; but some of the officers who were in the field for appointment had been accustomed to independent chief-officer status and might find it uncongenial to be formally relegated to membership of a team of equals. The district officers were being asked to carry very great responsibilities without the protection, support and backing of a parent committee at their level to take formal decisions. Again, it was important to study the process through which such officers were selected and prepared for their new responsibilities. A particular point of interest was the extent to which the new chief officers were found from within the Humberside area and from the hospital service which had always been 'big brother' in the tripartite structure. A related point was the acceptability of the appointments to staff farther down the line, some of whom lost status through the merging of small authorities.

(c) *Professional machinery* The adaptation of professional advisory machinery to the new structure, and to the new role of medical staff in health care management, was partly a matter of adjusting the constituencies and membership of existing bodies. But this, too, involved new roles and relationships: consultants and general practitioners had to join forces to form district medical committees, on which junior staff and public health doctors were also represented, and appoint representatives to sit with the four permanent officers on district management teams. The administrative load on some doctors was going to be very heavy, especially on management team members and on those who were nominated to represent their district on area and regional advisory committees. Professional participation carried (and was intended to carry) onerous duties and responsibilities as well as rights. We wanted to see how doctors, both in and out of the new machinery, reacted to the new situation.

(d) *Human relations.* Last among these general topics was the whole question of training, information and consultation with staff. The importance of maintaining morale is stressed in the literature of managerial change and was to receive corresponding emphasis in the documentation relating to health service reorganisation. Many safeguards for staff affected by the reorganisation were incorporated in the Reorganisation Act itself; others were to emerge during preparatory negotiations. Information about these and other aspects of reorganisation was communicated to staff through a variety of often competing media. A massive programme of training supplemented the written sources of information and, in addition, was intended to assist senior staff and authority members to appreciate the implications of their new roles. Participation in training schemes, both as members and as speakers, placed a heavy burden on senior officers who were also holding down responsible jobs, playing an active part in the interim liaison machinery, and acting as assessors for selection committees while themselves competing for posts with the new authorities. An estimate of the cost and effectiveness of this investment in training and information seemed likely to be important in any evaluation of the method of handling the change.

In addition to these general questions, we wished to examine the implications of reorganisation for some specific service areas. We finally selected ambulances, nursing services, geriatrics and orthopaedics.

(e) *Ambulance services.* Ambulances had previously been supplied by local county and county borough health authorities. In the new service, responsibility was to lie with area and (in the conurbations) regional authorities. In the case of Humberside, services run by six different local authorities, with different patterns of administration and often substantial differences in staff conditions of service, had to be fused together into a single service. Moreover, this had to be done quickly, since the old authorities would cease to exist on 1 April 1974; there was no possibility of maintaining the original pattern on an interim basis through agency arrangements, for there would not be any agents!

(f) *Nursing.* Community nursing services would also be affected by the abolition of the local health authorities by which they had been administered. Hospital nursing management would be affected, but to a lesser extent, by realignment of the former hospital groups with area and district boundaries. Both in local authorities and in hospital groups, a more hierarchical system of nursing management had recently been created by the appointment of chief nursing officers and intermediate managerial grades. The main points of interest were, therefore, the steps that would be taken to integrate these separate hierarchies and their implications for the allocation of nursing resources. The principles behind the reorganisation suggested that there would be some redeployment between hospital and community, to the latter's advantage. At the very least, the separate branches of the profession were going to lose some of their autonomy, and we expected this prospect to occasion some fear and anxiety.

(g) *Geriatrics.* The care of the growing numbers of aged persons was still a relatively neglected area of health provision. Not only was greater priority needed, but a more integrated pattern of care in which the (often substitutable) services offered by institutions, day centres and domiciliary care were coherently planned so that each could make its most effective contribution to a comprehensive and balanced system of care. There had, of course, been many successful schemes for joint working between hospital and community services; but they lacked the support of a unitary administrative structure. In spite of the exclusion from health service control of essential supporting services like residential homes, home helps and social services (collaboration with which was to be secured by the joint liaison machinery and joint participation in health planning teams), the wide responsibilities of the new health authorities offered some hope of constructing more sensitive patterns of provision, with a higher claim on available resources.

(h) *Orthopaedics.* This specialism offered a contrast to geriatrics. It is true that the post-hospital care and rehabilitation of orthopaedic patients presents many unsolved problems of coordination (e.g. the provision of continuing nursing advice and adaptations to houses). But we did not expect these to be priority questions for the new service; it was hard to see how reorganisation would help with some specific local problems. The specialty was selected mainly because we thought it would be slow to adapt to the new system and because, from the point of view of an orthopaedic consultant, reorganisation would be irrelevant or have mainly nuisance value.

A detailed brief was prepared for each topic. For example, the specification for the ambulance study was:

(i)   to produce a description of the organisation of ambulance services before and after the change;

(ii)   to produce a study of how arrangements developed for coordination on the ground (e.g. the location of 'cross-over' points to resolve problems between ambulance and other personnel);

(iii) to record the consequences which key ambulance personnel and some major users (including nurses, geriatricians and orthopaedists) expected to follow from the reform and their subsequent experience of it.

RESEARCH METHODS

Our choice lay among (a) the use of instruments to test a limited number of hypotheses specified in advance, (b) sustained observation of developments in the fields which we had singled out for special attention, (c) more directly participative observation. A word is needed about each.

A good example of a highly systematised approach to the study of organisational change can be found in the methods adopted by Greenwood and Hinings to study the 1974 reorganisation of local government.[1] Drawing on a range of organisational concepts such as specialisation, centralisation and formalisation, which had been developed over a substantial period by a team with which Hinings had been associated, they employed sophisticated instruments to plot the position of old and new local authorities on these parameters, as well as on readiness to innovate, interpersonal aggression and several others of the same sort. By distinguishing between authorities (like the Isle of Wight) which were not being altered and others which were either being expanded to take in bits of neighbouring authorities or (like Humberside) being fused into a completely new structure, the team hoped to isolate the effects of reorganisation from general management trends that were affecting local government at the same time.

In the health service, none of the existing authorities was being left unaltered (although admittedly the change was going to affect some parts of the existing service more than others). In the absence of a control group, a study on these lines would have been less fruitful. Moreover, our own research had to be confined to a single health area, in which there was not much room for internal variation.

It would still have been possible to take some of the implicit hypotheses underlying the reorganisation which were listed earlier in this chapter, construct an index to measure relevant changes in attitudes, and concentrate the research effort on these particular points while using a mixture of observation and judgement to decide how far the changes were in fact associated in the expected manner with the intervening structural variables. Gilbert Smith has constructed a research scheme along these lines to test the assumptions of the Seebohm Committee on personal social services.[2]

Our main reason for not structuring the main body of our work in this way was the belief that there would be a lapse of time before the effects of the new structure became fully apparent, and that the more subtle effects would be so obscured by transitional difficulties (adapting existing machinery, learning how to live with new formal systems and so forth) that they would be unlikely to reveal themselves within the period covered by the research.

Another source of hypotheses was unaffected to the same extent by these considerations. We could have drawn on established organisation theory and devised instruments to test, for example, the relevance in the health service setting of the hypothesis that resistance to change is minimised by the use of participative methods,[3] or the contrary hypothesis that change is always accompanied by a period of over-democratisation.[4] We discarded this possibility, partly because it seemed too limiting and partly because some of the theoretical material did not seem to fit the situation too well (a point discussed further in chapter 9) but also for more pressing reasons of time. By the time we started work, the first steps to set up transitional machinery had already been taken, and events on Humberside were moving very fast. It seemed important to get in and start recording events as they took place rather than spend several months clarifying our theory and sharpening our research instruments. While trying, therefore, not to lose sight of the wider considerations in the background we decided, perforce, that the systematic testing of preconceived hypotheses was not appropriate as a primary research technique. A strategy of sustained observation seemed more suitable in the circumstances. By rejecting more systematic methods of data-collection, we hoped to gain breadth at the expense of depth and (possibly spurious) precision.

In our case, sustained observation meant taking every opportunity of observing what was going on, recording what we saw, trying to identify the key issues as we went along and reserving analysis to later. We were aware of the pitfalls inherent in this procedure, notably the possibility that we might remain unaware of assumptions and expectations that were unconsciously guiding our selection of material and its interpretation; this is a well-known difficulty about field studies.[5] The compensating advantage is that the research can be adapted to take account of unexpected data. Another difficulty is that the observer may imagine that he is obtaining a representative picture from those aspects of the situation to which he has access (both intellectually and physically).

Our own data was drawn from four main sources. First, we identified over one hundred people, mostly at managerial level, who seemed likely because of their position in the NHS to be affected personally by the change. These were interviewed in the winter of 1972–3, about a year before integration day. The interviews were semi-structured, using an agreed set of headings (arrived at after pilot interviews outside the main study area) which concentrated on the respondents' place in the existing structure and on their feelings and expectations about the changes to come. The interviews were tape-recorded and the main points subsequently transferred to more structured summary sheets, which were themselves constructed by agreement among team members who had listened independently to the first tapes. Although necessarily selective, the summary sheets simplified the process of analysis later, and their employment was probably unavoidable. As a general rule, the summary was completed by a team member who had not conducted the original interview, although with the latter's agreement. Since members had different perspectives, this reduced the amount of subjectivity.

The results of this initial survey helped to clarify the main issues and from early 1974 we became much more selective about whom we asked what. For example, thirty medical staff were interviewed in March about advisory machinery and the impact of the reorganisation on them; the geriatricians and orthopaedists in this sample were interviewed again a year later. We obtained information about the immediate impact of the changeover in April 1974 from a dozen middle-managers whose position made them particularly vulnerable to disturbance. We also felt able to identify points on which we could usefully collect systematic material by questionnaires. A questionnaire was sent in March 1974 to members of four expiring authorities (not included in the original population) and repeated, with modification, for members of the area health authority and community health councils early in 1975. Similarly, questionnaires were issued in June 1974 to thirty-eight officers and clinicians holding key positions in the new structure, and in the autumn of the same year to over two hundred middle-management staff. Each questionnaire enquiry was followed by selective interviews and supplemented by informal contacts with senior staff concerned with particular issues. (The tape-recorder had by this time been discarded, but a note of any discussion, however informal, was made available to each member of the research team.)

While our data-collecting methods became more structured as the project went on and the need for comprehensive information on specific points (such as participation in training schemes and mutual role-expectations) became apparent, our overall strategy remained reactive in the sense that each phase in the research was determined in large part by what we had learned in the preceding one. The emphasis moved naturally from expectations and apprehensions to teething troubles and perceptions of the emergent structure. Gradually, profiles began to emerge which, after intensive discussion and further testing, formed the basis of the material in chapters 5 to 8.

The second source of data was attendance at meetings. Preparations for change on Humberside included the establishment of a joint liaison committee, consisting mainly of chief officers from the merging authorities. The committee spawned a large number of specialist working parties to examine the implications of reorganisation for particular services: one dealt with communications and information for staff. In addition, special conferences were called to identify key problems. We attended such meetings of the joint liaison committee itself and of its working parties as we considered relevant (e.g. those on ambulance services, nursing, health districts and accommodation), as well as meetings of an experimental child health care planning team.[6] This machinery was gradually disbanded as integration day drew closer and the shadow authority began to take over the reins and to appoint permanent officers. We kept in touch with developments by attending meetings of the authority itself, the family practitioner committee, community health councils, the joint consultative committee, the area team of officers, the nursing advisory committee, and special conferences that were held from time to time. We also saw minutes and agenda papers relating to meetings that we could not attend.

A third source was the flow of documents relating to the reorganisation. Many of these were generated locally by the joint liaison committee, its working parties and, later, the area health authority itself. In addition, there were documents emanating from the Department of Health and Social Security and the Staff Commission. We kept up with all of these in so far as they dealt with problems in which we had decided to take an interest.

Finally, members of the research team had been invited to play a part in the programme of training to prepare health service staff for integration. As individuals, we lectured to senior officers attending various national training centres and to newly-appointed members of community health councils. Collectively, we organised courses for middle-managers and seminars for senior clinicians within our own area; there were about 250 participants in the Humberside courses. These contacts provided opportunities for discussion and feedback on our developing picture of what was going on. Most of the courses were inter-professional, so that they enabled us to see how different occupational groups reacted to talks about reorganisation both from ourselves and from visiting senior health service officers. For teaching purposes, we administered a questionnaire on the first morning to most of those attending the management course; this gave us valuable material about the effectiveness of the channels established within the service to keep staff informed and to maintain their morale.[7]

Our participation in training courses did, of course, involve us to some extent as 'change-agents', which was close to the third possible research strategy, that of active participation in the events being observed. It would, in principle, have been possible to go beyond the training role and contribute more actively to the handling of the change as well as merely observing it. This had its attractions, if only from the point of view of access to data. As individuals we had a commitment, if not to the reorganisation itself, at least to seeing it implemented smoothly. Our surveys were bound to reveal some information about attitudes and rumours at lower levels that were not otherwise accessible to top managers. There were, therefore, strong temptations to place ourselves at the disposal of those who were responsible for implementing the change and to supply them with immediately useful information and advice. At one time, indeed, it seemed as if it would be useful to station one of the team in a participative role in the headquarters of the joint liaison committee. (This was not followed up, but because of time-pressure rather than research methodology.)

But there were also strong arguments against adopting a more active role. We were not trained in social consultancy methods; nor did we want to be restricted to the deep examination of a limited number of relationships that typically concerns social consultants. There were obvious objections to taking a stance that might lead us to be identified, at lower levels, with 'them'; and the fact that our funds came from an independent foundation implied a certain detachment. There were still more fundamental doubts about maintaining objectivity, and finding useful lessons for the future, if we became too deeply involved in helping management to solve its problems. Moreover, many of the matters that concerned management were inevitably short-term and we should have wasted a great deal of time trying to master the details of urgent problems of no lasting significance, to which our potential contribution would have been grossly outweighed by the detriment to our main job of observing and recording the means through which the managers themselves sought for (and generally found) solutions.

In practice, while rejecting an active participative role and avoiding the temptation to offer gratuitous advice on matters on which we had unavoidably reached a view, we could not wholly escape the obligation to supply information, not otherwise available, when it was specifically sought. Our periodic interim reports provided some feedback on the success of the arrangements being made, and were widely read by people at all levels in the service. One of us could not refrain from submitting evidence to the Secretary of State on her proposals to widen the membership of area health authorities.[8] We do not feel, however, that our interventions had more than a marginal effect on the development of events, at least on Humberside.

ASSESSMENT

What we have produced is a case-study based on three years of continuous observation, punctuated by nine separate programmes of data-gathering by questionnaire and interview. The results are open to the same objections as any case-study: the case may be atypical; local sensitivities inhibit full and frank publication; there is too much detail (or too little); the material is too selective in content or too restricted in time; the interpretation is subjective. There is some truth in each of these points. But it has been possible to round off the project material in two ways. First, by good fortune, contact with the health authority was maintained beyond the period covered by the main study, so that more can now be said about the 'latent hypotheses' than was possible in late 1975. Second, the Humberside material has been related wherever possible to the national picture, which also took some time to emerge. This suggests that, while Humberside has some unusual features, there is very little in the following chapters that will surprise anyone who has read evidence to the Royal Commission or the parliamentary committees which considered the national health service in 1976–7.[9]

Choice of topics. Of the four topics initially selected for exploration in depth, the four which were directly related to the reorganisation process proved apposite and manageable within the research framework. The new authority was complete by March 1974, and the main officer teams and professional structures were completed then or soon after. By mid-1974, too, the main thrust of the training and retraining programmes had been spent and it was possible to estimate their effectiveness. We were able to plot developments and study the slow emergence of a new organisation, which did not always conform to the role-structures prescribed in the 'Grey Book'. It was fairly easy to focus this part of the enquiry on three questions:

What did people expect to happen? What actually happened? What were people's reactions after the event? By 1975, however, new topics were emerging, notably the introduction of the planning system and new concepts in resource-management as well as the developing role of the community health councils. By following these up for a number of years it became possible to escape from 'nuts and bolts' and start to assess the viability of the concepts underlying the reorganisation.

It was therefore disappointing that there was little to report from the four special service areas—ambulances, nursing, geriatrics and orthopaedics. Apart from structural changes in ambulance and nursing management, very little happened within the time-span of the research. Ideally, we should have undertaken three complete surveys of operational effectiveness: one of each service as it was in the unreformed NHS; another shortly after reorganisation when the disruptive influences of the change might be at their height; a third some time later, when the service had settled down and the benefits of reorganisation (if any) had had time to appear. Even by restricting this part of our investigations, as we did, to two out of the four health districts on Humberside, this was too much for our collective resources.

On the nursing side we were helped by the generosity of the Hull 'A' Group Hospital Management Committee, which seconded a qualified nurse to the team, with the status of honorary research assistant, for six months. Mrs Stevens was able to review the pre-reorganisation pattern of coordination and attitudes among front-line nurses at ward-sister, district-nurse, midwife and health-visitor level in one district where four independent community nursing services were, until April 1974, cooperating in varying degrees with two separate hospital groups.[10] This is part of the study which could be repeated in some future year to see what changes have occurred at the operational level. In the other fields, we were obliged to rely on subjective impressions from key personnel (who are not necessarily aware of what is happening at the front line) supplemented by evidence from official working parties of senior officers, which it would be difficult to compare systematically with subsequent material collected in a before-and-after study.

Nevertheless, the failure of these services to develop along significantly new lines allows some generalisation about the relevance of administrative change unaccompanied by either additional resources or a reorientation of professional priorities. For this purpose, the chosen services were sufficiently representative. What was true of geriatrics seemed also to be true of psychiatry, while orthopaedics seemed for this purpose to be a weather vane for the other acute specialties.

Research methods. Here again, the research strategy seemed to be right. It was certainly fruitful. Our open-mindedness did lead into a number of blind alleys. We found ourselves over-reacting to whatever was most concerning our immediate contacts at the time: for example, there was much preoccupation in the early months of 1974 with the assimilation into common conditions of service of the fringe benefits enjoyed by many local authority staff. It was useful to note that such problems existed and could take up a great deal of valuable time; but it was not desirable for the researcher to become too immersed in the details. Our strategy did enable us to take account of factors that we would not have anticipated in a more structured approach. The salience of salaries and conditions of service, especially for staff transferring from local government, and their implications for staff attitudes to the new integrated service, was certainly one aspect of which we became fully aware only when we reviewed our findings halfway through the project. It is also true that we then became painfully aware of points that we had missed. One of these (which we were just in time to remedy) was a comparison between the work of the old committees and that of the new area authority and community health councils as seen by members. There were other points, like the relative importance and pervasiveness of different sources of anxiety among middle- and lower-grade staff (a key concept in the study of local government change by Long and Norton[11]) which, in retrospect, could have been investigated more systematically.

Access did not present a problem. Documents were made freely available both by the joint liaison committee and by the new bodies. Very few of the people whom we approached were reluctant to be interviewed, or showed a lack of frankness in answering a questionnaire (although one or two, understandably, reserved indiscretions until the tape-recorder had been switched off). We were freely admitted and made welcome at nearly all the meetings we sought to attend; and we were usually (not invariably) invited to attend important discussions that we should not otherwise have known about. On the whole, people were very ready to talk, either about their worries or because they felt they were making a contribution to the reorganisation which deserved independent recognition, and we were willing listeners. Many of these officers were in the field for senior appointments in the new service, and our research became more marginal to them after these posts had been filled. But the only real moments of tension came in early interviews when we realised that we were inviting views on details of the new structure with which some respondents were themselves unfamiliar.

This freedom of access did, however, cause some difficulties at publication stage and thereafter. Four interim reports were issued while the research was in progress. These were intended partly to monitor what was going on and enable mistakes to be corrected in time. It is doubtful if they did; but from our own point of view they provided a useful discipline, forcing us to concentrate on concrete issues and make sure we had a complete picture before moving on to something else. The first three reports were mainly factual. But the last attempted to draw the threads together and indicate the emerging strengths and weaknesses of the new structure (few of which were specific to Humberside). Although the report was drafted with great care—to an extent that many researchers would have had qualms about—and was discussed with influential participants at that stage, it was sensationalised in the press. It was even quoted, as an indictment of the Tory-inspired structure, in the House of Commons by the Secretary of State.[12] The press comment was undoubtedly damaging to the health authority and to our subsequent relationships with it.

Research in context. There is almost no way of winning the publication game. The research team that stays on the outside can publish what it likes; but its scope will be limited. The team that has access must obviously respect confidence, refrain from identifying individuals without their consent, take full account of any criticisms of draft material, and so on. But in the last resort, if individuals are concerned, there is an unhappy choice between suppressing evidence and risking hurt feelings. Organisational research is particularly difficult because of the demands it makes on the time and tolerance of those who are being studied, who must be uneasily aware that the final report could be a source of embarrassment. It can only be carried out in an atmosphere of trust, confidence and reciprocity.

The present research was possible because these conditions existed. In the pre-reorganisation period, the main participants were fairly sure of where they were going and were confident that the results of an independent investigation would not reflect discredit on them (as indeed it did not); but much of this confidence was eroded in the unhappy confusions and disappointed expectations that followed the reorganisation. As for reciprocity and trust, the research team was enormously helped by the pattern of relationships that had built up between the university and health service staff, particularly in Hull, over the years. Two of the team had worked with senior hospital officers on committees, sometimes in the context of specific projects to which the university was making a research contribution, and at management courses which the university had provided for hospital staff since 1968. In some parts of the service, therefore, the researchers were already known and their motives well-understood: they did not, for example, have to go to great lengths to establish confidence and to emphasise their respect for confidentiality. This reciprocity was maintained through the pre-integration courses which the research team offered in the run-up to reorganisation. In turn, experience gained in teaching the courses was relevant to the research. This combination of circumstances is not easily obtained.

Every research project, however, is itself an investment— in knowledge, in expertise and in goodwill. It provides the basic capital for further studies which, in an important applied field like the NHS, must involve the operating authorities as well as the academic community. The Humberside study has supplied a knowledge base for other research, notably on information requirements for decision-making at health area level and on the whole structure of decentralised administration in the reorganised NHS.

NOTES

1   C. R. Hinings, Royston Greenwood and Stewart Hanson, 'Contingency Theory and the Organisation of Local Government', *Public Administration,* London, Spring and Summer 1974.
2   Gilbert Smith, 'Research After Seebohm', *SSRC Newsletter No. 12,* Social Science Research Council, London, Nov. 1970.
3   L. Coch and J. P. R. French, 'Overcoming Resistance to Change', *Human Relations,* London, 1948, pp. 512-33.
4   C. Sofer, *The Organisation from Within,* Tavistock, London, 1961, pp. 161-2.
5   W. R. Scott, 'Field Methods in the Study of Organisations' in Amitai Etzioni (ed.), *A Sociological Reader on Complex Organisations,* Holt Rinehart, New York, 2nd ed., 1969.
6   B. Edwards, W. Ferguson and D. Jackson, 'Planning the Child Health Services', in G. McLachlan (ed.), *Bridging in Health,* Oxford University Press for Nuffield Provincial Hospitals Trust, 1975.
7   S. C. Haywood and S. Griffin, 'Informing Staff about Reorganisation', *Hospital and Health Service Journal,* London, April 1974, pp. 119-22.
8   R. G. S. Brown, 'Democracy in the NHS: an Open Letter to Mrs Castle', *Health and Social Service Journal,* London, 10 Aug. 1974, p. 1799.

9   *9th Report from the Public Accounts Committee for 1976–77* (HC 532); *9th Report from the Select Committee on Public Expenditure for 1976–77* (HC 466—V), 'Spending on the Health and Personal Social Services': both HMSO, 1977.

10 Marjorie Stevens, 'Integration of Nursing Services in Scunthorpe', University of Hull, 1974.

11 J. Long and A. Norton, *Setting up the New Authorities,* Charles Knight, London, 1972, pp. 85-97.

12 *House of Commons Debates,* 27 October 1975, col. 1043 (Mrs Barbara Castle), HMSO, 1975.

Chapter 5

The Structure: Humberside and its Districts

The next three chapters are concerned with the way Humberside's health services were amalgamated into a new four-district health area. This chapter deals with the preliminary work carried out by a joint liaison committee, with the establishment of new statutory bodies and with the division of the area into districts. Chapter 6 describes the development of new staffing structures and chapter 7 the creation of professional advisory machinery. First, however, it is necessary to say something about Humberside and its antecedents.

HUMBERSIDE

Until April 1974, Humberside had no legal existence. It was one of the new counties created by the Local Government Act, 1972. The county was formed out of two county boroughs, Hull on the north bank of the river Humber and Grimsby on the south, as well as most of the East Riding of Yorkshire and parts of the West Riding and North Lincolnshire (Lindsey).

Ten years earlier, the affinity of interest among the estuarial towns on both banks of the Humber had been considered sufficiently important to justify the south bank's inclusion in the Yorkshire and Humberside planning region. But the river had been regarded as a formidable barrier to administrative integration. In 1969, the Royal Commission on Local Government advised that separate authorities should be established for North and South Humberside. The Commission's main objective had been to create viable local government units linking towns with their surrounding countryside:

> The potential for industrial growth on both North and South Humberside led us also to consider whether these two areas should be combined into a

single unit for local government purposes. We decided however that . . . the river divides rather than unites North and South Humberside . . . we do not think a single authority for both banks would be feasible without a bridge. In our view the existence of a bridge would not, in itself, be a decisive consideration in favour of one authority for both banks, but after a bridge has been built the possibility of amalgamating the North and South Humberside units should in due course be looked at again.[1]

About the same time, the Royal Commission on Medical Education came to the conclusion that in the absence of a bridge the catchment area of the Hull hospitals was too small to support a medical school.[2]

The Labour government proposals of 1970 envisaged separate authorities.[3] So did the Conservative government proposals of February in the following year (which suggested that, subject to local agreement, the south bank should simply stay in Lincolnshire).[4] But the draft Local Government Bill, published in November 1971, specifically contemplated a new county of Humberside. Many changes were made in the Bill before it finally reached the statute book. But Humberside survived more or less as proposed.

No doubt a decisive factor was the firm decision to build a Humber bridge, then due to be opened in 1976. This bridge, which had been a dream for a century, came to reality in an odd way. Early in 1966, when the Labour government had a majority of one in the House of Commons, there was a by-election in a marginal Labour seat in North Hull. There was an intensive campaign, in the course of which the Minister of Transport promised that, subject to the necessary economic studies, 'You shall have your bridge'. The late Richard Crossman alleged in his diaries that Ministers decided to honour the promise for political reasons, even though traffic forecasts suggested that the bridge would not be viable for another decade.[5] The city of Hull and two small local authorities agreed to underwrite the bridge's finances (a decision which their successors came to regret) and work duly started. Although the new Humberside County Council adopted a sketch of the bridge as a motif for its notepaper, work was delayed and the bridge is unlikely to be open before Easter 1979 at the earliest, five years after the administrative reorganisation which largely depended on it. In the intervening period, Grimsby has been connected to the north bank only by a vintage and unreliable ferry service or by a circuitous road journey, and communication problems have seriously affected administrative functioning.

Locally, the main support for the proposed county came from the industrial towns of Goole, Grimsby, Hull and Scunthorpe. Cleethorpes and the county councils of the East Riding and of Lindsey were strongly opposed to it. On the north bank, relationships between Hull and the surrounding East Riding had for years been coloured by typical town-versus-country disputes centred on the city's need for additional housing land. Throughout 1971 and 1972 the county council fought a long and bitter campaign to maintain its separation. A referendum was held to demonstrate the degree of public opposition to amalgamation with Hull, and another to mobilise opinion against going into Humberside. One of the arguments which obtained a substantial measure of public support was that the East Riding had more natural affinity with York than with Hull, let alone Humberside. Even in the last stages of the passage of the Local Government Bill, the county council made a last-ditch attempt to form an amalgamation with York and most of the North Riding, leaving only a narrow coastal strip for Humberside. The main effect of this was probably to harden opinion in favour of the boundaries proposed by the government.

There were parallel moves on the south bank of the Humber. A plebiscite in Cleethorpes found a large majority in favour of staying in Lincolnshire. Lindsey County Council organised two separate polls within three weeks, as a result of which an amendment was in fact made to the Bill in order to allocate certain parishes in Caistor Rural District to Lincolnshire instead of to Humberside.

The new county council became responsible for personal social services, education and other major services. But it did not become an all-purpose authority as the Royal Commission had recommended. The county was divided into nine local authority districts, whose councils became responsible for housing and environmental health. The district boundaries were drawn up by a Boundaries Commission in a way that conformed as closely as possible to the wishes of the local people; these wishes were ascertained mainly by consulting the existing borough and district councils. It was not therefore surprising that the districts looked remarkably like their predecessors: Hull, Grimsby and Scunthorpe emerged as districts with their old boundaries intact; the twenty-one smaller boroughs and districts were reduced to six by amalgamations. The new structure is shown on the map on p. 93.

The Humberside concept remained unpopular with many groups on both banks of the river. The district councils provided focal points for dissatisfaction which began to escalate towards the end of 1977. First, the landslide Conservative victories in the county council elections of that year had removed the slender Labour majority in the original Humberside council, to the distress and alarm of the Labour-controlled municipalities. The Secretary of State for the Environment (Peter Shore) fuelled the fire by suggesting that education and personal social services might be restored to Hull and eight similar cities which had lost them to the new counties in 1974. Second, the district councils were forming views on government proposals for a regional tier of government, which provided an opportunity for attacking over-administration and the alleged remoteness of the county council (although it is fair to add that the overall view was that the new county should have a chance to prove itself).[6] Third, there was a popular campaign to rebel against administrative 'labelling' (aggravated by some official insensitivity about postal addresses) and restore old attachments to Yorkshire and Lincolnshire: a petition to have 'East Riding' recognised by the Post Office attracted over 100,000 signatures in the old county area. Some bodies, like the East Riding Division of the British Medical Association, have never changed. In spite of continued support for the Humberside idea from local radio and newspapers (both of which served the two banks) it did not seem to be increasing its hold on the constituent communities.

The area health service, which was based on the county, did not escape these tensions. But it is time to return to the main reorganisation period.

THE EXISTING PATTERN

The logic of change required that existing health services within the new county should be brought under a single administration. For the community health services, this involved staff and functions administered by the health committees of Hull, Grimsby and Scunthorpe local authorities,[7] the great bulk of the East Riding county health service[8] and those elements of the West Riding and Lindsey services which covered Goole and parts of the south bank. For family practitioner services the pattern was similar, since the executive councils covered county or county borough areas, except that Scunthorpe was administered from Lincoln as part of Lindsey. The hospital pattern was more complex.

Hospitals in Humberside were administered by eight different hospital management committees and two regional hospital boards. On the north bank there were three management committees (HMCs) for hospitals in and around Hull and the adjacent market town of Beverley. Their responsibilities still reflected the pattern inherited in 1948: one HMC was responsible for a group of general hospitals based on Hull Royal Infirmary;

another was based on the former Hull city mental hospital; a third administered both general and mental hospitals in the county area. By the early 1970s, these hospitals were coming to be regarded as part of a common pool. The doctors had established a joint medical staff committee. There was a common supplies organisation, and two of the three HMCs shared a finance officer. The regional hospital board had attempted, unsuccessfully, to amalgamate the management committees themselves. The three groups appeared to offer a natural starting base for an integrated service on the north bank. But hospitals in Bridlington, in the north-east of the county, were administered by a hospital management committee based on Scarborough, in the North Riding, which was to become part of North Yorkshire. At the opposite corner, those in Goole were administered from Pontefract, which was going into Wakefield. Two specialist hospitals within the western boundary were part of the York hospital group. All six HMCs, however, came under the Leeds regional hospital board.

In south Humberside, there were hospital clusters at Grimsby and Scunthorpe. Their management committees came under the Sheffield regional hospital board. But the Grimsby HMC served a wide area, not all of which would be coming into Humberside. Conversely, neither Grimsby nor Scunthorpe was self-sufficient, since both depended on mental hospital facilities in Lincoln.

In total, then, if we exclude the regional hospital boards, nineteen authorities were administering services which, by the logic of reorganisation on geographical lines, would have to be transferred to the new Humberside area health authority. Only in six cases (four HMCs and the two county borough ECs) were services being absorbed 'lock, stock and barrel'. In the others, some disentangling would be needed: even in the three local authority services which were being wholly absorbed, headquarters officers would not necessarily transfer to the NHS rather than to the new county or district councils. Moreover, there were considerable differences in traditions, standards and (in the case of local authority staff) conditions of service among the merging services.

JOINT LIAISON COMMITTEE

The Department of Health and Social Security asked the merging authorities to set up joint liaison committees in June 1972. At that time, the Local Government Bill was still subject to amendment in Parliament. The definitive White Paper on the NHS reorganisation was not ready until

August. The management study group did not report until September, and the partial acceptance of its recommendations was not announced until January 1973. The NHS Reorganisation Bill was not published until November and did not complete its stages until the summer of 1973. By that time, most of the work of the Humberside JLC had been completed.

In spite of these uncertainties, the DHSS was confident enough to announce that there probably would be a Humberside area health authority, that it would be included in 'Region 2' (later to be confidently named 'Yorkshire' without much regard to Lincolnshire susceptibilities) and that it was desirable for existing bodies to undertake 'as much preparatory work as possible, short of pre-empting decisions that can appropriately be taken only by the new authorities', which would be set up in shadow form by the late spring or summer of 1973.[9] The main mechanism for this preparatory work was to be a joint liaison committee of senior officers, reporting back to their own authorities as necessary. The JLC could set up working parties and coopt specialist officers as required.

The Humberside area JLC was inaugurated on 27 July 1972, when the Department's principal regional officer called a meeting of representatives of eighteen authorities (excluding one peripheral HMC which had been overlooked) with RHB representatives in attendance. The local authorities were generally represented by their medical officer of health and his chief administrative assistant; in one case the second representative was a director of nursing services, and the administrator came too, as an observer. Executive councils sent their clerks and (for this first meeting) a second administrator; two of the latter were later replaced by general practitioners who were EC or local medical committee chairman. HMCs were represented by their group secretary and either his deputy or a treasurer or in one case by the chairman of the medical executive committee. This initial composition did not change much. In March 1973, the JLC consisted of twenty-six non-medical health administrators, four medical officers of health, two consultants, two general practitioners and a community nursing administrator, all representing merging authorities. At that time, the DHSS requested that membership should be broadened to include representatives of medical and nursing interests. The JLC responded by coopting a chief hospital nursing officer and inviting organisations representing general practitioners and hospital consultants to nominate two members each, one from the north bank and one from the south.

At the first meeting, the medical officers of health for Hull and

Grimsby had been elected chairman and deputy. The group secretary of the main Hull HMC became secretary. The chairman and deputy chairman were appointed to the regional JLC, with a south-bank group secretary as a third, optional, representative. (The regional JLC consisted of members appointed by the regional hospital board and up to three nominees from each area JLC, two of whom had to reflect non-hospital interests; the chairman of the Yorkshire JLC was the medical officer of health of the West Riding.)

By the second meeting, in September, the chairman and secretary had coopted immediate colleagues from their own authorities to form a coordinating group of four. All were Hull-based. The chairman's co-member was an administrator who was active in the (now defunct) Association of Health Administrative Officers and editor of its quarterly bulletin. The fourth member of the team was a deputy group secretary who had research experience and was putting the finishing touches to a short book of his own on the forthcoming reorganisation.[10] This quadrumvirate kept in regular touch and accepted collective responsibility for the conduct of JLC business. By September they had assembled a set of maps, a summary of available background information about the area and detailed proposals for the creation of thirteen working parties with provisional membership and terms of reference. Two further working parties were established in October.

The DHSS circular setting up JLCs had envisaged the establishment of uni- and multi-professional working groups. Nine of the fifteen Humberside working parties were confined to members of one profession, such as finance officers, supplies officers, medical staff, nursing staff and ambulance officers. Inter-professional groups were set up to deal with questions like accommodation, computer services and the division of the area into districts. Like the JLC itself, the working parties were given a two-part brief, consisting of (a) principal tasks, largely connected with information-gathering, and (b) provisional tasks which 'are broader in nature and as they involve an element of future planning may be dependent on decisions made elsewhere'.[11] One of the objectives was to involve as many staff as possible in the preparations. The briefing document described the situation as 'unique . . . in the sense that never before in the history of social evolution had the staff in the field been presented with such an opportunity for guiding events. The fact that the JLC itself and in consequence the working parties had merely a persuasive influence does not diminish the value of the opportunity.' The working parties were free to coopt and to elaborate on their terms of reference as they thought fit. About 150 staff were directly involved in working parties.

Most of the working parties went about their work with great enthusiasm. Some, meeting weekly, had covered their principal tasks by the end of October and proceeded to draw up blueprints for their sector of the new service. When their reports were presented at the JLC meeting in February 1973, it was no surprise to find a preference for arrangements that would maximise the power, status and influence of the relevant professional group in the new structure. For example, the works officers drew up organisational charts in which there was no mention of the district administrator; they also recommended a planned maintenance scheme which would require an extra 115 staff. The ambulance officers put in their bid for a new central control unit; the social workers said that twenty-eight more staff were needed if they were to play their full part in the new service; and so on. The amount of paper produced was vast: the nurses' report ran to 177 pages, while the supplies officers produced a massive report in two volumes. Some of this, of course, was immediately relevant: the finance and supplies officers had to go into a great deal of detail to make sure that services did not break down on the appointed day because of some unforeseen contingency. But other reports, equally detailed, read more like five-year programmes for incoming chief officers with no financial worries. Even these, however, were treated as useful background documents by JLC members and working-party convenors who later became chief officers in the new authority.

The immediate problem was what to do with the material. Few of the reports were, or could be, adequately discussed by the full JLC, or presented as they stood to the new authority. Eventually it was decided to hold a special conference ('Operation Survival') in October 1973 where the chairman and secretary of each working party would be asked to identify the essential steps that would have to be taken to maintain continuity in the relevant services after 1 April 1974. The main outcome, so far as the new authority was concerned, was a six-page document listing about fifty points for action, mostly on matters of detail. A great deal of technical skill was in fact applied to compressing and digesting this and other JLC material into a manageable form for authority members.

Bearing in mind that all his work had to be done in officers' spare time, or at the expense of their existing jobs, one has to ask how valuable the exercise was. Much of the information about existing resources, methods of administration and varying conditions of service had to be gathered somehow, and the JLC working parties offered as good a method as any. There would not have been time for this in the hectic six months when the shadow authority was in existence, and there was a double bonus for participants who secured senior posts in the new structure. Equally important was the spadework which allowed rapid decisions to be taken later, for example on the location of pay points, the integration of family practitioner records and office accommodation. (The district question raises other issues and deserves a section on its own.) It was probably better, too, that this should be out of the way before senior officers became too preoccupied with their own futures during the protracted appointment procedures in the second half of 1973.

The scale of their efforts reflects great credit on the participants. At first sight, the circumstances were unpropitious. The key officers were, in a sense, exceeding their duties to their employing authorities, who were understandably more concerned with the old structure than with the new. There was something of a lacuna in accountability, which could have been avoided only by appointing a reorganisation coordinator, relieved of his other duties, at an early stage, or if the work could have been carried out under the authority of a shadow chairman: this happened in Scotland, where the reorganisation bill reached the statute book early enough to enable health authority chairmen to be appointed early in 1973, prior to the establishment of 'study groups'. But, certainly in Humberside, the English JLC did what was expected of them. There was some administrative confusion on the appointed day, but no serious breakdown affecting patients.

An incidental benefit of the exercise was that it brought together fellow professionals and administrators from all parts of the new area, and thus helped to build relationships which would be invaluable later on for those who stayed in the area. The JLC deliberately tried to foster 'Humberside-consciousness', not only in the working parties but also by issuing its own information bulletin *Humberside Health*. This was particularly necessary because of the unfamiliar nature of the new county.

The JLC's attempts to build morale through participation, however, were less successful. Part of the difficulty here was that local enthusiasm became out of phase with what was happening nationally, and this engendered a good deal of frustration. The DHSS circulars setting up the JLCs seemed to provide a clear invitation to experienced officers to carry out as much preliminary analysis as possible of the management questions which would have to be settled well in advance of April 1974. Yet by the end of

1972, when the Humberside working parties had already completed much of their work, the DHSS was still issuing advice (which might have been more welcome had it come earlier) and warning JLCs not to waste time on matters which were under study by departmental teams. From this point of view, much of the Humberside effort was premature; a definite feeling of anticlimax, which was to persist for many months, began to set in early in 1973. Attempts to rekindle the original enthusiasm proved unsuccessful. When senior officers began to take up their new posts, the JLC machinery itself became redundant. The last meeting of the Humberside JLC was in December 1973.

DISTRICTS

The division of Humberside into districts caused the JLC machinery some of its greatest problems and remained a source of contention for over five years. The health district, based on a district general hospital, had emerged as the most suitable level for community representation and for day-to-day management. Some of the smaller areas might serve as districts in themselves; but those matching the larger counties, like Humberside, would have to be divided. Accordingly, one of the original tasks set for JLCs was to advise on the appropriate health districts.

The Humberside JLC set up a strong working party to address itself to this problem, which was rightly seen as a major factor affecting management structures, accommodation needs and much besides. By September 1972, the report of the management study group had indicated the probable nature of a district structure.[12] But it was not until February 1973 that the DHSS confirmed that these recommendations had been accepted. A circular emphasised that the final decision on districts must rest with the shadow area health authority but invited area JLCs, within two months, to submit proposals for a district pattern that satisfied certain criteria and to consider methods of dealing with 'natural' health districts which could not be reconciled with the new area boundaries. The timetable seemed to envisage that any difficulties would be ironed out well in advance of the appointment of shadow authorities.[13]

The management study group suggested that the ideal health district should contain the smallest population for which integrated services could be planned realistically to meet the majority of health needs. It would be relatively self-contained and detached, taking account of existing patient flows. It should have a population of 200,000 to 300,000 and should correspond to the boundaries of local authority districts and also to the operational 'divisions' of the local authority social service departments. Few of these criteria helped in Humberside. Over half its population (500,000) was served by the hospital nucleus within a ten-mile radius of Hull. The remaining 350,000 was spread along fifty miles of the south bank, with three separate population centres at Grimsby, Scunthorpe and Goole. Only three of the nine local government districts (Hull, Grimsby and Scunthorpe) contained major general hospitals. The social service divisions retained the old boundary between Hull and the East Riding. The only relevant criteria seemed to be self-sufficiency and patient flows. The DHSS circular of February 1973, indeed, suggested that the first concern of JLCs should be to identify 'natural' health districts, without regard to local government boundaries, either at district or at county level, or to population numbers. Special arrangements could be made for parts of an area which belonged more naturally to districts in adjacent areas.

On that basis, a logical structure for Humberside might have been centred on a large district based on Hull and a smaller district based on the catchment area of the Grimsby hospitals, taking in part of Lincolnshire. Bridlington and Goole would have been surrendered to preserve their existing links with Scarborough and Pontefract. Some other parts of the old East Riding would have fallen naturally into a district based on York. Scunthorpe would have been linked, rather unsatisfactorily, either with Lincoln or with Grimsby, both about thirty miles away. The composition of the district working party, which included both general practitioners and consultants based on Goole and Bridlington, suggested that the main problem was initially seen in terms of these marginal cases. Hiving off on this scale would, of course, have played havoc with the Humberside concept. However, the working party recommended that Humberside should be administered as an entity, subject to temporary arrangements with adjacent areas to maintain services for Goole and Bridlington. This was accepted by the JLC and later by the regional JLC, with the proviso that two small hospitals should continue to be administered from York. (They were taken over by Humberside in 1976.) Although the North Yorkshire JLC made a bid for Bridlington, this was quashed by the DHSS. The peripheral problems soon became less salient than those internal to Humberside.

Starting from the existing authority structure, the working party found little difficulty in identifying two smallish but natural districts based on Grimsby and Scunthorpe. The Goole practitioners, once it had been

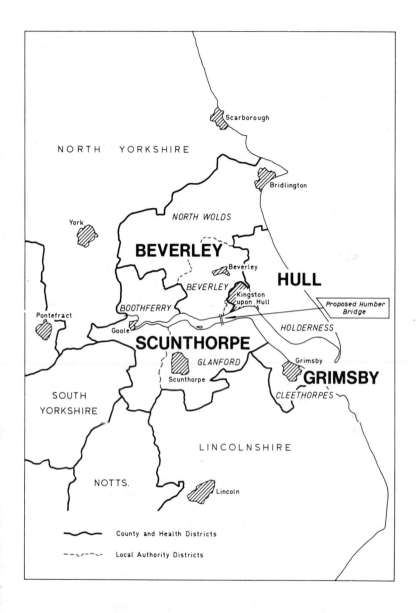

Fig. 4 Humberside Health Area with its Nine Local Authority and Four Health Service Districts

decided that they should come into Humberside, expressed a wish to be associated with Scunthorpe rather than with Hull; this was agreed without difficulty. There remained the problem of the north bank, comprising Hull and most of the East Riding. This caused intense controversy, which was only temporarily resolved by the DHSS guidance.

The essential problem was that nearly the whole of the north bank was served by the acute hospitals in Hull itself. There was no other hospital to provide a natural centre for a second district. Yet a single district would be very large and difficult to manage: the general practitioners were particularly unhappy at the prospect of having only one representative on the district management team to represent some 250 colleagues, working in a great variety of practice conditions. There was also a fear that the smaller centres outside Hull would not get a fair crack of the whip from a district administration which would inevitably be based on the city. This was aggravated by the old political tensions between the city and the county. On the other hand, the hospital medical staff were wholly committed to integration and saw a two-district structure as a threat to the efforts they were making to develop a comprehensive service and attract a medical school.

Although the composition of the working party produced a technical majority in favour of two districts, the discussions ranged far beyond. Two mass meetings of north bank doctors revealed a complete split between the GPs and the consultants, not one of whom was in favour of a two-district solution. Impasse had been reached when the DHSS circular arrived with its strong emphasis on 'natural' districts. This seemed to settle the matter, and with some murmurs about 'the best of a bad job' the JLC agreed in March 1973 that there should be a single North Humberside district. This was approved by the regional JLC two months later and forwarded to the DHSS in the expectation that it would be formally approved when the area health authority met in the autumn.

In July, however, the DHSS expressed concern at some of the district proposals for Yorkshire, including North Humberside. It was suggested that such a large district would not permit the adequate representation of interests and that a management team would have difficulty in managing 'a district of such size, variety and complexity'. The Humberside JLC was invited to reconsider the feasibility of two districts based on an east–west division of Hull and its hinterlands. This caused intense irritation, partly because so much earlier work had gone for nothing; but the JLC voted by a majority to accept the two-district principle. When it came to details, however, no satisfactory way could be found of splitting Hull. Two proposals were finally sent forward, with a rider from the consultants' representative that either scheme would impede the development of acute hospital care. One scheme followed local district boundaries by separating Hull and Holderness from the remainder of the East Riding ('Beverley'). The other made some show of dividing Hull by allocating the western part of the city (which happened to contain no hospitals and few other facilities) to the 'Beverley' district.

That was in August 1973, and at that stage it was still assumed that the AHA would make a final decision in the light of the preparatory work done by the JLC and of guidance from the DHSS. In September, the newly-appointed chairman addressed the JLC; he indicated that the DHSS was recommending a division of the north bank and that he would advise the AHA not to oppose this, partly because of the representational aspects, at its first meeting in the following month. A few days before the meeting, however, the Secretary of State wrote to each area chairman to say that in the interests of speed he had taken personal responsibility for deciding the initial district pattern and boundaries for the new authorities, although the AHA would be free to suggest changes later in the light of experience and developments. In the case of Humberside, there would be two south-bank districts, as proposed by the JLC, and two on the north, constructed on the basis of dividing Hull.

The district pattern is shown in heavy lines on the map on p. 93. Except in Hull, it follows local district council boundaries. Except in Hull and Holderness, it also fits reasonably well with local authority social service and education divisions.[14] What it does not follow is the pattern of health service usage. Almost by an accident of local government geography, all the mental-handicap hospitals happened to end up in one district and nearly all the mental-illness beds in the other. More serious from the viewpoint of integrated care is that most of the acute specialties in North Humberside are based in the 'Hull' district, although many of the consultants also work in hospitals which have been assigned to 'Beverley'.

District management structures, professional machinery and community health councils had to be organised on this rather artificial basis. Difficulties were experienced in each respect. But although the hospital doctors repeatedly drew attention to the problems which the administrative structure caused for them, it was not seriously reexamined until 1977, when the regional health authority asked the AHA to review the district structure both in the context of its administrative cost and in terms of the viability of each district for comprehensive planning and development; the RHA was particularly anxious to avoid expensive developments to make the Beverley district self-sufficient. This reopened all the old controversies, with the added complication that district management teams and community health councils were now in existence and jealous of their territories. By 1977, also, opinion was moving away from multi-district areas towards a simpler pattern of administration which matched health needs, even if it entailed sacrificing the advantages of coterminosity between health and local authority services at area/county level. At the time of writing, it is difficult to predict the outcome, except that there is a distinct possibility that North Humberside will eventually become a single-district area. But if this does occur, it will not be until any relevant recommendations from the Royal Commission have been taken into account. In November 1977, Humberside AHA decided to retain the two districts but to review their boundaries and management structure.

THE AREA HEALTH AUTHORITY

Subject to the requirements in the Reorganisation Act, the composition of health authorities was a matter for the Secretary of State. It was announced in August 1973 that areas with up to three districts would have authorities consisting of fifteen members. A four-district authority would have seventeen. Originally conceived as a three-district authority, Humberside AHA would therefore have a chairman appointed by the Secretary of State, four members nominated by Humberside County Council, one nominated by the University of Leeds (the medical school serving the area) and nine appointed by the Yorkshire Regional Health Authority after consulting various bodies which represented professional and community interests. At that time, neither the county council nor the RHA existed.

As early as April 1973, the DHSS undertook 'informal consultations on behalf of the regional health authority'. Nominations were invited from existing health service authorities in each area and from national organisations ranging from the BMA and the Association of Nurse Administrators to the British Red Cross Society and the National Association of Leagues of Hospital Friends. (Since the list of national bodies provides an unusually full picture of the processes through which members are recruited for voluntary service on statutory bodies, it is reproduced in Appendix B.) After Parliament had passed the Reorganisation Act in July, the relevant nominations were sent to the chairman of the RHA, who had already been selected, so that informal consultations could be ratified on the statutory basis:

> On this occasion, the requirements of the Act will be met if each RHA sends a letter to all the organisations, both national and local, listed in the appendix ... and request them to reply within ten days confirming or varying the recommendations already made.... On future occasions, RHAs will no doubt wish to undertake more extensive local consultations after they have established contact....[15]

(The Yorkshire RHA covered seven health areas, including Humberside. One of its eighteen members came from Hull and another from Scunthorpe: both were prominent local councillors with wide experience of health administration.) By September, when the Yorkshire RHA met to consider the nominations, the Secretary of State had also appointed the AHA chairman, who was thus available for consultation.

Over a hundred nominations had been received for the nine places originally available on the Humberside AHA. The task was to find nine members who could look at the problems of Humberside from various viewpoints and apply different sorts of experience and knowledge— of the work of existing authorities, of different parts of the area, and of different professions. They also required to have management abilities. Each AHA was intended to include at least two doctors and one nurse or midwife. A latent constraint was the need for the new authority to be broadly acceptable to established interests whose support and confidence would be needed in the early stages of its work.

Given the nature of Humberside, it was not surprising that considerable emphasis was placed on geographical representation. The AHA chairman himself lived on the south bank, where he was a county councillor and chairman of a hospital management committee. The two doctors appointed by the RHA included a north-bank consultant (then chairman of the medical executive committee) and a south-bank general practitioner (then chairman of an executive council). The six 'lay' members appointed by the RHA came equally from north and south: they lived in Grimsby, Scunthorpe, Goole, Bridlington, Hull and a small East Riding village. All but one had previously served on a hospital management committee; but none were members of a local health authority or executive council. One was a well-known trade-union organiser.

The Humberside County Council also respected the geographical principle by filling two of its four places with councillors from Hull, one from

Grimsby and one from Scunthorpe. Three of them were members of the local authority social services committee; at least two had experience of local health authority work and two had served on hospital management bodies. On the other hand, all four were members of the same dominant political party and all represented industrial constituencies; it was left to the RHA appointees to reflect the interests of residents in the former county areas.

These thirteen members had been appointed in time to meet as a shadow authority in October 1973. Four more were to be appointed over the next few months. The University of Leeds appointed a social scientist. A former director of nursing services from the north bank became the nurse member. The two additional seats which arose from Humberside's promotion from a three- to a four-district authority were also filled from the north bank — one by a headmistress from Bridlington and the other by a Hull University professor who was interested in medical research. These appointments brought the north/south balance to 10:7, which almost exactly matched the population distribution, and filled some gaps in expertise.

This then was the authority which took over the reins in Humberside and steered it through reorganisation. (Additional local authority representatives were added in 1975 and there were substantial changes in 1977 when the county council changed colour and half the appointed members came to the end of their term of office.) Its seventeen members replace nearly 300 Humbersiders on the old health authorities, although appointments to community health councils and the family practitioner committee later brought the number of 'involved part-timers' up to around 150.[16] Together they represented not only the main communities being absorbed into Humberside but also the majority of the expiring authorities, especially on the hospital management side.

At the outset, the authority had no staff apart from an administrative assistant and a clerk, whom one of the hospital management committees had made available to help with the mechanics of the business. The authority's own staff still had to be appointed. There were no senior officers until the third meeting, in December 1973. The JLC machinery was of course still in existence and the AHA chairman was able to attend the 'Operation Survival' exercise. There was plenty of documentation, including the JLC background papers, DHSS guidance about tasks and priorities, and Staff Commission arrangements for selection procedures. But these had to be translated into action. An area team of officers had to be appointed, closely followed by the formation of a family practitioner committee and district management teams, to take over existing services in the following April.

A good deal of this burden fell on the chairman himself. Unlike his predecessors in hospital management committees and local authorities, he drew a part-time salary and was expected to spend between one and two days a week on the business of the authority. During the initial period, the commitment was much heavier. By way of preparation, he had been briefed at meetings with the Secretary of State and the RHA chairman, and had been introduced to the new theories of health service management at a Brunel University seminar. Most of the other members took part in a two-day seminar at the Nuffield Centre for Health Service Studies at Leeds University.

The main task of setting up an infra-structure was simplified by the preparatory work that had already been done. The JLC, for example, had identified the accommodation needed for new area and district headquarters; the AHA simply endorsed these arrangements and spent some time deciding what the main headquarters building should be called. Again, the JLC had produced a document listing the essential steps that would have to be taken to effect a smooth transition on 1 April 1974. The AHA was able to accept the suggestions, commend the authors and authorise them to take all necessary steps, including any necessary and reasonable expenditure. On staff appointments, too, the AHA had little choice but to fall in with the procedures and timetables worked out by the Staff Commission.

Between mid-October 1973 and the end of May 1974, AHA members were involved in selection panels for thirty-five posts, fifteen at area and twenty at district level. The busiest months were January and February, when twenty-one appointments had to be made. By then, however, the most senior officers were in post, and the conduct of business began to centre on proposals from the permanent management team. A formal scheme of delegated authority was adopted in March. Members were able to relax a little, and some devoted a good deal of time to familiarisation visits.

FAMILY PRACTITIONER COMMITTEE

A family practitioner committee had to be established to take over the work and records relating to Humberside of executive councils based on Hull, Beverley, Grimsby, Lincoln and (for Goole) Wakefield. Again, the details were worked out within the JLC machinery, and by October 1973 preparations for the transfer to new offices were well in hand, the main outstanding problem being the recruitment of staff. Applications for the post of FPC Administrator were already in the pipeline.

For the committee itself, Humberside County Council had to find four members and the AHA eleven, at least one of whom should be a member of the authority. The other fifteen members had to be appointed by local professional committees of general practitioners (eight members), dentists (three), opticians and retail pharmacists (two each), who therefore had to organise themselves on a Humberside basis.

The general practitioners (who, of course, had been involved in the argument about districts in late 1972) were quick off the mark. After discussion among the chairmen of the five merging local medical committees, a steering committee was formed to decide on the shape of a Humberside local medical committee. The shadow LMC was able to meet in September 1973 and agree on its nominations to the FPC. Eventually, by a similar although less formal process, the dentists, opticians and pharmacists also produced their nominations.

The AHA set up a sub-committee to consider how to fill its quota of eleven places. Like the RHA in the previous section, the sub-committee was able to draw on a list of nominations collected by the DHSS from interested organisations, including the expiring executive councils. On the sub-committee's advice, the AHA appointed three of its own members (the general practitioner member, one of the local councillors and a member with HMC experience) and selected eight others, having regard to broad experience and geographical representation, from the list of nominees.

The Humberside FPC met for the first time in December 1973. One of the four county council representatives, who was chairman of an existing executive council, became chairman. Its first task was to appoint a panel of members to help select an administrator.

COMMUNITY HEALTH COUNCILS

CHCs could not be established until the district pattern had been settled. Moreover, their mixed composition had been the subject of some controversy and of amendment to the Reorganisation Bill. Consequently, preparations were much less advanced than those for the main statutory machinery. A DHSS guidance circular was not issued until January 1974.[17]

Regional health authorities were invited to set up machinery for securing representation from local authorities and voluntary organisations as well as appointing their own quota of members. It was hoped that this would be done in time for an inaugural meeting by the end of April 1974. The Yorkshire RHA followed the guidance by inviting voluntary organisations, through press advertisements, to declare their interest. Conferences were then held with voluntary organisations in various parts of the region to clear the ground. These helped to produce some ground rules about the size of CHCs and the kind of organisations that should be represented on them. The RHA then designed a model constitution for each of the seventeen CHCs. This made it possible to ask the relevant local authorities to nominate their fifty per cent of the membership and to make a fairly arbitrary apportionment of the remaining places among representatives of various organisations.

A CHC had to be set up for each of the four Humberside districts. The largest (Hull) was given a membership of thirty and the smallest twenty-four: the figure had ideally to be divisible by six because of the require-ments in the Act. The first meeting (convened by a representative of the RHA) were held in May 1974. These were very exploratory, and one of the CHCs did not feel able to elect a chairman until the following meeting. Others immediately set about appointing a chairman and a selection panel to find a secretary. But one CHC was without a secretary until May 1975; temporary arrangements were made by the relevant district management teams.

Unlike the AHAs and FPCs, the CHCs did not inherit a package of functions and plans for taking them over from expiring authorities. The emphasis was very much on 'do it yourself'. Their first annual reports, covering the year ending May 1975, show how preoccupied they were with finding their feet and establishing some sort of organisation. Not only had they to find their own staff and accommodation; even their budgets were initially very hit-and-miss. But most CHCs organised themselves fairly quickly into special interest groups, or visiting panels, and tried to establish a working relationship with the district management teams as well as with the local community. The RHA organised a series of one-day introductory seminars, which were well attended, in June 1974, and offered what help it could with finding staff and accommodation. The chairmen of CHCs within the region were given facilities to meet at the RHA headquarters and the RHA chairman gave them his personal support. This led naturally to the development of a regional association. Towards the end of 1974, national seminars were arranged for CHC secretaries. Within Humberside, the AHA chairman took an early opportunity to meet each CHC, and tried to ensure that they were receiving sufficient help from the district officers. Joint meetings between the AHA and each CHC were arranged in March 1975. It was not until then that the CHC could be described as firmly established.

The composition and early work of CHCs has been described elsewhere.[18] Within Humberside, a third to a half had previous experience on a health authority—usually a hospital management committee. The main new blood came from local councillors (many of whom found the work unfamiliar and unrewarding and resigned after a period of poor attendance) and from the voluntary organisations. The latter group included representatives of leagues of friends, all-purpose voluntary groups like the British Red Cross, the WRVS and the Yorkshire Council of Social Service, as well as special interests like Age Concern, the Society for Mentally Handicapped Children and the Family Planning Association.

SUMMARY AND COMMENT

As soon as the broad outlines of the new area, and later its districts, were known, preparations started locally for the creation of new machinery and the transfer of existing services in April 1974. These preparations began nearly two years ahead of the change, and a good year ahead of parliamentary approval of the NHS Reorganisation Act, 1973. For most of the time, therefore, they were wholly non-statutory. Even the establishment of shadow authorities, which had to await the passage of the Act, was anticipated by a process of informal consultation which enabled action to be taken very quickly when the time came. The main exception was the establishment of community health councils, which was several months late. Partly because there was not much to build on, it was not until 1975 that the CHCs became fully operational.

The main responsibility for preparing for the change rested with the expiring authorities. In practice, it fell to the senior officers on the area and regional joint liaison committees, with a wider involvement of doctors and other professional groups on key issues. Although participants in the JLCs were still acting as representatives of their own authorities, they acquired the status of a self-actuated change group, accountable mainly to the central department and to their own vision of the reorganisation. The work was done well; but it need not have been, and may have been done less well elsewhere. There was some tension and frustration when conflict arose between self-motivation and upward accountability, as when the DHSS issued more and more detailed instructions and guidance on matters which the officers felt able to settle for themselves. There might also have been tension between the officers' responsibilities on the JLCs and their duties to their employing authorities; but we did not hear of any.

On Humberside, the preparatory work was vitally necessary, both because of the number of merging authorities and because of the need to establish the concept of the new county. The reader has been spared a full list of the things that absolutely had to be done: some indication will be gleaned from examples in the text and from the list of circulars in Appendix A. Two things perhaps stand out.

One is the amount of effort that was contributed voluntarily, almost unpaid, and without statutory cover, both by administrators and by professionals.[19] Not all of them believed in the need for reorganisation. Not all had a stake in its success; many of the leading participants did in fact obtain posts in the new structure they helped to establish, but they had no guarantee that this would be the outcome of the centralised short-listing procedures; others were planning on early retirement or hoping for posts elsewhere.

The second point is that there was so little political involvement in matters which would fundamentally affect the structure of the service, and the structure of consumer representation, for years to come. The most striking example of this was the determination of the district pattern, with its implications for CHCs. Even the decision that 'No. 2 Region' should be named 'Yorkshire', rather than 'Yorkshire and Humberside' or some such equivalent, was taken by the regional JLC and approved by the DHSS well in advance of the constitution of a regional health authority. The arrangements for filling posts, to which we come in the next chapter, also had political implications which failed to attract much attention.

NOTES

1   *Report of the Royal Commission on Local Government in England 1966–69,* HMSO, Cmnd. 4040, 1969, p.203.
2   *Report of the Royal Commission on Medical Education 1965–68,* HMSO, Cmnd. 3569, para. 393.
3   *Reform of Local Government in England,* HMSO, Cmnd. 4276, 1970, p.39 (map).

4   *Local Government in England: Government Proposals for Reorganisation,* HMSO, Cmnd. 4584, 1971. (An all-Lincolnshire authority was proposed for the south bank, subject to local agreement, in the Department of Environment's explanatory circular 8/71.)

5   Richard Crossman, *Diaries of a Cabinet Minister* (vol. 3, 1968–70), Hamish Hamilton and Cape, London, 1977, p.449.

6   *Devolution: the English Dimension,* HMSO, 1976. This consultative document suggested the establishment of some form of regional assembly (which might assume responsibilities for the NHS) and a review of local government boundaries and functions.

7   As a municipal borough, Scunthorpe was able to exercise an option to administer certain health and welfare services on behalf of Lindsey County Council.

8   Small parts of the former East Riding were transferred to North Yorkshire.

9   DHSS, *Health Service Reorganisation,* circular HRC(72)3, para. 3.

10 B. Edwards and P. R. Walker, *Si vis pacem. . .: Preparation for Change in the National Health Service,* Oxford University Press for Nuffield Provincial Hospitals Trust, London, 1973.

11 HRC(72)3, para. 5.

12 DHSS, *Management Arrangements for the Reorganised National Health Service,* HMSO, 1972, appendix 1.

13 HRC(73)4.

14 The local authority social services and education departments, like the health authority, subdivided the county into 'divisions' based on Hull, Beverley, Grimsby and Scunthorpe. But in each case the Hull division coincided with the *local government* Hull District, which was substantially different from the 'Hull' *health* district. Moreover, the 'East Riding' education division followed the old county boundary and included part of Boothferry in the west, in which both social services and health were allocated to Scunthorpe. The Scunthorpe/Grimsby boundary also differed marginally.

15 HRC(73)24.

16 There had been ninety Humberside members on the seven main HMCs serving Humberside until March 1974, including Goole members of Pontefract HMC and Bridlington members of Scarborough HMC. Ignoring Lindsey and the West Riding, the four main local health authority committees had ninety-three councillor members and twelve coopted members. There were also places for twenty-four local authority nominees, forty-five professional members and twenty-one additional members on the three core executive councils (compared with four, fifteen and eleven on the new Humberside family practitioner committee).

17 HRC(74)4.

18 Jack Hallas, *CHCs in Action,* Nuffield Provincial Hospitals Trust, London, 1976; see also ch. 3, note 13, above.

19 Local government staff received a percentage increase on their salaries for work on reorganisation. NHS officers did not become entitled to supplements for JLC work until November 1973.

CHAPTER 6

Filling the Posts

The reduction in the number of lay management committees implied an increase in the power and responsibility of permanent officials. One of the objectives of the reorganisation was to strengthen management and clarify lines of accountability within health authorities. It was therefore important to identify officers with the relevant calibre as soon as possible. But promises had been made that the interests of existing staff would be fully safeguarded. Under Staff Commission rules, the search for talent was at first confined to the merging services.

The first part of this chapter deals with the filling of senior posts in the new structure. Later sections explain the arrangements for assimilating other staff, including the attempts to sustain morale through training, consultation and information.

THE TOP POSTS

The Management Study Group had sketched a management structure for the new authorities and drawn up role-specifications for twenty-seven key posts (seven at district, ten at area and ten at region level) which incorporated its rather sophisticated ideas about inter-managerial relationships.[1] These ideas were communicated and discussed on the training courses for existing senior officers which began towards the end of 1972. Discussions with the staff associations about appropriate salaries were instituted about the same time; but so many difficulties were encountered that the Secretary of State had to announce provisional salaries unilaterally in May 1973, so that arrangements for recruitment could be put in hand. The NHS Staff Commission (at that time still a non-statutory advisory committee) then placed display advertisements in the '£4,000+' sections of the quality newspapers inviting officers from a prescribed field to submit multiple applications for the new posts. On behalf of the still non-existent regional and area health authorities, the Commission sifted the applications, drew up short lists for each post, scheduled interview dates and nominated assessors.

The first posts to be advertised were those of regional and area administrator, treasurer and nursing officer. Applications for a maximum of five regional and five area posts in each profession had to be submitted by 30 June. Only those serving in merging health authorities in England and Wales were eligible. Interview dates for each post were announced in August and September. Those for the regional posts came first, since regional health authorities were appointed some six weeks earlier than the area authorities. The regional interviews were scheduled for September 1973, and interviews for area posts started in the following month. At its first meeting on 5 October, the shadow Humberside AHA had to appoint selection panels to choose its administrator on 15 October, its treasurer on 26 October and its chief nursing officer on 2 November. The Staff Commission 'proposed' named assessors to assist each selection panel. It was also suggested that each panel should consist of not more than five members, including the chairman of the authority.

At that time, as noted in the previous chapter, the authority was incomplete. Few of the available members can have had more than the haziest notion of the duties of the new posts, although nine of the thirteen did attend a two-day introductory seminar in the following week, and the Staff Commission had prepared some background literature. Some of the assessors were equally at sea. The Humberside authority formally accepted the suggested procedure, and nominated selection panels whose composition reflected a balance of interests, both between the north and south banks of the Humber and among different types of merging authority, so that no candidate could feel disadvantaged. For these early appointments, an attempt was made to ensure that none of the candidates was personally known to the selection panel: this proved unworkable and was later abandoned. It was also decided that the interviews should be held on 'neutral' territory; facilities were provided in the Guildhall at Hull.

The selection panels could only express a preference among the short-listed candidates. The final matching was made by the Staff Commission, after taking candidates' own preferences into account. As a result, the outcome of the Humberside interviews was not known until mid-November, along with those of other areas which had been able to make appointments at this stage. After a selection process lasting nearly five months, the most senior group secretary, HMC finance officer and chief nursing officer in the merging authorities learned that they had been appointed to the corresponding posts in the new area. Their employing committee raised no difficulty about early release, and they took up their new positions on 1 December 1973.

The appointment of an area medical officer followed a similar procedure, except that the selection committee had to include a majority of medical members (four out of seven, including the medical members of the area authority) and a local government representative with a right of veto. Interviews were held in November, and the appointment became effective on 1 February 1974, only two months ahead of the appointed day. The choice fell on the county medical officer of health for the East Riding. The medical officer of health for Hull later secured the senior medical post in Hull district.

This completed the area team of officers. A number of other senior area posts were filled by national competition. The area personnel officer (again from the leading HMC) took up post in February 1974, the family practitioner committee administrator in March and the ambulance officer on 1 April; both the latter came from outside Humberside. The area works officer did not appear until February 1975. However, like the area dental and pharmaceutical officers, his was a new job, concerned initially with policy advice, and it was less essential that he should be in post on the appointed day.

Another quartet of officers had to be appointed to each district management team before the district structure could become operational. The Staff Commission advised that competition for appointment as district administrator, finance officer, nursing officer and community physician should be restricted to NHS staff serving within the appropriate region, and that each region should set up a regional appointments unit to process the applications. This could not be done until the outcome of the earlier competitions was known. The regional appointments unit also dealt with applications for less senior posts, which were open to competition on a regional basis; posts below that level were filled by transfer. The Yorkshire appointments unit had to deal with applications for about 200 posts within a four-month period. Candidates were allowed to apply for up to five district posts.

On Humberside, none of the four district teams was complete before the appointed day. The earliest appointments took effect on 1 February 1974, usually when a local candidate was available. All four district community physicians (who held posts with the expiring local authorities) took up their new duties on 1 April. One team was short of a finance officer until 1 May. Supporting staff structures took much longer.

Humberside was perhaps unusual in being a relatively isolated area. The existing cadre of senior officers had local affiliations which would have been severed if they had moved to posts elsewhere. Only six of the twenty-three main area and district posts were filled from outside Humberside—one by a former administrator returning. Conversely, only two of the twenty-one 'old' chief officers (one HMC treasurer and one executive council clerk) sought and obtained a post elsewhere; another nine retired. The outcome might have been very different if the new area had been carved out of a conurbation, with a range of other posts within easy travelling distance. Nevertheless, the degree of continuity is striking. All four members of the area team had been active in the joint liaison committee: the area administrator had been its secretary and his medical, nursing and finance colleagues had chaired relevant working parties. At least one member of each district team had been involved in the JLC working parties, and two had been members of the main committee. For them at least, there was a direct progression from the old authorities, through the transitional machinery, to senior posts in the new structure.

Where there was discontinuity, it was due to a shortage of local candidates which had to be made up either from outside Humberside or by very rapid promotion. For example, the Humberside family practitioner committee was a 'natural' successor to three merging executive councils, each with its own clerk. Two retired and the third obtained a post elsewhere. This threw the field for the FPC administrator's post wide open, and an executive council clerk from the Midlands was appointed to the vacancy. On the general administrative side there were, in theory, five group secretaries and four local authority chief administrative officers competing for five new chief officer posts. Three of the group secretaries retired; the remaining two were appointed as area and district administrators. One of the local authority administrators retired; another took a post with the social services department; a third became a district administrator; and the fourth was content with a second-in-line post. This left two gaps which were filled by appointing younger men, who had been deputy group secretaries, as district administrators.

One test of continuity is the extent to which the new officer elite had been identified for advance training courses to prepare them for their new roles. The DHSS arranged national courses on the management of integrated health care for senior officers and clinicians from all branches of the merging services at designated university and other centres. Eligibility was defined partly by grade and partly by salary. All medical officers of health, with their deputies and chief administrative officers, were eligible from the local authority side, but only group secretaries, treasurers and their deputies above a certain salary level from HMCs. Four of the five deputy group secretaries on Humberside (one of whom later became a district administrator) were therefore eligible only for shorter courses which were arranged regionally. By September 1973, when most of those concerned were bracing themselves for selection interviews, twenty-four senior Humberside officers (nearly all the eligible officers who were not retiring) had attended or been accepted for one of the national courses. But when we checked with the senior officers who had actually been appointed by June 1974, we found that seventeen had attended the relevant course and seven had not, usually because they were too junior. Seven of the senior officers who did attend, later decided to opt for early retirement.

Nationally, there were some absolute shortages in technical areas like personnel, finance, works and community medicine, and problems of quality in the field of nursing.[2] The Staff Commission procedures were intended to ensure that fair consideration was given to existing staff but were not intended to give them absolute preference for posts for which they were unsuited, although the procedures might have tended in that direction. Applications for each post were sifted by a panel of assessors, which drew up a short-list. There was a national outcry about the construction of these short-lists—particularly about the exclusion of candidates already occupying senior positions in the merging authorities. The Staff Commission replied that the new jobs demanded qualities for which success in the old jobs was not necessarily relevant. But its attempt to maintain standards encountered fierce opposition from the health service staff associations.

Nursing provides an interesting example (there were plenty of qualified nurses; but how many of them had the management ability to play an effective part in the new teams?). In spite of suggestions from the DHSS and the professional associations that there would be good candidates for the new nursing administrative posts outside the NHS,[3] the Staff Commission advised that the principle of limiting the field to the staff of merging authorities should be followed. The short-listing was done by a panel of eleven senior nurses, all but three of whom had recently held NHS posts and none of whom apparently possessed a degree or any managerial qualification. The assessors decided that only thirty-four of the ninety nurses who had applied for the fourteen regional nursing officer posts were suitable for short-listing; fourteen of these were duly appointed. Of the 379 applicants for the ninety senior area posts, only 131 were short-listed; seventy-three of these found appointments in the first round. The field was then opened to all candidates remaining in the field, whether or not they had originally been thought suitable for short-listing; seventeen of the latter were appointed to the remaining vacancies.[4] At that stage there were still over 1,200 district, divisional and second-in-line nursing posts to be filled at levels higher than the existing pinnacles of nursing administration. Even if, as seems likely, some well-qualified nurses did not offer themselves for regional and area appointments, the remaining field cannot have been very large. (As late as June 1975, one in nine divisional posts was still unfilled.) The position on Humberside, as we have seen, is that the area and district posts were filled with local candidates on the first round. But only two of the five authorised supporting posts were filled at area level, and one of these was dropped when a vacancy arose three years later.

It was accepted from the outset that there were insufficient qualified finance, personnel and works officers within the NHS, and that it might be necessary to look outside. Again, the first round failed to produce enough acceptable candidates, and most of the remaining posts were filled with candidates whom the assessors had originally considered unsuitable. Eventually, three regional works officers and four area personnel officers were appointed from outside. Humberside filled all its posts, eventually, from NHS applicants, although not from within the area. Finance was a particular problem, since none of the local authority finance staff was interested in the NHS. Of the three eligible hospital treasurers, one retired, one went elsewhere and the other became area treasurer. The district posts were filled with relatively junior applicants. The lack of financial expertise caused recurrent difficulties, exacerbated in the early months by the withdrawal of local government support for staff transferred from the community services.

So far as Humberside was concerned, the national appointment procedures were merely a cause of delay in cases where a suitable local candidate was available: in one case, when the assessors argued for an external candidate they were over-ruled. Nationally, too, in spite of the initial anxiety over short-lists, 'In the majority of cases the obvious candidate has been appointed and there are some enterprising appointments among the less obvious'.[5] The main contribution of the Staff Commission (and later of the regional appointments unit) seems to have been as a recruitment agency for posts which could not be filled locally.

Parallel arrangements had been made to deal with the local government reorganisation; but they were much simpler. Only the chief executive posts were open to national competition. The Local Government Staff Commission advertised the vacancy and sent the relevant applications to joint committees, composed of members of the expiring authorities, with an indication that they could initiate the selection process if they so wished. The other chief officer posts were open only to candidates from the authorities which were being merged in each new county. As early as February 1973, the joint committees were advised that they could invite applications before the new county councils were elected in April.[6] The outcome was very similar to that in the NHS: in Humberside, for example, the Town Clerk of Hull became chief executive, and the new directors of education and social services had been chief officers of the East Riding and Hull services.

INTERIM MANAGEMENT ARRANGEMENTS

Early DHSS circulars emphasised that the disturbance caused by reorganisation should be reduced to the minimum. For the great majority of NHS staff, the only change on 1 April 1974 would be a change of employing authority.

In general, this was true. The majority of staff, especially in the hospitals, were transferred to the new authority without change in their pattern of work or conditions of service. Even they, however, could not be completely protected from the consequences of changes in the top structure. From early 1973, the normal arrangements for filling vacant posts were suspended in order to protect the position of existing staff. With the approach of the appointed day, there were more and more discontinuities in the chain of command as senior officers left to take up their new jobs: 'acting up' became the name of the game, and the main Hull HMC had three acting group secretaries in six months. In the family practitioner services, a good deal of upheaval was inevitable, since two of the existing executive councils (in Grimsby and Beverley) were being abolished and their functions transferred to the new Humberside FPC office in Hull; in fact, the Grimsby office remained open, with a nucleus of staff, for a couple of years and provided a convenient local contact point for both public and practitioners during that time. The most serious disruptions occurred in the local authority services, where lines of communication with town and county headquarters had to be severed and reconnected with integrated NHS headquarters services.

In November 1973, the DHSS advised that blocks of staff should be 'latched on' to the embryonic area and district management structures, retaining their existing management arrangements as far as possible until the new ones had been fully introduced. It was accepted that this might mean retaining structures which did not conform to the new area and district boundaries. But the DHSS stressed that the interim arrangements should provide for clear lines of accountability. Nobody should be left 'free-floating'. On the advice of their area team of officers, the Humberside AHA endorsed a policy of minimal change, in the short term, at their meeting in February 1974. One attraction of this policy was that it would allow the district officers a breathing space to collect their districts together. Another was that it would avoid immediate traumatic changes for the majority of staff.

The essential ingredient of this policy was the identification of focal points to which existing organisations could be 'latched on'. In some cases, these lay outside Humberside. Agency arrangements were made with the North Yorkshire and Wakefield health authorities to continue supplying Bridlington and Goole hospitals from their existing headquarters in Scarborough and Pontefract. Conversely, the old East Riding health department remained an entity, under its existing headquarters at Beverley, although it would later have to be split among three of the Humberside districts and lose some staff and services in the north of the county, where there was a boundary change, to North Yorkshire AHA.

Within Humberside, the treasurers of the expiring authorities had identified four hospital finance departments which would progressively take over responsibility for the preparation of payrolls. These were the main hospital group finance offices in the area; and it was convenient that one fell within each of the four new districts. These bases were then extended to provide a nucleus for each district headquarters. The East Riding health department, for example, was 'latched on' to the Beverley district management team, which was originally based on the relevant hospital finance department.

These arrangements worked well when blocks of staff were already organised under self-contained service structures. Within nursing, for example, both hospital and community services were themselves becoming structured under hierarchies headed by a chief nursing officer for each hospital group, and a director of nursing services for each local authority.

Again, there were chief nursing officers in the four principal hospital groups. One became area nursing officer and the other three were appointed as district nursing officers. They simply retained their old jobs, with the addition of any groups of staff who could be latched on (like hospital nursing staff at Goole, whose senior nursing officer was asked to report to the 'new district officer at Scunthorpe rather than retain his links with Pontefract) until the intermediate structure could be filled up. The directors of the community nursing services in Hull, Grimsby and the East Riding were asked to report to the most relevant district nursing officer. Only in the Scunthorpe district, which contained loose ends of the former West Riding and Lincolnshire (Lindsey) county services, was it necessary to restructure the line of command below director level at that stage.

Like the community nursing services, ambulances had been the responsibility of county and county borough authorities, serving patients within their defined boundaries. Reorganisation meant a reduction from 120 to forty operating authorities in England: regional health authorities were to take over ambulance services in the new metropolitan counties like West Yorkshire, and area authorities were to take over those in shire counties. Interim DHSS guidance suggested that ambulances should be 'latched on' at district level until the regional and area chief ambulance officers had established themselves. In Humberside, the ambulance working party had been one of the most active in suggesting changes that would follow reorganisation. A chief ambulance officer for the area was appointed from outside Humberside and took up post on 1 April. At that time he had no experience of the area, no support staff and no approved budget for 1974–5. Initially, therefore, he handled only policy matters and questions requiring a reference to the area health authority. The 'old' ambulance services of Hull, Grimsby and the East Riding remained intact, drawing on the appropriate district headquarters for pay and rations. The Lindsey service had been based on Scunthorpe, and a chief officer there took over responsibility for such parts of the county service as were not transferred to Lincolnshire. As an interim measure, the Goole services (formerly part of the West Riding) were latched on to Hull. At this stage, existing links were preserved where possible, like those with county council engineering and servicing stations. Over the succeeding months, the chief ambulance officer gradually took over the reins of control. But the difficulty of integrating the old services has persisted to the time of writing.

But, if blocks of staff and services could be kept intact during the interim period, this was not necessarily true of the administrative services on which they depended. Some of the best officers on the local authority side opted for posts with the new local government authorities, which were advertised earlier than NHS posts and were known to be well paid. Of the twenty-one local health authority administrators who attended middle-management courses before the reorganisation, seven had left for local government posts by October 1974. Those who remained had to cope with a crushing burden of work during the interim period, when their support on the local government side had largely disappeared and the ex-hospital officers who staffed the new headquarters had little experience of their problems. It was in this area that breakdowns occurred (for example in paying travel and subsistence allowances). But staff on the ground had made their own arrangements (e.g. by stockpiling supplies) to ensure that patients did not suffer. Their own position was helped by the issue to all NHS institutions in Humberside (and in some cases to individual officers) of an information card showing a point of contact for supervisory and financial services, and sources for general and special supplies and any necessary maintenance and emergency services. An information service was set up at area health authority headquarters, and individual staff were invited to consult it on any points of difficulty concerning the changeover.

PERMANENT MANAGEMENT STRUCTURES

Early in 1973, the DHSS advised that, once the senior regional, area and district officers were in post,

> subject . . . to such directions as the Secretary of State later issues, it will be for the new authorities to decide on the pace and extent to which they introduce changes in the organisations and processes which they take over from the present National Health Service Authorities.[7]

On Humberside, the JLC working parties had given some thought to the pattern of organisation within districts, basing their ideas on models in the 'Grey Book'. In fact, the process of filling up the new structures was to be tightly controlled; guidance and authorisations trickled out from the centre over a prolonged period, which is not yet complete.

In November 1973, the authorities were given permission to fill some additional permanent posts, such as area supplies officer, before the appointed day. In April 1974, a batch of circulars authorised (but did not necessarily require) authorities to make a number of additional senior appointments to support the chief area and district officers; these included area nursing and medical liaison officers for child health and social services. The circulars also asked the authorities to confirm in posts all existing officers below a stated rank in middle management, on the basis that there would be places for them in the new structure. Finally, authorities were asked to draw up permanent management schemes, in consultation with staff interests, for administration, finance and nursing; the schemes were to be submitted to regional health authorities by the end of September for approval by the end of the year. Authorities were reminded that resources, both of money and of manpower, were limited, and were warned against excessive generosity.

By June 1974, therefore, some top costs had been filled, the great majority of staff had been confirmed in their existing posts, and there remained a narrow band of staff who were still occupying temporary posts under the interim arrangements. They were understandably anxious to know what opportunities there would be for them in the permanent structure: some were hoping to become heads of divisions at area and district level, others were looking for sector posts within the districts. Of the eighty reasonably senior officers employed by the old health authorities coming into Humberside, eleven had by then decided to retire, twenty-five had obtained senior posts in the new structure, six had left, and thirty-eight were still waiting for a place in the new management structure. Their anxieties were communicated to staff below them (some of whom were hoping for 'dead men's shoes') and caused frustration among their seniors and authority members, who wanted to see things settled and were power-less to help. At national level, too, there was pressure to get on with the job. The timetable had to be speeded up. The submission date was brought forward to June, with a view to issuing approvals in September.

The effect on Humberside is best expressed in papers presented to the authority by its officers at meetings in July and October 1974:

The long-delayed progress on the approval of substantive schemes of management came to a remarkable climax in the middle of June when we received less than a week's notice to make our submissions ... in a situation where much of the essential guidance was still outstanding. The submissions were in fact made in time, but without reference to the Authority or full discussion with district management teams or discussion with staff organisations. The outcome of the submissions is so speculative that we feel that it would be a waste of time to go into any further detail about them at this stage. There can, of course, be no implementation of these until the Authority has given formal approval to whatever establishment emerges. (July)

> Any resemblance the proposed allocation of posts to Humberside bears to our actual submissions is entirely coincidental, and the present task is to devise a management structure to fit an establishment of staff, rather than the other way round. (October)

What seems to have happened is that some authorities put in extravagant bids for new posts, so that some arbitrary rationing criteria had to be applied.[8] Paradoxically, the effect was that Humberside obtained fewer posts, but at higher grades, than the officers had requested. The controls were in terms of numbers and grading. The authority was advised to accept the allocations, in order to avoid further delay. Actual structure charts for administration, finance, nursing and community medicine were presented to the authority in November and approved in the following month. In January 1975 it was possible to report that appointments were being made, under the auspices of the regional appointments unit, and permission was granted to advertise outside the health service to fill the gaps left by people who had left the area or left the NHS.

In April 1975, twelve months into the new service, the Humberside AHA held a special stocktaking meeting. Concern was expressed that some groups of staff were still uncertain of their position, because either the salary scale or the authority to make appointments had not yet been confirmed; this applied to groups of remedial, catering, ambulance and dental staff. Concern was also expressed at the effect of the reorganisation on the basic level of administration. It was pointed out that sector administrators, divisional nursing officers and others at this level had only recently been appointed and were still working themselves into their new jobs. For many, in fact, the only new feature of their job was its enhanced grading and salary. Some senior officers had gone through a complicated selection process simply to stay where they were. But until mid-February few had been certain enough of the outcome to set about establishing new approaches and contacts.

1975 was indeed a year of reckoning. It was known that local government reorganisation had increased the number of administrators by nearly five per cent and the salary bill by nearly ten per cent.[9] Figures were not yet available for the NHS, but examples of apparent extravagance were beginning to be quoted. In a speech to their national association in July, Mrs Castle asked authorities to try and bring their administrative costs back to the pre-reorganisation level. In fact, the number of administrative and clerical staff in England and Wales increased by twenty per cent in the eighteen months from April 1974 to September 1975. Senior and middle-grade posts increased by thirty per cent. Nearly half the increase was attributed to the new management structure. A standstill was ordered for 1966–7 and in the following years authorities were asked to cut their total management costs by five per cent. A two-per-cent cut had in fact been achieved by the end of 1976, mainly by leaving vacancies unfilled. By this time, the structure itself was considered over-elaborate.[10]

It is not easy to make exact before-and-after comparisons, partly because some of the cost of administering the former local authority services was 'lost' in the general expenditures of local government. (But this was the minority partner in the NHS amalgamation, most of whose administrative functions were directly inherited from the hospital service; it was estimated nationally that ten per cent of the additional NHS administrative posts were required for the community services.) On Humberside, there were in fact some savings. The replacement of the old executive councils by the family practitioner committee initially produced a saving of two senior and middle posts out of fifteen. The number of senior community medicine posts was about the same—a total of eight senior posts (four district community physicians, one area medical officer and three area specialists) against four MOH and three deputy MOH posts in the merging authorities (excluding Lindsey and the West Riding).

On the nursing side, the main increases were in salary and status. The seven top posts (four district, one area and two area specialists) were one down on the chief nursing posts in the merging services. But fifteen divisional nursing officers were also appointed, making a total of twenty-two nursing administrative posts carrying salaries (and therefore presumably responsibilities) considerably in excess of the most senior chief nursing officer in the merging services.

The large numerical increases were in administration and finance. In administration (which includes supplies and personnel) the number of posts carrying salaries in excess of £4,400 (at July 1975) rose by a quarter, with proportionately larger increases in the highest grades. The corresponding finance staffs increased by nearly forty per cent, including a five-fold increase in the number of posts in the top bracket; but this has to be set against the extra work inherited from local authority finance departments and the under-development of the finance function in the old hospital management committees.

The new structure, combined with the loss of experienced senior officers, created opportunities of very rapid promotion for staff in the merging authorities, who were the only contestants in the early rounds. No systematic evidence on this point was collected in the Humberside project. But national figures collated by the DHSS suggest that the great bulk of the increase in administrative staff between 1974 and 1975 took place in the grade of principal administrative assistant (c. £5,000 per annum) which covers most sector administrators, two levels below the management teams. In June 1975, twenty-one per cent of those holding posts at this level were under the age of thirty; although a quarter of these were graduates, seventy per cent did not possess any professional qualification related to the health service management. Of all NHS administrators holding posts in that grade or above, only fourteen per cent were graduates, and only thirty-three per cent held any professional qualification; even in the very highest grades (£10,000+ per annum) less than a quarter were graduates and thirty-seven per cent were unqualified.

MORALE-BUILDING

While this was going on, we tried to assess the effects on staff morale, and the success of attempts to sustain morale through training, consultation and information.

The impact of training courses for senior staff has been discussed, largely in terms of take-up rates, on p. 105. Candidates for senior posts in the new structure had a positive incentive to attend these courses in order to familiarise themselves with what lay ahead and to prepare themselves for competitive interviews. Enthusiasm began to falter after the senior posts began to be filled and, quite properly, more emphasis began to be placed on local conferences and seminars to deal with immediate local problems. When those who had attended the original courses were asked how useful they had been, a general criticism was that they had been too general and did not provide all that much help with specific problems.

For less senior staff, in Humberside, ten one-week courses were organised by the University of Hull between March 1973 and January 1974. There were 330 applications, of which 220 were catered for. Membership was restricted to heads of department and staff at middle-management level who would be personally affected by reorganisation. Over a third of the course members were administrators and just under a third were nurses, with the emphasis on the community side. The objectives included the supply of information about the merging services on Humberside and about the principles of the reorganisation. A secondary objective was 'to help managers to . . . develop in their staff a positive attitude towards change and to gain their commitment to its objectives'.[11] The involvement of the research team in the courses provided an excellent opportunity to observe how far these objectives were being achieved, both by the courses themselves and by other information media.

During this period, DHSS circulars about the reorganisation were receiving a wide circulation. The DHSS was also issuing *NHS Reorganisation News*, and the Staff Commission its *Staff Information Bulletin*. The policy was one of maximum information. Locally, the same policy was followed. The Joint Liaison Committee issued a news-sheet called *Humberside Health* until it was disbanded at the end of 1973. Thereafter, the AHA took over a weekly information sheet (*Monitor*) from one of the constituent authorities and made it available throughout Humberside as its official news medium. (*Humberside Health* was restarted early in 1975, but later abandoned for economy reasons.) Moreover, managers were encouraged to make local arrangements to keep their own staff in the picture. A film and a training kit, with flip-charts, were supplied for their use.

We tested the impact of these arrangements in various parts of the research. About half the managers who attended the one-week courses said that they had made some arrangements for training their own staff. Early in 1974, we discovered that just over half the nurses at ward-sister or district-nurse level in the most complex of the nascent districts (Scunthorpe) had received some local training, usually in the form of a talk. But by the end of 1974, only eighteen managers had used the film, and thirty the training kit, out of a total of 183. The managers themselves expressed satisfaction with the amount of information they were receiving. the most helpful sources were stated to be DHSS circulars and *NHS Reorganisation News*. There was some decline in satisfaction between the time they attended the courses and the time of a follow-up questionnaire in October 1974; by the second date, many of them were worried by the lack of specific information on their own position; there had also been some disruption of communication flows in the immediate aftermath of reorganisation.

Altogether, the investment in training and information as a means of generating commitment and goodwill was very considerable. Was the expense justified? We can only hint at an answer. In the follow-up questionnaire, a majority of those who had attended the one-week course said that it had been helpful both in increasing their knowledge and by helping them to cope with anxieties among their staff. But well over three-quarters said that the training had not reduced anxiety about their own position. Nor had it altered their attitude to the objectives of the reorganisation: the majority said that training had increased their knowledge and interest in the details, but that it had made no difference to their enthusiasm or willingness to accept change. These are, of course, subjective statements. It is harder to assess the effects of attitudes on behaviour. The only overt resistance to change arose out of industrial disputes (as when hospital engineers refused to service community health buildings during the latching-on period). Otherwise, acquiescence in the change was virtually complete, and the majority of staff worked very hard to minimise its disruptive effects. But it would be an act of faith to claim that training had any direct influence here. Certainly, not many of the senior officers who had taken on new roles felt that the general training courses had provided much help in coping with new problems.

It is easier to test the success of the information system in generating knowledge about the new service. Both at the one-week course and in the follow-up questionnaire, managers were asked to give off-the-cuff answers to a number of factual questions which had featured a good deal in the information sources to which they had access. Even in October 1974 (six months after reorganisation day), there was considerable uncertainty about the services now included in the NHS: over a quarter thought that the NHS included home helps and residential accommodation for old people, and over a third thought that it included both general and medical social work. At the time of the courses, a remarkably high proportion were misinformed about the composition of management teams, about the division of functions between areas and districts, about the authorities that would be affected by the Humberside merger, and even about the NHS Staff Commission. All these points had been covered by national and local sources of information. If they had failed to convey knowledge about key features of the reorganisation to the relatively senior officers who had been selected for the course, the impact on more junior staff was presumably slight.

In addition to training and information, consultation with staff interests was intended to play a major part in the reorganisation strategy. For example, the right of staff associations to be consulted about transfer schemes was written into the Reorganisation Act. Throughout the reorganisation process, consultation with staff associations at national level considerably influenced the final shape of the change procedures and indeed of the final management structures. This was meant to be mirrored locally: almost every circular enjoining the joint liaison committee or the shadow AHA to take the reorganisation a step further contained a paragraph urging maximum consultation with the staff concerned. One of the eleven primary tasks specified for the joint liaison committees was to arrange for staff consultation.

On Humberside, the JLC was approached about consultative machinery by two of the larger unions in November 1972. In the following January the JLC chairman and secretary, with the personnel officer of the largest HMC, met representatives of all the major unions. It was agreed to set up five consultative committees, on a Humberside basis, where staff representatives could meet representatives of the JLC. The committees would cover: administrative and clerical staff; nurses and midwives; professional and technical staff; ancillary staff; ambulancemen. At its meeting in February 1973, the JLC confirmed the arrangement and nominated nine members to represent the management side. The JLC working party reports were made available to the staff-side secretaries. All this was done before DHSS guidance about consultative machinery arrived in May. But it took the unions several months to agree on membership of the staff sides. A constitution was finally agreed at a joint meeting in June 1973. The staff representatives secured the right to approach the JLC independently if they wished, and insisted on further meetings with management. By October, all the staff-side committees had held preliminary meetings, and the ambulancemen and the administrative and clerical staff had submitted items for discussion.

By this time, however, the JLC was on the way out and the shadow AHA had been appointed. At its second (November 1973) meeting, the AHA agreed to take over the consultative machinery and to replace the JLC representatives with its own nominees in due course. This was overtaken by a decision, in July 1974, that new consultative bodies should be set up on an area and district basis. This decision had still not been implemented by June 1975, partly because of the difficulty of agreeing on staff-side membership. (At this time, the unions were refusing to recognise consultative machinery which included representatives of professional associations like the Royal College of Nursing.) In the meantime, the JLC bodies for ambulancemen and administrative and clerical staff remained in existence.

Among the items on which staff interests should have been consulted were staff transfer schemes, acting-up arrangements, interim management arrangements and the permanent management structure. By October 1975, just over half the managers in Humberside (who were personally concerned about all these issues) recalled having been consulted about the interim management arrangements. About half thought they had been consulted about the permanent management structure, and considerably less than half about staff transfer schemes and acting-up arrangements. Moreover, 'consultations' generally meant a brief personal chat with one's superior. The formal arrangements were seldom mentioned spontaneously and were confused with staff meetings, the professional advisory committee for nurses, the JLC working parties, the JLC itself, meetings of heads of departments, and even the joint consultative committee between the NHS and local government.

About half these middle-ranking officers felt that the efforts made to consult them about important matters had been inadequate. Most of the dissatisfaction came from one district, which suffered more than the others in discontinuity among senior staff, and from the administrative and finance officers who had borne the brunt of the changes. Nevertheless, out of the total sample, just under half felt that staff had generally been treated fairly in the run-up to reorganisation; a third felt that they had not and the remainder were unsure.

SUMMARY AND COMMENT

The comment was made at the end of the last chapter that quite important decisions about the shape of the new service in Humberside were made technocratically, with the minimum of involvement by lay authority members. This was almost as true of the substantive arrangements for staffing the new service which have just been described. The arrangements for filling senior posts, and the restriction of competition for the less senior (which in Humberside persisted from the beginning of 1973 to the beginning of 1975), were deliberately designed to restrict the freedom of the employing authorities in the interests of the staff. Nationally, this policy had the effect of depriving the NHS of some of the talent that was available at a time of recession in industry. On Humberside, it led to difficulty in filling some very senior posts, especially on the finance side.

Chapter 10 considers some other strategies that could have been adopted. An important point to be made here is that the NHS arrangements were very complex—certainly in comparison with those that were made to deal with parallel situations in local government—and may well have been too elaborate for their purpose. For example, the complicated arrangements adopted by the NHS Staff Commission for short-listing candidates for the most senior posts caused a great deal of unhappiness, mainly because of the delays and uncertainties built into the procedures. But their outcome, in Humberside, was that the obvious local candidate (where there was one) got the job. It is difficult to point to a single appointment at this level which would have been made differently if there had been no Staff Commission. (This is not, of course, to depreciate the need for some body to process applications so that the AHA could proceed quickly to the actual selection procedure, or for experienced assessors to advise the selection committees.) The difficulty arose when there was no suitable local candidate. Here the authority was seriously restricted by the Staff Commission rules, compounded by the loss of experienced senior officers under the provisions for early retirement.

The continuity among senior officers compensated in many ways for the delay. But there is no doubt that the delay and uncertainty was felt, not only by those directly concerned, but also by managerial subordinates, who themselves were to have to wait an unconscionable time before being allocated to posts in the new structure. Once given the all-clear, Humberside completed their assimilation with great speed. But this was not until the beginning of 1975 for the main groups of staff and even later for some. There was a serious problem of morale among key groups, especially in administration and finance. This was not diminished by the outcome, which was in many cases far more advantageous than the incumbents could have expected at the outset.

That said, the central authorities perhaps exaggerated the scale of the morale problem and the scale of the measures needed to deal with it. Low morale was associated with personal insecurity, and this was limited to certain groups, even within the managerial strata who attended preparatory courses. For the great majority of NHS staff, the reorganisation was a non-event until later, when deficiencies began to appear in the new structures. The expensive measures to create awareness and acceptance of the change (in which we have to include costly concessions to the NHS staff associations and unions) did not seem all that relevant. The consultative arrangements did not really work, and were not particularly salient. Nor did the newsletters and training courses have a great deal of success in transmitting knowledge or modifying attitudes (although they may of course have helped to scotch rumours). They were not intended to equip people for new jobs and could not remove the anxieties of those who were unsure about their own position. Again, it is possible that they prevented people from becoming anxious who had no need to be; but these were not the people training courses were aimed at and the limited evidence is that information sheets were not widely read at lower levels.

By contrast, latching-on was a great success. Although there were pressure points, especially in the administration of community services where there was not much left to latch on to, the policy of attaching whole blocks of existing staff and functions to the most convenient point in the new structure allowed the provision of services to continue with the minimum of immediate disturbance. It was a pity that pressures exerted on behalf of relatively small groups of staff made it impossible to continue with latching-on until there was time to prepare adequately for the introduction of the new structures. As it was, the latching-on period was brought to an abrupt and hasty end.

The main lesson of this chapter is that, while steps can be taken to reduce the extent of upheaval, any major administrative restructuring is likely to involve heavy costs, delays and discontinuities in the ongoing processes of management. In Humberside, they were most clearly seen in the loss of momentum in the expiring authorities, which lost their most experienced officers, and in the difficulty of establishing financial controls and information bases for the new administration. How they affected the professional staff will be seen in the next chapter.

NOTES

1   DHSS, *Management Arrangements for the Reorganised National Health Service*, HMSO, 1972, appendix 3. The main recommendations were accepted in Health Service Reorganisation Circular HRC(73)3. More specific advice relating to staffing structures was contained in HRCs(74)29, (74)31, (74)34 and (74)35.
2   DHSS, *National Health Service Staff Commission Report (1972–5)*, HMSO, 1975, paras 6.19–6.25.
3   Some of these might have been found among the headquarters staff of the DHSS: in his *Diaries* (vol.3, p. 692), Richard Crossman comments that the DHSS had creamed off the best matrons without having a great deal for them to do.
4   *Op.cit.* (note 2) pp. 67–8.
5   *Hospital and Health Services Review*, London, editorial, Jan. 1974.
6   Local Government Staff Commission Circulars 6/72 and 8/73.
7   HRC(73)3.
8   The Public Accounts Committee of the House of Commons commented that health authorities had aspired to develop their management capacity more quickly than resources would allow. The DHSS had restricted the total number of senior and middle posts in England to 5,330 (556 fewer than the health authorities had requested) and allocated quotas to each region. See *Ninth Report of the Public Accounts Committee for 1976–77* (HC 532), HMSO, 1977.
9   *Survey of Local Authority Salaries*, Local Authority Conditions of Service Advisory Board, London, May 1974.
10   Public Accounts Committee, *op.cit.* (note 8).
11   HRC(73)11.

CHAPTER 7

Professional Machinery

One of the objectives of reorganisation was to involve the professions more directly in the management of the health service. The Reorganisation Act made provision for professional advisory committees at area and regional levels. In addition, the medical profession was required to set up non-statutory machinery at district level which would bring together the different branches of the profession and from which would emerge two clinical members for each district management team.[1]

Detailed guidance on the composition and role of advisory committees was issued in February 1974. This covered model constitutions, agreed nationally with representatives of the professions concerned, for area and regional advisory committees to represent doctors, dentists, nurses and midwives, pharmacists, and ophthalmic and dispensing opticians; the possibility of additional committees for other professions was not ruled out.[2] The circular also dealt with medical machinery at district level.

General medical and dental practitioners, retail pharmacists and opticians already had representative committees within the executive-council system; these were retained in the new service, although they had to be realigned on an area basis to match the new family practitioner committees. Senior hospital doctors had a separate representative system, normally based on specialty divisions serving the hospitals administered by a hospital management committee;[3] these, too, would be preserved, but adapted to the new pattern of health service districts, which (at least on Humberside) did not coincide with the former hospital groups. What was new was the concept of a district medical committee, on which general practitioners and hospital specialists would sit together with representatives of junior medical staff (both in general practice and in hospitals) and of community medicine, and develop an integrated approach to the planning and operation of medical services in their district; the elected chairman and vice-chairman of the district medical committee would become the clinical members of the district management team, playing an equal part in team decision-making with the four official members appointed by the AHA.

A similar balance of interests was to be reflected in the area and regional medical advisory committees. The area committee was to be created separately from the district committee, but in much the same way. Membership of the regional advisory committee would come partly from the area committees and partly from groups of staff, such as specialist groups and educators, which were felt to need separate representation at regional level.

The result is a complex network of medical committees, outlined diagramatically in fig. 2 on p.35. The machinery for dentists, nurses and other professions is less complex, since it does not include a district tier; but it is based on similar principles and similarly intended to formulate coordinated advice after discussion among representatives of the different branches of each profession.

This chapter is concerned mainly with the way medical machinery was developed in Humberside, with a brief reference to other professional groups at the end. Comments made by practising doctors are drawn upon to illustrate the problems and advantages of both the old and the new system.

THE TRANSITION

General practitioners. Prior to April 1974, Humberside was served (in whole or in part) by five executive councils, and its GPs were therefore represented on five local medical committees. These committees dealt with professional matters affecting general practice, such as allegations of excessive prescribing or undue care in the issue of medical certificates, as well as the interpretation of regulations about fees and conditions of practice. They consisted mainly of elected general practitioner representatives, plus a medical officer of health and one or two hospital consultants for liaison purposes. Their total size was usually about twenty-five; but the Grimsby LMC had only twelve elected members to represent its thirty-four doctors, and the West Riding (which covered Goole) had forty-one. The LMC members we spoke to tended to complain about their limited influence on hospital policies, such as access to physiotherapy departments; consultant representation was not always regarded as productive, and the GPs did not always have reciprocal membership of the hospital medical committees. There was also a feeling of remoteness about the larger LMCs;

for example, there was only one member on the large West Riding committee to represent the thirteen Goole GPs.

The tasks were first to reconstitute the LMCs on a Humberside basis and then to nominate GP representatives to the family practitioner committee and the new district and area medical committees. The chairmen of the five existing committees agreed to form a steering committee of twelve members (four from the East Riding, three from Hull, two each from Grimsby and Lindsey and one from the West Riding) to decide the shape of the new LMC. They agreed that the Humberside LMC should have thirty members, of whom twenty-two should be elected by the 356 doctors practising in the area. The constituencies were based on local government district boundaries, and representation was to reflect the number of practitioners in each district. This system gave predominance to urban doctors; twelve of the twenty-two places went to Hull, Grimsby and Scunthorpe. Of the eight remaining places, one was allocated to the area medical officer, and the others (which were not in fact filled) to consultant staff and coopted GPs, to include one assistant. The amalgamation also reduced the number of places available: the representation of Grimsby doctors fell from twelve to two. Except in one district, which was formed out of parts of three old LMCs, elections were avoided. The new LMC met in September 1973. It elected the chairman of the Hull LMC as its chairman, and the chairman of the East Riding LMC as its vice-chairman.

Nominations for the eight GP places on the family practitioner committee were agreed at the same meeting. But arrangements for representation on the main medical committees had to wait until the consultants had made up their minds about their representation: the model constitutions drawn up by the BMA stipulated that all these bodies should have equal numbers of GPs and consultants, with additional provision for doctors working in community health and for juniors in training. But the LMC did agree to split into four district sub-committees to nominate representatives on the district medical committees in due course.

By the end of March 1974, it became clear that there would be six consultant members on three of the district medical committees, five on the fourth, and eleven on the area advisory medical committee. Corresponding numbers of GPs were nominated under the machinery already set up. Of the eleven GPs on the area committee, seven came from the north bank (three from Hull and four from Beverley) and two each from Scunthorpe and Grimsby.

From discussions with them a year earlier, we know that many GPs approached this new structure with some trepidation. Most of this concerned the size and possible unrepresentativeness of the new LMC: country doctors were particularly worried about its dominance by urban colleagues who might know little about rural practice problems. But there was some enthusiasm for the district medical committees, so long as they did not disintegrate into separate sub-committees for general practice and hospitals. By March 1975, however, there was some disillusionment among GP members, since consultants were tending to bypass the DMC machinery.

North-bank consultants. The history of medical machinery for the North Humberside hospitals is long and involved. It is worth going into some detail because it helps to explain why the consultants were consistently opposed to the division of the north bank into two administrative districts. It also illustrates some of the problems of representational machinery.

Until 1974, there were three management committees serving the population around Hull and Beverley. (Bridlington hospitals formed part of a group based on Scarborough; a bid by their medical staff to have Bridlington hived off from Humberside to North Yorkshire was over-ruled by the Department of Health and Social Security.) From 1948 to the late 1950s, each of these HMCs had its own medical advisory committee. But this became increasingly unworkable as the three hospital groups began to provide an integrated service; many consultants had contracts covering hospitals in more than one group. Some machinery was needed to achieve a more coordinated approach to medical policy. The solution found by the doctors was to establish a joint hospital medical staffs committee (JHMSC) for all established medical staff working in any of the three groups. The executive arm of this body was a small medical advisory committee, consisting of five consultants (one for each HMC and two elected on a personal basis) and two general practitioners representing the Hull and East Riding LMCs. In addition, there were three sub-committees—one for each HMC—mainly to assess priorities for the purchase of medical equipment.

In 1967, the first report of a working party on the organisation of medical work in hospitals[3] recommended that consultants working in specialty groups should form themselves into 'divisions' to discuss matters of common interest and that representatives from the divisions should meet as a medical executive committee (MEC) to deal with overall policy for each hospital group. In applying this to Hull and Beverley, the JHMSC decided to retain the integrated structure and form divisions covering the whole Hull and Beverley area. After a number of experiments, a new structure became fully operational in 1972. It consisted of six divisions, a standing committee on community medicine, and a medical executive committee. The MEC consisted of the chairmen of the divisions and the standing committee, the chairman of the JHMSC and the chairmen of the three sub-committees (which had to remain in existence so long as the HMCs remained financially independent). The divisions varied greatly in size: those for surgery and medicine had thirty-five members each; those for psychiatry and pathology had twenty-five members each; anaesthetics had twenty members; and the radiology and nuclear medicine division had twelve. The main division consisted exclusively of hospital doctors: contrary to advice from the national working party, there was no involvement of administrators or nursing staff.[4] The standing committee on community medicine consisted of representatives from the six divisions, six general practitioners, and the medical officers of health and their deputies from Hull and East Riding. Its relationship with the divisions had been strained. It had been demoted from divisional status after heated discussions about whether it should rank equally with the hospital-based divisions. Its chairman (the Medical Officer of Health for Hull) was, however, a member of the MEC.

Many consultants felt that these bodies were mere talking-shops and achieved very little. The greatest dissatisfaction was expressed by members of the large surgical division, who claimed that no one person could represent all the sub-specialties on the executive committee and pointed to the case for proportional representation. Members of the executive committee regretted the absence of a senior nurse and an administrator and felt that it was unfortunate that the committee had been established just at the time when more substantial reorganisation was beginning to be discussed.

Nevertheless, the 1972 structure would have offered a good basis (with or without the addition of Bridlington consultants) for consultant participation in the new structure, if it had been decided to create a single district for North Humberside. As we have seen in chapter 5, however, the DHSS decided with some local support to insist on a division into two districts, in spite of the unanimous opposition of the consultants who had invested so much energy in overcoming the pre-1974 administrative boundaries. (This opposition was not, incidentally, mollified by experience: when the district structure came under review in 1977, the consultants were the only group to express whole-hearted support for amalgamation.)

The immediate task was to adapt the newly established structure to the even newer requirements. In particular, it was necessary to devise some machinery through which hospital representatives could be nominated to the two North Humberside district medical committees and to the Humberside area medical advisory committee. The JHMSC appointed a small sub-committee to consider the alternatives. Its report was considered at two full meetings (with attendances of fifty-two and twenty out of a possible 150) in February 1974. The outcome was a decision to retain the unified JHMSC and the unified divisional structure for Hull and Beverley districts, with the addition of consultants from Bridlington. The community medicine committee, however, was abolished. Each of the six divisions would appoint a representative to both district medical committees — thus settling the number of places, both for consultants and for GPs. In addition, the chairman of each division, along with the chairman of the JHMSC, would form a coordinating north-bank medical committee. (This committee found itself with little to do and was abolished in 1975.)

These arrangements were not acceptable to the surgeons, who were pressing for larger representation, proportional to their numbers, on the district medical committees. This the JHMSC was unwilling to grant, and for some months the surgical division failed to nominate representatives to the district committees. The other consultant (and GP) representatives took up their places in time for a meeting in March; this was a joint meeting, convened by a local BMA representative.

The north-bank JHMSC also took the initiative in forming an area medical advisory committee. Here again, the model constitution stipulated a membership of between twenty and thirty, to include equal numbers of GPs and consultants, with a third category of junior doctors and doctors in public health or community medicine. The JHMSC decided to convene an area *hospital* medical committee, with equal representation from north and south banks, to act as an electoral college. The north-bank divisions, and the medical committee chairmen in Grimsby and Scunthorpe, were invited to submit nominations for consideration. In fact, the meeting was convened at very short notice; only seven consultants out of a possible twelve (two per division) attended from the north bank, and two out of a possible six from each of Grimsby and Scunthorpe. The south-bank representatives felt out-numbered and out-manoeuvred. But eleven names were agreed, giving a fair spread of hospital specialties (including a north-bank surgeon) and a reasonably fair reflection of the distribution of consultants north and south of the river: seven of the eleven came from the north bank, and two each from Scunthorpe and Grimsby. At that time there were about 150 consultants on the north bank and seventy on the south.

South-bank consultants. Arrangements on the south bank were more simple and more straightforward. There were obvious nuclei of hospital staff in the two district centres, and the main problem was assimilating Goole into Scunthorpe.

At this time, Grimsby consultants had just set up a fairly simple divisional structure. There were three divisions, covering surgery, medicine, and psychiatry with child health. The medical executive committee consisted of the chairman and one other member from each division, with the chief nursing officer and deputy group secretary as non-voting members. Every third meeting was an open meeting, which any consultant could attend with full voting rights; this was Grimsby's equivalent to the north-bank JHMSC. When it came to appointing members to the district medical committee, it was decided not to follow the divisional pattern but to elect six consultants on their individual merits. The outcome was a reasonable spread of specialties, including a gynaecologist but no general surgeon. Nor was a surgeon among the two Grimsby representatives on the area medical advisory committee.

Until February 1974, the twenty-six consultants working in Scunthorpe hospitals met as a medical advisory committee, with the group secretary initially as secretary and latterly as a non-voting member. At the suggestion of the regional hospital board, the consultants then formed themselves into six divisions, including the four consultants based on Goole. The divisions were small and somewhat artificial: one consisted of only two surgeons, and another contained two obstetricians, one X-ray specialist and two radiologists. In addition, a group medical committee, consisting of all consultants and medical assistants, was established as a general medical forum. The chairman of this committee joined the chairmen of the six divisions to form a medical executive committee, of which the group secretary became a non-voting member; there was no nurse representative, although nurses attended some of the divisional meetings. It had been difficult enough to maintain interest in the original advisory committee, and most of the consultants felt that the new structure was too elaborate. (The divisions were later abandoned in favour of an all-purpose hospital medical committee.) However, they now had to cope with the additional complexities of district and area medical committees.

In fact, the district arrangements for Scunthorpe were made by the old advisory committee in its last months of life. It was decided late in 1973 that there should be five consultant members and that they should be directly elected instead of emerging from the new divisional structure. In January

1974, the advisory committee chairman, who had been a member of the Humberside joint liaison committee and had kept Scunthorpe doctors well abreast of developments, wrote to all the thirty consultants in Scunthorpe and Goole to invite nominations. A few weeks later he wrote again, since nine nominations had been received and it was necessary to take a vote. The result was a somewhat unbalanced specialty representation, consisting of two physicians, an anaesthetist, an obstetrician and an ophthalmologist; a surgeon just missed being elected.

Some weeks later, at the meeting convened by the north-bank JHMSC, it was agreed that Scunthorpe would be represented on the area medical advisory committee by an obstetrician and an anaesthetist. South-bank consultant representation was completed by a paediatrician and a physician from Grimsby. Two of these were also members of the district medical committees.

TRAINING

The general programme of training for reorganisation was intended, in part, to meet the needs of medical staff. At least one Humberside consultant attended the four-week senior management course. Several general practitioners and public health doctors attended the shorter course for middle management at Hull University. The leading medical officers of health took part in longer courses specifically intended to provide some crash training for their new roles as community physicians.

But it was recognised that many general practitioners and consultants would find it difficult to get away for a week or more. Special two-day courses were therefore arranged for them. These concentrated on the roles and relationships of clinicians in the new service, with a particular emphasis on the district medical committee and the district management team. The intention was to prepare a nucleus of four consultants and four general practitioners in each district for the work of a clinical member of a district management team. On this basis, Humberside would have had places for thirty-two doctors. But by the closing date in September 1973, only four consultants and seven GPs from Humberside had applied for places. After discussion, it was agreed that Hull University would arrange a residential seminar, exclusively for Humberside doctors, in March 1974. Twenty-one doctors attended, including all the eight original district management team members. A second seminar was arranged a year later for members of the area and district medical committees. This was less well-attended, as it coincided with a consultant boycott of all committee work.

During a round of interviews in July 1974, most specialists in community medicine and clinical members of management teams said that the courses they had attended had been either helpful or very helpful. However, it was evident at the second seminar in March 1975 that there was still a good deal of confusion about the new structure and in particular about the new medical advisory machinery.

THE NEW STRUCTURE AT WORK

By March 1974, the consultant and general-practitioner members of the area committee and the four district medical committees had been appointed, except for surgical representatives on the two north-bank district committees. Under the model constitution, there was a third category of membership to include junior staff in training, representatives of public health staff, the area medical officer or district community physician, and any other interest which it might be felt necessary to coopt. The consultants and GPs agreed that each district committee should have four places in this additional category: one for the district community physician, one for an elected clinical public health officer, and one each for junior hospital doctors and assistant or trainee general practitioners. The area committee should have eight such places: one for the area medical officer, two for community physicians from the north and south banks, one for each group of junior staff, and three for representatives of the regional postgraduate committee for medical education.

Lacking the machinery of their seniors, the junior staff were slow to nominate their representatives. There were no assistant or trainee general practitioners at all in Grimsby. The names of junior staff and medical education representatives on the area committee were still not known when the area health authority approved its constitution, so that it could be recognised under the Act, in April. In fact, only two of the ten places available for junior staff had been filled.

Nevertheless, all four district committes were able to meet in March. All four elected a general practitioner as chairman and a consultant as vice-chairman. These two doctors thus became the clinical members of the relevant district management teams. For this (but not for associated work on the medical committee and its parent bodies) they received an extra payment of about one-eleventh of a consultant's basic salary.

The district committees were, as intended, broadly representative, except for the absence of surgery due to the temporary boycott on the north bank and the electoral system adopted by the south-bank consultants. An interesting point was the representation of the peripheral areas of Goole and Bridlington, which were being grafted on to older organisations in Scunthorpe and Hull/Beverley. The geographical system of representation employed by the GPs ensured that such areas were represented. It was perhaps more by good chance that one of the six consultants on the Beverley committee came from Bridlington, and one of the five Scunthorpe consultants from Goole. In addition, Bridlington provided an assistant GP and Goole supplied a clinical public health officer (who neatly balanced the district community physician, based on Scunthorpe).

During their first year of operation, attendance at district medical committee meetings was around seventy per cent. Some became very active, settling down to serious discussion of questions like the hospital waiting list. Others seemed to see themselves more as a brake on the district management teams: the practice developed of holding committee meetings immediately before a team meeting so that the clinical representatives could brief themselves on the views of their colleagues. Initially at least, the committees became responsible for filtering and allocating priority to requisitions for medical and surgical equipment. But much of their business consisted of reviewing the minutes of other committees. It has to be remembered that district medical committees are intermediate between the management teams and bodies representing the constituent groups of doctors—the district sub-committee of the local medical committee for general practitioners, and either (on the north bank) the specialist divisions of hospital doctors or (on the south bank) a coordinating medical executive committee of a committee consisting of all hospital doctors. It was not surprising that they should be feeling their way.

At the time of the research, there seemed to be two main threats to the district committee structure. One was that, to hospital consultants, it represented yet another obstacle to getting quick decisions. Many felt that purely hospital matters should go straight to the district management team without passing through the district committee, whose other members would be tempted to interfere in matters they did not understand. On major questions, the area medical advisory committee looked a better route to the area health authority.

The second threat arose from the two-district structure on the north bank. The consultants had never been happy about the creation of two districts and had retained their own divisions spanning both districts. It seemed increasingly artificial to have to deal with two separate district medical committees and management teams. In a sense, the consultants made matters worse by abolishing the divisional chairmen's committee in 1975, since there was now no means of reconciling differences between the specialty divisions on the north bank. The north-bank consultants campaigned for the amalgamation of the two districts and in 1977 began to boycott the district committees.

The north-bank consultants were by that time beginning to see the area medical advisory committee as a possible answer to their problems. Even in the preliminary stages, some doctors saw the area committee as the key medical body, because of its prestige and direct access to the health authority. But it was slow to get under way. Its first meeting was not until May 1974, and by June 1975 it had met only three times. Like the district committees, it was affected by the consultants' boycott during their industrial action in the early part of that year. Even so, it took time to find a role: it was not thought worth reporting the outcome of these early meetings to the area health authority.[5] Indeed, the AHA cast around for things for it to do, like advising on kidney donor cards. More substantial issues arose in 1976, when the committee had to be consulted about the area strategic plan and about a commissioned report on waiting lists. By this time the original chairman (a GP) had been replaced by a consultant in geriatric medicine.

But the increasing salience of the area committee was associated with problems on the north bank. Of its twenty-two consultant and GP members, fourteen came from the north bank. Its agenda tended to be mainly concerned with north-bank matters. Some doctors regarded it as a 'North Humberside' body. Understandably, the district structures remained more salient for the south-bank consultants in Grimsby and Scunthorpe. But in at least one of these districts, there was evidence that the district medical committee as such was becoming less important than the hospital-based medical executive committee.

The area health authority was unhappy about the kind of assistance it was receiving from the area committee. In December 1977 it approved proposals to reconstitute the committee with a smaller and more district-grounded membership, with one consultant and one GP from each district, one junior staff representative, one district community physician, one representative of the postgraduate education committee and the area medical officer. Its terms of reference were redefined to cover only matters affecting all doctors on Humberside.

NURSING AND OTHER PROFESSIONS

While the medical committees were being set up, parallel committees at area level were being set up for nurses, dentists, opticians and pharmacists, under the same Act and the same DHSS circular. In each case, the professions themselves were required to form the committee, and the area health authority was required to recognise it if certain requirements were met. The most important of these was that the committee should represent different branches of the profession, with particular emphasis on the balance between hospital and community representation. These professions had an easier task than the doctors, since they did not have to set up machinery in each district.

The dentists, opticians and pharmacists were in the same position as general practitioners. Local committees already existed to represent those who were in contact with executive councils. They had to be reconstituted on a Humberside basis to match the new family practitioner committee. Hospital interests then had to be brought in to form a balanced professional advisory committee which could be recognised by the AHA. The area optical committee was in effect the local optical committee with the addition of one ophthalmic optician and one dispensing optician elected by their respective colleagues in the hospital eye service. In contrast, the pharmacists set up separate area committees for retail and hospital pharmacy, which nominated four members each to form the area pharmaceutical advisory committee. The dental and optical committees were formed by the appointed day, but the pharmacists were not ready until June 1974. None of these bodies had anything like the same stake as the doctors in overall health policy, and nothing much was heard from them over the next three years.

The nurses, however, had to create an organisation from scratch. The nurses' working party which had been set up by the joint liaison committee might have provided a model. But it was decided nationally that a model constitution was needed which reflected the wide diversity of nursing and its representation by a variety of trade unions and professional nursing associations such as the Royal Colleges of Nursing and Midwifery. A national steering committee was formed, consisting of thirteen representatives from the eleven main nursing associations and unions.[6] They agreed that each organisation should obtain nominations from its local branches and, after consideration, put forward the names of those they wished to sit on advisory committees for final decision by the steering committee. The result looks more like a staff consultative committee than a professional advisory body since the emphasis is placed on lower-grade staff, and over a third on the steering committee consists of trade unionists (albeit with a statutory qualification). The Humberside AHA was informed in May 1974 that sixteen places had been allocated, with ten still to be filled. Most of the gaps were in Scunthorpe district, where the communication system with local branches had apparently broken down. The authority approved the committee subject to rectification of the omission.

In spite of its curious composition, the nursing advisory committee set about its work with considerable enthusiasm. Regular meetings were held and by June 1975 a report on hospital discharge procedures had been submitted to the health authority. This was the first report on any subject to come from any of the advisory committees.

The Act provided that regional and area health authorities could recognise advisory committees formed by professions not specifically mentioned in the Act. It was thought in some quarters, for example, that advisory committees for paramedical staff (radiographers, physiotherapists and the like) would be needed, since the development of community services might considerably alter the nature and organisation of their work. But it proved very difficult to find the right place for paramedical staff in the new organisation, partly because the original idea, that they should normally be managed by designated clinicians,[7] was vigorously resisted and partly because internal dissension among the various professional groups frustrated any viable alternative. No ideas for representative machinery had emerged by February 1977, when the Secretary of State ruled that, in order to economise on administrative costs, no further advisory committee should be recognised for the time being. On Humberside, however, some of the groups established as working parties during the joint liaison committee phase, including medical records officers and members of the remedial paramedical professions, remained in existence as non-statutory advisory committees. They confined their advice, however, to matters of administrative detail.

SUMMARY AND COMMENT

By or shortly after the appointed day, the Humberside doctors had established new machinery at area and district levels, and the other four professional groups listed in the Reorganisation Act had formed area advisory committees. One or two other groups remained in being from the joint liaison working party phase. With some conspicuous exceptions, these tasks were accomplished in a good-humoured atmosphere of constructive cooperation. But certain difficulties began to appear.

Apart from the doctors and nurses, it was difficult to see what the new machinery had to offer its participants. Certainly, there are important issues about, for example, the most suitable balance between hospital dispensing for out-patients and retail pharmacy, or between hospital and independent dental services; but there is some incentive to keep them under the carpet. At any rate, they do not seem to have been discussed by (or referred to) the relevant committees. Moreover, there are area dental and pharmaceutical officers, with direct access to the AHA, to deal with such problems, while 'community' dentists and pharmacists have direct access to the family practitioner committee on questions which concern them directly. The new committees did not command much interest.

Nursing is interesting, because nurses are hierarchically organised under nursing officers who represent the profession on all management teams. Each health authority includes a nursing member. There is also a staff consultative committee for nurses and midwives. The establishment of a rather similar committee to advise the health authorities may therefore seem redundant, and there was indeed some tension between this committee and nursing officers who felt that it was usurping their role. Nevertheless, the Humberside committee carried out some useful work. This seems to have been partly because nurses were enjoying their new, vastly enhanced, status as a power group and partly because they were more enthusiastic than other professional groups about the opportunity to build bridges between hospitals and the community services.

But the main objective was to build similar bridges between hospital and non-hospital doctors, and to involve both groups of autonomous clinicians in the processes of management and planning. The other professions were simply swept up in the arrangements made for doctors. How successful have they been?

The first question here concerns the reality of involvement through several layers of representative machinery. Representation involves some surrender of power to the representative, and it was clear from our interviews that many doctors could not accept this. Even in the smaller divisions, some felt that a chairman from another, albeit related, specialty could not adequately represent their interest on a medical executive committee. The difficulties increased with the size of the divisions, and they were compounded as the pyramid of indirect representation sharpened to the single consultant member of the management team. Some clinical team members were equally doubtful about their ability to represent several hundred colleagues—hence the frequent referrals back to the medical committees. The less political did not much like what they saw, and regretted that these layers of machinery were in fact cutting them off from the real decision-makers. (They did not, perhaps, realise quite how elusive any executive authority had become in the reorganised system.)

The second point is that these complex structures could make enormous demands on the time of those who were willing to give it. There were over 120 places on the five main medical committees for the 1,000-odd doctors on Humberside. The consultants did their best to share the load: only two of the original consultant members of the area medical committee sat on district committees, although they could not avoid commitments in their own divisional or hospital committee structures. But there were fewer willing horses on the general-practitioner side. Ten of the eleven GP members of the area committee were also members of district medical committees; three of them also sat on a district management team, the area local medical committee and the family practitioner committee; one, who was vice-chairman of the FPC, also became chairman of the area medical committee and thus automatically a member of the regional medical advisory committee.

Even so, the hospital consultants seemed to have the greatest difficulty, possibly because of the complexity of their internal arrangements. In each district (or pair of districts) the consultants felt the need for a committee which included all senior members of the medical staff. On top of this was grafted the divisional structure, with a coordinating medical executive committee. On top of this again came consultant representation on the statutory area committee and on the district medical committee and management team. It was not surprising that some parts of the machinery failed to operate. In the smallest district, the divisions and the medical executive committee soon disappeared, leaving the district medical committee in a strong position. In another, the medical executive committee was retained, but the district committee tended to become redundant, since the GPs felt adequately represented by their man on the management team. On the north bank, the divisions (which straddled both districts) remained strong, but the coordinating committee disappeared, leaving a vacuum to be filled by the district and area committees. Impatience with the two-district structure caused the consultants to boycott the district committees, largely on the grounds of duplication and extra work. Some expected the area committee to take over. In the early stages this had looked like the fifth wheel on the coach. But the area health authority was determined to make it work and tried to prevent it becoming a 'North Humberside' committee.

The reader who has persevered with all this may still need to be reminded of the theological significance of the district and area committees as meeting points for consultants, GPs and junior and public health staff. If the DMC is bypassed on questions of hospital development, the GPs and other groups lose, in theory, the opportunity to influence them and build an integrated service. But the GPs who do want to influence these developments are sure of a spokesman on the district management team, whch is one of the reasons why GPs were in favour of retaining two teams on the north bank. (A GP representative for one of the teams had to be found during the consultants' boycott of the district committees; he was appointed directly by the local (FPC) medical committee.) Yet another channel of influence for GPs is through the local medical committee to the family practitioner committee: an amendment to the Reorganisation Bill ruled out the possibility that the LMC might be fused with any of the all-purpose medical committees. It is also possible to lobby the GP member of the area health authority. Public health staff, too, have their spokesmen in the district community physician and area medical officer. So, perhaps, short-circuiting the district committee would not be a great loss.

The architects of the reorganisation certainly under-estimated the practical difficulties of running four medical structures (local medical committees, hospital divisions, district committees for integrated clinical management, area and regional committees for integrated policy advice) side by side. The professional organisations which negotiated the representational arrangements seem equally to have over-estimated the enthusiasm of their local members for committee work.

This ends the discussion of the transition to new structures in Humberside. The next chapter will consider how far they contributed to comprehensive planning, coordination and rationalisation of services.

NOTES

1 DHSS, *Management Arrangements for the Reorganised National Health Service*, HMSO, 1972, ch.4.
2 Health Service Reorganisation Circular HRC(74)9.

3 Ministry of Health, *First Report of the Joint Working Party on the Organisation of Medical Work in Hospitals*, HMSO, 1967; DHSS, *Second* and *Third Reports of the Working Party*, 1972 and 1974.

4 In their second (1972) report, the working party stated that they knew of only two instances where a senior administrator did not attend MEC meetings. In about three-quarters of the structures on which they had information, a nurse also attended. In North Humberside, one of the group secretaries had been invited but felt that his presence would be inappropriate.

5 While the BMA was pleased with the way these committees had been established generally, there was concern that in some parts of the country, the area committees had failed to attract much interest from hospital doctors, who were accordingly under-represented. See *British Medical Journal*, 27 April 1974, pp. 29–30 'Annual Report of Council for 1973–74'.

6 HRC(74)9.

7 *Management Arrangements for the Reorganised National Health Service, op.cit.* (note 1), ch. 7. The problems of paramedical staff are too complex to be discussed here, and are the subject of a separate research project at Hull University.

CHAPTER 8

New Bottles: Old Wine?

The test of the reorganisation is not whether it was successfully carried out but whether it produced the intended results. On balance, was the new service better able than the old one to operate efficiently, to coordinate hospital and community care, to draw up and implement comprehensive plans, and to reallocate resources in accordance with local need and national priorities?

These are not easy questions to answer, even from a close acquaintance with the workings of one authority. Too many other things were happening at the same time. There was a change of government a few weeks before reorganisation day, and the incoming administration was out of sympathy with the managerialist philosophy embodied in the new structure. The country was passing through an economic crisis which considerably reduced the scope for health service growth and development: an attempt to cushion the service from the results of inflation led first to a spending spree, and then to attempts to recover some of the lost ground. Old patterns of authority and control were breaking down as one group after another, from the doctors and nurses to the maintenance workers and ambulancemen, flexed their industrial muscles in pursuit of pay and power. Some of these events directly impeded the progress of reorganisation. All consumed time and energy which might have been used to exploit it.

The reorganisation itself cast a long shadow. For at least a year beforehand, the normal development of the service was affected as officers and members of the old authorities were drawn into the new system. During the first two years after reorganisation, the key people were preoccupied with filling gaps in the structure and with learning how to make it work: this period was punctuated by special seminars and closed meetings to examine roles and relationships. The Humberside area health authority did not really get into its stride until 1976, when it began to get the information it needed for financial control and strategic planning.

The research project on which this analysis is based was concerned with the reorganisation process. Most of the fieldwork was completed by June 1975.[1] At that time, the problems seemed more salient than the benefits. To give a more balanced picture, the story has been carried forward as far as possible to the end of 1977. It starts with a description of the psychological climate in which the new structure was born.

ATTITUDES TO REFORM

In the first quarter of 1973, 134 key officers and medical committee men, whose roles seemed likely to change as a result of reorganisation, were identified and interviewed. At that time the impending restructuring had not had much impact on staff outside the network of the joint liaison committee and its working parties. There was, in fact, a good deal of ignorance of the details. Professional, technical and nursing staff seemed fairly satisfied that their own work would continue regardless of the administrative changes and that April 1974 would be relatively unimportant for them. The best-informed groups, and the most critical, were medical and lay administrators (medical officers of health, divisional medical officers, chief clerks, executive council administrators, senior hospital administrators and treasurers). But criticisms tended to centre on details, like the abolition of hospital management committees, the possible remoteness of the new Humberside authority or the risk of too much bureaucracy. The general feeling was that the amalgamation of the services themselves was logical and desirable. Even the local authority nurses, who were to become increasingly anxious about their own position, approved of the change in principle. Some local authority medical staff feared that their services would suffer in what they saw as a hospital takeover. Only a small minority, including some influential general practitioners, regarded the change as misguided and irrelevant. The general attitude could be described as qualified approval. Over the ensuing months, a great deal was heard of low morale; but this was attributable to the process of reorganisation, and its side-effects, rather than to the change itself.

Members of authorities were more pessimistic. Shortly before the appointed day, only one-third out of a sample of hospital management committee and local health authority members thought that reorganisation would benefit the services with which they had been concerned.[2] This view was understandable, coming from members of authorities which were about to be abolished. But it was shared by members of the new bodies: one year after reorganisation day, only a third of area health authority members, and even fewer from community health councils, were sure that reorganisation would mean a better service for the patient; the majority of CHC members (many of whom had served in the old system) thought it would definitely mean worse.[3]

By this time, attitudes towards the reorganisation had become coloured by feelings towards Humberside. The new area had few supporters. Many officers and members felt that it would have made more sense, at least for the health service, to have had two separate authorities for the north and south banks. As a small illustration of the feeling, ambulancemen who had been part of the Lincolnshire service took a poor view of the decision to have a white rose on their uniforms. The antipathy towards Humberside came out, too, in a question to members of the expiring authorities about the composition of the area health authority. In spite of the care with which the authority had been constructed, only three out of thirty-eight respondents agreed that its membership was fairly balanced as between different groups. Follow-up interviews suggested that most of the fourteen who positively disagreed were really expressing their resentment at the loss of local autonomy. Among the officers, too, there was more identification with the district than with the area.

This emerged from a questionnaire and interview survey of thirty-five top managers in the new service in June 1974 and a postal questionnaire, followed by selective interviews, with 183 less senior managers in October. Asked about the effect of the reorganisation on services to patients, over two-thirds of the senior managers thought that these would improve, the remainder being unsure. But less than a third of the middle managers thought that reorganisation would improve services for patients; rather more than a third thought that it would not make much difference. (At this stage, nearly half the middle managers thought that the new management structure promised to be little more than a re-titling of jobs — a view which was most emphatically not shared by their seniors.)

In the same survey, the managers were asked what they thought priorities should be for the next twelve months. Very few (mostly medical administrators) mentioned anything to do with forward planning. Nearly half suggested a 'wait and see' approach: 'before we change things, we must first examine the opportunities presented by reorganisation'. One in five agreed that 'the most important thing is to keep the machine ticking over and minimise change in the next twelve months'. Slightly more took the view that 'we must work hard to minimise the damage caused by reorganisation to the service'. Only one in five thought that 'we must move quickly to reap the benefits of reorganisation'.

These attitudes were attributable to many factors, including the sheer difficulty of completing the transition in an unfamiliar and in some ways unnatural new area. But they contrasted sadly with the enthusiasm shown by the joint liaison committee and its working parties in the winter of 1972–3. Several months into the new system, it seemed that the soil was distinctly inhospitable for some of the more visionary ideas behind the reorganisation. The preoccupations were with nuts and bolts, and interest in comprehensive planning and reallocation of resources was ebbing fast. There was also a tendency (especially among former hospital administrators) to interpret new roles in terms of old ones, possibly because at that time there was little reinforcement of the impetus for change that had been generated during the intensive training period.

In this unpropitious climate, the central Department of Health and Social Security, with minor exceptions, had to provide the initiatives from which some progress was eventually made to achieve the objectives of the reorganisation. As we shall see, that does not imply that DHSS interventions were necessarily well-judged or well-timed to elicit the maximum response at the periphery.

MANAGEMENT EFFICIENCY

One of the express purposes of the reorganisation was to streamline the management system. Within clearly defined role-structures and chains of command, responsibility was to be delegated so that decisions were taken as close to the patient as possible.[4] Higher-level authorities would refrain from interfering in the detailed affairs of the next down, and the authorities themselves would delegate executive authority to their permanent officers. On the other hand, authorities would concern themselves with setting broad objectives for their officers and with monitoring their achievement, and so on back up the line.

But there was a disconcerting amount of evidence that things were not working out as intended. A number of national surveys revealed considerable confusion and uncertainty about what people were supposed to be doing, with prejudicial consequences for the efficiency of day-to-day management.[5,6,7] Those outside the management structure complained that it was top-heavy. Those within it talked hopefully of abolishing a tier of administration (seldom their own) or complained about the diversion of administrative energy to consultation—the community health councils were a favourite target here. Some of this was to be expected during the settling-in period; but the volume of criticism continued unabated during the time when evidence was being prepared for the NHS Royal Commission in 1976 and 1977. Some of it was perhaps scapegoating: the reorganisation coincided with economic measures to restrain expenditure and, later, to restrict incomes, which caused much frustration. But, at face value, the complaints concerned the structure itself.

One explanation for the uncertainty might be that the new role-structure was insufficiently defined: this is hard to accept, in view of the amount of preparation and descriptive paperwork. An alternative explanation is that, in spite of the sometimes rather arid specifications, the structure was not fully understood. This links with three other possibilities, all of which seem to have some truth in them. First, the peripheral organisations of the NHS may not have had the administration capacity to translate the specifications into reality: we have already drawn attention to the loss of experienced managers and to the problematic calibre of those who moved up to fill the gaps. Second, there may have been a lack of incentive to make it work, which would be reinforced by a failure to apply philosophy at key points, such as the relationship between the controlling department and the NHS authorities. Finally, the structure may have been unrealistic, in terms of the way the NHS actually works and its inherited assumptions, or may have entailed unforeseen consequences.

In Humberside, we were told (and accept) that reorganisation did not of itself directly affect services to patients. But it was also clear there was a deterioration in management support. During the fieldwork period, this observation was made by the managers themselves, who drew attention to the long period of uncertainty and interregnum, and by doctors who complained that it had become impossible to locate centres of power and executive authority. This kind of evidence was not available after the middle of 1975. But anecdotal evidence supported by the accounts of two out of the four community health councils of their experience with district management, suggested that the situation did not change a great deal during the next two years.

The main problem seems to have been at unit or sector level within the districts. Equivalents could be found for the pre-1974 hospital secretary (with his direct access to the group secretary) or local authority chief clerk (with direct access to the medical officer of health). But their successors had much less power. The nurses now had their own administrative structure, culminating in the district nursing officer: their divisions, which were roughly equivalent to administrative sectors, had been worked out independently and did not always coincide. Engineering and maintenance staff also had a separate organisation and were ultimately responsible to the area works officer. Even the 'support services', like laundry, catering and domestic services, whose coordination with clinical services is the essence of unit administration, were separately managed by an officer who was directly responsible to the district administrator. It was only at district level that most of the threads came together, and the emphasis on inter-professional consensus meant that district management teams had to deal with matters that could have been settled more quickly lower down. Moreover, in the larger districts the district officers, while themselves too remote from day-to-day management, were often regarded as weak substitutes for the powerful officers on the area team. Unit management suffered from too little authority and too much fragmentation.[8]

There was not much the health authority could do about this. Their immediate contacts were with the area officers who, under the new structure, were meant to act as advisers without exercising direct authority over their district counterparts. It was some time before the authority members established direct contact with district team representatives. Even by late 1977 no effective reporting system had been established: except on financial matters and progress reports on specific questions, supplemented by site visits, the main sources of information about the quality of management within the districts were the doctors and the community health councils. Nor did the authority have much opportunity to influence the district management structure. The main management arrangements were set by the national study group, and their application to Humberside was influenced by the desire of senior officers to make appointments as quickly as possible to the available posts. Only when this had been settled did an authority member ask, somewhat despairingly, what a 'support services manager' was supposed to do.

Whatever the authority might have done, given the time and energy, there was not much evidence of a dynamic approach to internal management. The old hospital service had developed a habit of looking upward for guidance, and this was carried into the new service. The Yorkshire regional health authority did make a serious attempt to give areas as much scope as possible (although this may not have been evident to the areas). But the Department of Health and Social Security was reluctant to relinquish its controls. Often there were good reasons. Health authorities proposed a complement of managerial posts which the service had not the capacity to supply, and had to be allocated a quota. Others who wanted freedom to buy off industrial action had to be reminded that national wage and salary agreements were universally binding. But it seemed unnecessary to discourage the Humberside authority from taking breach of contract proceedings against engineers whose industrial action was clearly affecting patients. (Perhaps the significant part of that incident was that the authority felt it wise to consult the Department before exercising its managerial responsibility.)

FINANCIAL MANAGEMENT

One of the things a supervisory authority can do is enforce financial discipline. Two of the main themes in the post-reorganisation period were the need to redeploy resources in favour of neglected services and districts and the need to release resources for new development by curbing extravagance in existing services. These, of course, are not easy tasks. They call for fairly sophisticated tools (such as population-based indices of service availability, comparative cost analyses, and other measurements of efficiency which are naturally unpopular and disputed by those who come out badly) and the expertise to handle them. Like the NHS generally, Humberside emerged from the reorganisation with very weak capacity on the financial side. In spite of considerable increases in finance staff and the AHA's determination to recruit qualified officers, there were only six qualified accountants to deal with a budget of £33 million in 1974–5.

In any case, financial control during 1974–5 and 1975–6 presented great difficulty. Health authority allocations are made by the DHSS through the regional health authorities. Humberside inherited hospital services on the south bank which had previously been in a different region and it was some time before the financial implications had been sorted out. There was great uncertainty about the true cost of running the community services taken over from local authorities. Nobody was very clear about the implications of the Ministerial promise to protect the NHS from inflation during these two years, over and above the obvious commitment to meet the full cost of large salary awards. The service lurched from desperate attempts to contain expenditure to equally desperate attempts to use up its allocation in the last few months of the year. It was not, in fact, until September 1975 that Humberside learned that its allocation for the year ended in March had been finally calculated at £33.5 million (including pay awards funded in arrears), compared with an original £23.2 million. The provisional financial allocation for the year starting April 1975 was not announced until June.

There were explanations for this, including changes in government economic strategy and their effects on the public sector and the inability of the Treasury system of financial control to cope with rampant inflation. But that is another story.[9] Additional difficulties arose within the NHS because of the failure of local authorities to supply adequate information about the cost of community services in the year before reorganisation, and the inability of many health authorities to maintain the flow of routine statistics in 1974–5.[10] But the confusion made it difficult for health authorities to take the economic crisis seriously. Over-spending was easily redefined as 'under-financing'. It came as a sharp jolt (although also as a relief to uncertainty) when more rigorous financial discipline was imposed from April 1976; in common with most of the public sector, health authorities were told that their allocations for 1976–7 and later years would include a percentage addition for inflation and that their total spending would have to be contained within these 'cash limits'. At least, they now knew where they stood.

Humberside was rebuked by the regional health authority at one point when its spending pattern looked like taking it well above the allocation. After a review, a finance advisory committee was set up to monitor expenditure in conjunction with the area treasurer and the four district finance officers. By 1977, with the help of a new treasurer with local government experience, the advisory committee was receiving high-quality financial information on which it was possible to make recommendations about expenditure planning and the allocation of area money among the constituent districts. This was clearly essential if the authority was to stand on its own feet and accept, within its allocation, the incidental consequences of new building and new senior medical appointments. An important task was to persuade the management teams that money which was available in one year might not be available in the next, so that it was necessary to distinguish between non-recurrent expenditure and expenditure like the appointment of additional staff which implied commitments for future years. (A great deal of resourcefulness was employed in using non-recurrent funds for the temporary employment of school-leavers in order to carry out programmes of painting and cope with bottlenecks in administrative records.) But the authority was still not receiving information which would enable it to monitor the efficiency with which the resources were being used.

A new impetus to financial discipline was the government's decision to make allocations to regions on a formula which was based partly on the population served (weighted for age and sex) and partly on mortality rates (on the assumption that variations from national rates would reflect differences in health needs).[11] Regions were intended to apply the same principles in making distributions to areas, and areas to districts. The objective was to move as fast as possible towards parity without actually lowering standards in the better-off regions, areas and districts. Both the Yorkshire region and Humberside benefited from this formula. But within Humberside there was a special problem, in that services on the north bank, and especially in Hull, were already well-developed, expensive, and poised for still further growth. Those on the south bank started from a lower base; but it was not until comparative figures were presented that the extent of the inequality became evident and the subject of some bitter arguments. The problem was how to allocate a fair share to the south bank without causing severe difficulties in Hull, where the super-specialties serving the whole area were concentrated. The story is still incomplete, and it would be difficult to explain the issues in more detail without going into an impossible mass of detail. The point is that, three years after reorganisation, some of the tools became available to enable the authority to consider a strategy for evening out inequalities.

There had not been the same success in developing financial tools for the other major task of the authority—to reallocate resources among services. Progress in that direction is best described in the next section.

COMPREHENSIVE PLANNING

The lack of integrated planning had been one of the great weaknesses of the health service before 1974. In the hospital service, planning had been geared to expansion and improvement, within a broad strategy of replacing small, out-of-date and badly-sited units with modern district general hospitals. In essence, planning meant deciding on priorities for new construction, with the implication (not always achieved) that older hospitals would have to be closed as they were replaced. For local authority services, planning also meant growth towards rather unrealistic 'norms' (e.g. health visitors per thousand population) recommended by the Department of Health and Social Security. The only planning in the primary care services was an attempt to improve the distribution and practice organisation of general practitioners by a system of positive and negative incentives.

From 1974, all that was to change. Area health authorities were to prepare comprehensive plans to meet the total health needs of the populations they served, within guidelines and resource-assumptions provided by the DHSS. Apart from these guidelines, the building blocks for planning were to be proposals for each patient group (elderly, mentally ill, etc.) worked out by inter-professional health care planning teams and woven by the district management teams into coherent district plans, together with the comments of community health councils, professional advisory committees, staff consultative committees, and the matching local authorities. When the plans had been agreed and approved by the regional authority, success in carrying them out would be the main criterion by which the AHA's performance would be judged.[12]

It did not work out quite like that. The first serious exercise in strategic planning took place in the summer of 1976; and the first attempt to apply the plans operationally was made in the following year as a basis for concrete developments in 1978–9. The change of government in February 1974 played some part in the delay. The incoming administration regarded the original planning system (devised by a firm of management consultants) as too elaborate. After reconsideration, it was decided to separate the broad look forward (the strategic plan, covering objectives for ten or more years ahead) from proposals for short-term development (the operational plan, covering a rolling three years). This was spelt out to health authorities in the early summer of 1975, in a series of documents which incidentally prescribed in some detail the consultative process which they should follow locally, with a detailed timetable, and suggested a method of documentation which would enable everybody to see what the gaps were and how far the plans tried to remedy them. Health authorities were asked to prepare a profile of services in each district.[13] The planning guidelines were not issued until March 1976, in the form of a consultative document.[14] They emphasised the government's policy of improving services for the elderly, mentally ill and handicapped, and showed that, within the resources available, this could only be done by holding back the development of acute hospital services and *reducing* expenditure on maternity care, which had continued to rise in spite of a decade of declining birthrates.

Not all areas succeeded in producing strategic plans in time. Most of the plans that were produced suggested that the concept of strategic planning had not taken root: some were extremely vague, simply echoing the sentiment of the consultative document without applying them to local situations; others were not strategic plans at all, but lists of new hospitals, health centres and ambulance stations which the authority would like to build (shades of pre-1974 hospital 'planning' here); some attempted to do both, without any attempt to relate the two. Overall, there was great reluctance to put objectives in some order of priority and cost.

The regional health authorities had to submit an overall regional plan to the DHSS. But they often had to build bricks without much straw from the constituent areas. In a brief commentary issued in 1977, the DHSS noted the general patchiness of the plans and the authorities' intention to try and do better next time. As for the strategies themselves, it seemed that the health authorities generally subscribed to the national guidelines but saw serious difficulties about putting them into practice. But, again, that is another story.[15] Up to and including 1976–7, developments continued to be submitted and approved on a piecemeal basis, without reference to strategic plans.

In Humberside, a fairly comprehensive 'profile' of the merging services had been prepared by the joint liaison committee well in advance of reorganisation. As early as July 1974 the new authority held a special 'where do we go from here?' meeting. This was essentially a brain-storming session, and the upshot was that each district management team was invited to review the services for which they were responsible and to suggest six priorities for development. The lists tended to follow the prevailing fashion by placing some emphasis on the development of community services. They were discussed at special meetings of the full authority and the full management teams—one of the rare occasions when such a meeting took place—in the autumn. No decisions were taken; but some comments were offered and it was left to the area officers to discuss the priorities in more detail. In each case, the district teams were asked how far they could achieve their priority objectives by their own efforts; it turned out that some were relatively modest (like schemes for up-grading wards), and were met from the windfall money that became available towards the end of the financial year.

In the meantime, the Yorkshire regional health authority had been very active in producing guideline documents of its own. These consisted mainly of checklists and norms of provision, usually but not always derived from published DHSS sources, against which the area authorities were invited to compare their own levels of provision. Most of these documents were made available, although they were not discussed, at the special AHA meeting.

Individual area officers also used them as a basis for occasional papers, reviewing parts of the Humberside services, which were presented to the AHA for information. One of these, for example, dealt with nursing services in the community and another explained, point for point, how services for the mentally handicapped compared with the regional norms. When the first DHSS guidance on planning arrived in Easter 1975, all the documentation was brought together at a special weekend conference for all the area and district officers concerned with planning. It was agreed to produce a catalogue of needs and deficiencies which could be used as a basis for further planning. The catalogue was considered by a sub-committee of the AHA and, after some amendment, was referred for comment to the district management teams, community health councils, professional advisory committees, etc.

So, halfway through 1975, the Humberside AHA had begun to activate the planning and consultative processes for which the new structure was designed. The Yorkshire RHA was also in a good position to deal with the formal planning process when the time came. The regional officers had received copies of the Humberside papers and of similar documents from other areas within the region. In November 1975, they submitted to the regional authority a comprehensive review of regional needs and resources which was based partly on area papers and partly on their own appreciation of the needs of each area and of the region as a whole.

When, therefore, the consultative document arrived in the following year, it was debated in the AHA; but the basis for an area plan had already been established and it was a matter of seeing how the DHSS guidelines could be fitted in. This was done largely by adding some general expressions of intent to the existing paper, which was then reissued for comment through the prescribed consultative process. In consequence, it was possible in September 1976 to submit to AHA members a thick document consisting of the draft plan, interleaved with comments and suggestions from all the bodies that had been consulted and with comments from the area officers on those comments. During the discussion, there was some criticism of the DHSS priorities, but the main debate was about the implications of the plan for two particular parts of the area, which the relevant spokesmen had come briefed to oppose. The paper was referred back to the area officers so that agreed amendments could be incorporated in the main document which, after clearance through a planning sub-committee, was submitted to the RHA in October.

In its final form, the first area strategic plan was an impressive document.

For each of the main health care programmes (such as mental illness, primary care, maternity services) there was a statement of objectives and deficiencies in existing services, followed by a list of one-star, two-star and three-star developments desired within a three- and a ten-year period. There were also descriptive accounts of the problems and needs of non-clinical services like ambulances, works and supplies organisation. In spirit, if not in detail, the plan kept fairly close to regional and national guidelines with two interesting exceptions. The RHA had suggested that north-bank mental hospitals which served both districts should be administered as two separate units to facilitate liaison with other district services; this was rejected on advice from the psychiatric division of north-bank doctors. The RHA had also commended advice from the Health Advisory Service that the north-bank geriatric service could best be administered on an integrated basis; this was rejected by the AHA because it conflicted with the policy of making each district self-sufficient.[16] An introduction dealt with the main issues concerning the AHA, including its desire to see a medical school established in Hull and the north-bank district problem.

But detailed analysis suggested that, as a strategic plan, it had a number of deficiencies:

(a) Most of the specific objectives concerned new building, especially on the hospital side, which would call for the injection of additional capital money into the area; there was little or no reference to strategies which were within the AHA's own control, like the redeployment of existing manpower or the development of new methods of dealing with demand; there was not much attempt to concretise the grander rhetoric about, for example, giving priority to community services.

(b) While priorities were offered within programmes, there was no attempt to compare priorities between programmes, although this is what the whole exercise was about; nor was there any attempt to compare the costs and benefits of the different proposals, or to relate them to the morbidity profile of the population.

The lack of prioritisation was one of the main criticisms expressed by the RHA when it reviewed the plans. In defence, the AHA argued that there was no point in offering priorities until the amount of resources was known. In practice, priorities would be determined by what could be fitted into the available budget. This 'money first' approach, and the reluctance to engage in purely theoretical exercises, was to be revealed again when the first operational plan, covering the 1978–81 period, was required at the end of 1977; the area officers told the authority that they found it difficult to formulate specific proposals because of poor financial prospects and the lack of information from the RHA about the capital programme.

It would be wrong to criticise Humberside for its failure to come to terms with the planning concept: tremendous energy was deployed, and Humberside did much better than many other areas. But this section illustrates the extent to which the NHS had been conditioned to think of planning in terms of persuading higher authorities to approve proposals for expansion, and therefore to use these authorities as a scapegoat for local inadequacies. The story also illustrates how badly the DHSS (and the management consultants who advised them) over-estimated the readiness of NHS authorities to cope with uncertainty and to work out means of pursuing objectives through a range of possible futures.

COLLABORATIVE PLANNING WITH LOCAL AUTHORITIES

The area health authorities were deliberately constructed to facilitate joint planning with the local authorities responsible for education and personal social services. The Reorganisation Act specifically required health and local authorities to set up joint consultative committees as a forum for collaboration. In many parts of the country, however, the collaborative machinery failed to attract enthusiasm. Ministerial disappointment with its performance coincided with deepening awareness that national objectives for the elderly, handicapped and mentally ill depended on integrated health and local authority provision: the health authorities were responsible for hospitals, nursing support and medical care in the community, but local authorities were responsible for homes and hostels, day centres, sheltered housing, home help and other forms of social support. But many health authorities were preoccupied with acute medical services, while the local authority social service departments showed a consistent preference for child care over the medico-social groups. In an attempt to correct these imbalances, health ministers resorted to two devices. One was joint financing, which would enable health authorities to use an earmarked part of their own budgets as pump-priming funds which could be used to pay for developments on the local authority side to relieve pressure on health facilities.[17] The other was a redirection of health service planning activity so that, instead of placing the main emphasis on health care planning teams within health districts, the main effort would go on joint care-planning teams, which would include local government officers, at area level under the auspices of the joint consultative committees.[18]

The original circular requesting area health authorities to take the initiative on collaborative machinery was received in March 1974.[19] Characteristically, it hoped that the machinery would be working by 1 April. In fact, it was not possible to hold an exploratory meeting in Humberside until June. As well as the chairman of the AHA, the chairman of the county social services committee, the director of social services and an assistant county director of administration were present. On the basis of a paper prepared by the AHA, it was agreed to have a joint consultative committee for the whole county, to handle collaboration over social services and education, and two committees, one for the south bank and one for the north (the two committees later agreed to meet together), for collaboration with the district councils on housing and environmental health. On each of these committees, local government members were given key positions with the intention of enlisting their support. Four officer working parties were set up to deal with personal social services, child health, environmental health and general aspects of collaboration. It was subsequently agreed that the officer working parties would meet four times a year and the main consultative committee twice, at times which coincided with the main planning and estimating points in the year.

In spite of expressions of goodwill and good personal relations, the joint committees themselves were fairly peripheral for the first two or three years. At one time, it looked as if the main impetus was going to come from the community health councils, whose working groups on the elderly and mentally ill were acutely aware of the interdependence of health, housing and personal social services. Points raised at AHA meetings were referred to the consultative committees; but not much came back. Other commitments kept committee meetings short and not well-attended. In the autumn of 1977, some members of the environmental committee suggested its abolition on the ground that it was not serving a useful purpose. In fact, the main function of the committees during these years was to provide an umbrella for the working groups, which brought together key officers who were working at the points of interface and enabled a number of practical points to be sorted out (e.g. on responsibility for the classification of handicapped schoolchildren or for disposing of contaminated hospital waste). The working groups reported to the main committee, which also had an opportunity to comment on the development plans of various authorities. But the policy implications remained latent, in spite of much work behind the scenes.

From April 1976, the AHA received its share of 'joint finance' money. Suggestions for using this money were discussed on the joint consultative committee. But the county council was cautious about accepting the bait, mainly because the terms of the arrangement were that responsibility for jointly-financed schemes would, over some years, be progressively transferred to the local authority. County councillors were reluctant to commit their resources for future years in that way. Nationally, the joint finance initiative was only partially effective in 1976–7, and the conditions were somewhat relaxed in 1977–8. On Humberside, it proved impossible to spend more than half the money available in 1976–7. But additional home helps were financed, and money was allocated for a home for the elderly, a day centre and a training centre for mentally handicapped adults, to start in 1977–8.

The other DHSS attempt to vitalise the collaborative machinery resulted from fresh thinking about the fulcrum of the planning process. The original idea had been that planning for patient groups would be based on the work of planning teams within the districts. Humberside AHA had encouraged the district teams to think about planning teams, and had itself set up area teams on mental illness and mental handicap, for which provision was very unbalanced between the districts. Although this shift to an area basis anticipated later DHSS guidance, there was no immediate input from these teams into the 1976 strategic plan. By early 1977, however, the DHSS had realised that planning for the vulnerable socio-medical categories of patients was not likely to get very far on a purely NHS basis. Health and local authorities were therefore asked to set up a high-level joint care-planning team which would include district representatives, with subgroups for the elderly, mentally ill and mentally handicapped. Humberside reacted positively. The director of social services was invited to chair the planning team, which was able to draw on earlier work by the AHA. By the end of 1977, the joint consultative committee had received three impressive reports. Two of these reviewed the existing levels of provision, shortfalls, and the extent to which these were likely to be remedied by developments in the pipeline, for the elderly and the mentally handicapped across the whole range of services. The third report examined the criteria and information bases which were used for health and local authority planning, and suggested points where the two sides could help each other. The reports were endorsed by the joint consultative committee and referred with commendations to the parent authorities. Here again, after a long period of uncertainty, the analytic tools needed to identify problems and priorities were beginning to be forged.

FOUR KEY SERVICES

Part of the fieldwork on Humberside was intended to test the effects of reorganisation by assessing its impact on four services which might have been expected to be affected in varying degrees. The acute services were not expected to be much affected. But geriatrics was expected to benefit from the new framework of priorities. Better coordination between hospital and community nursing, and between ambulances and the health services to which they were ancillary, were anticipated as a consequence of bringing them under the same administrative roof. This part of the fieldwork was completed about a year after reorganisation day. Views at that time were often conditioned by short-term problems. But the more important factors affecting each service are summarised below.

Orthopaedics. The main problems facing the four Hull orthopaedists before reorganisation were pressure of work, long waiting lists, and unnecessary referrals from general practitioners. They were not enamoured of the medical advisory system: as members of the large surgical division they felt that much of the business was trivial and irrelevant to them.[20] When they wanted something done they went straight to the chief administrator, the hospital group secretary. They worked in two separate hospital management committees, which often had different policies, and found this a nuisance.

A year after reorganisation, the problems had not changed. The AHA was concerned about the waiting list, and tried to do something about it; but its scope for action was not different from that of a hospital management committee. Any advantage of working under one AHA rather than two HMCs was outweighed by the artificial division of the working area into two districts. The divisional machinery had not changed, but the superimposed professional machinery had become, in the consultants' view, even less helpful. The reorganisation had caused breakdowns in the supplies organisation (difficulties in obtaining the right size of orthopaedic screw were featured in a national Sunday newspaper).[21] A more permanent consequence was the destruction of their old relationship with administration: 'There is no-one to lobby any more . . . . The whole scale of operations has changed . . . there is more of a distance between us and those who make the decisions.'

Before reorganisation, plans were well advanced for a new orthopaedic and dental block in the main Hull hospital. Although one of the AHA's priorities, this was repeatedly put back by the RHA, and it is tempting to link this with the low priority given to acute services; but it would possibly have happened anyway as a result of cuts in the building programme. An additional orthopaedic post was among the many new consultant appointments sought and obtained by the AHA as part of its own policy of expanding acute services.

Geriatrics. Like the orthopaedists, the three Hull geriatricians worked in both hospital groups serving Hull before reorganisation. They had developed an active geriatric service (recognised in 1977 as a 'centre of excellence') with good supporting links with community services. Their main complaints concerned ambulance facilities for day-patients and the difficulty of getting enough recognition for their specialty in the various medical committees.

A year after reorganisation, a talk with the chief ambulance officer had brought some improvement in that area. But geriatrics did not seem to be getting any more priority generally. A paper outlining the need to develop the service to cope with the growing number of elderly had been sent to all relevant district and area officers, but had elicited no response. It had been widely circulated because, like the orthopaedists, the geriatricians were no longer certain who made the decisions. They intensely disliked the district structure and wanted to continue to develop an 'area' (i.e. north bank) service.[22] In this they were supported by a visiting team from the health advisory service and by the RHA; but the AHA rejected the proposal as inconsistent with their policy of making each district self-sufficient.

The AHA was required to give special consideration to the elderly in its strategic plan, but did not accept the DHSS doctrine that the rapid expansion of geriatric services was the best or most practicable way to deal with demographic changes. Nevertheless, the Hull service gained a new day centre in 1978. Meanwhile, one of the geriatric consultants was elected chairman of the area medical committee. The salience of services for the elderly in joint planning with local government has already been noted.

Nursing. The structure of nursing management was profoundly affected by the reorganisation. All nursing staff, both hospital and community, were brought under the unified command of district and area nursing officers, who had a seat at the top table and enjoyed new status, responsibility and salary. The opportunity now existed to create a more unified profession and to tackle the problems of rational redeployment to make the best use of available resources. (For ten years, committees investigating the nursing 'shortage' had been pointing out that the real problems were inefficient management and deployment.[23])

On Humberside (and no doubt elsewhere) the community nurses and midwives had been very apprehensive about the reorganisation. It was perhaps wise, therefore, to retain their identity under separate divisional nursing officers. Mental handicap and psychiatric nursing also retained their identities where appropriate. But this meant that there was no crossover point below the district nursing officer. While AHA policy was to improve community nursing services, there was little evidence of redeployment in the staffing statistics and redeployment was not discussed at all in the strategic plan. Nursing was also badly affected by the district structure on the north bank. A good deal of disruption to the community service was caused by the transfer of part of Hull county borough to the Beverley district.

There were some changes within the community sector. Some rationalisation was achieved within the school nursing service. The system of attaching nurses to GP practices, which had been gradually adopted in the merging authorities with the exception of Hull, was extended to that city. It would be difficult to attribute either development to the reorganisation except in the sense that a larger scale of operation created an incentive to deal with anomalies. (Ironically, one of the community health councils criticised the attachment system as leading to a waste of the nurse's time.)

More progress was made with the unification of the profession. The work of the nursing and midwifery advisory committee has been discussed on pages 136–7. Its first report was concerned with the continuity of care after a patient had been discharged from hospital. A survey carried out by the research team in October 1974 disclosed that almost the only effect of reorganisation on services to patients was in communications between hospital and community nurses: over a third of the respondents claimed that they had improved.

Ambulance services. Until 1974, ambulances had been supplied by local county and county borough authorities, although most of their work consisted of transporting patients to and from hospital. Their reorganisation on a new county basis (under area health authorities in shire counties, and regional authorities in the metropolitan counties) should have led both to internal rationalisation and to better integration with hospital needs.

Although Humberside's chief ambulance officer took up post in April 1974, not much progress was made with either objective. At the end of 1976, the strategic plan devoted a separate section to the ambulance service and commented that little progress had been made towards the integration of the merged services. The grandiose schemes of the ambulance working party in 1972–3 had come to nothing. There was no money to build new stations and central control facilities. There was no national pay settlement which would have sorted out pay anomalies and established a career structure. The ambulancemen's grievances made theirs the most active of the staff consultative committees and consumed a good deal of the area personnel officer's time. The grievances were not within Humberside's power to rectify. But while they remained, there was little hope of rationalisation. The absence of a bridge, of course, made it difficult to plan services on an area basis. Of all the occupational groups covered in the October 1974 survey, ambulance officers were most enthusiastic about a suggestion that there should have been separate health authorities for the north and south banks. Those on the south bank complained that the area ambulance headquarters was too remote. This left the area ambulance officer in a somewhat isolated position, in which he had to work very hard to make himself known and accepted.

In the meantime, the operational problems continued. There was a general consensus among middle-managers (including nurses) that reorganisation had made no difference to ambulance services for out-patients, day hospitals, accident and emergency cases, or discharged patients. Early in 1975, the consultants had detected no significant change, apart from an improvement in the arrangements for one day hospital. There had been no serious discussion about the place of ambulance transport in an integrated health care system, which might have covered (for example) the relative costs and benefits of taking the patient to the service or the service to the patient, the opportunity costs of providing free door-to-door transport for nearly-fit patients, and the very substantial implications for the ambulance service of a switch from in-patient to day-patient care.

SUMMARY AND COMMENT

Reorganisation was intended to be much more than an amalgamation of different types of health authority; it was taken as an opportunity to introduce new concepts of the administration of integrated health care. But if these concepts carried lip-service, there was not a great deal of understanding or enthusiasm for what they entailed. Here again, as was suggested in the last chapter, it seems that those on central working parties either over-estimated innovative capacity at the periphery or misinterpreted the pattern of incentives. (It is a strange fact of official life that when representatives of various groups are brought together on a working party to explore some new idea, they often become too easy converts and forget the realities of the world they are supposed to represent.) They could not, of course, have anticipated the sheer difficulty of cobbling the new structure together in an atmosphere of staff militancy and uncertain financial prospects for the NHS as a whole. Planning, for example, may be just as necessary in times of shortage as in times of abundance (almost certainly more so); but it does not offer the same rewards and is not much fun. But if the reluctance to get involved in 'speculative exercises' which has been described in this chapter is at all general—and other evidence suggests that it is—some fundamental questions are raised about the structure of the NHS and the expectations that have been based on it.

In one respect, reorganisation seems to have made matters worse. There is a lack of clarity and authority at administrative levels below the district management teams. This seems to be a direct effect of the doctrine of consensus management at team level, and perhaps of an exaggerated deference to the doctrine by the executive officers who sit on the teams. Authority drains upward. Of the teams themselves, much could be said. Some teams seem to consume inordinate amounts of time without accomplishing very much. When consensus breaks down, on contentious issues or because of a clash of personalities, management comes to a dead stop. Some cases have already been reported.[24] Indeed, it is surprising that more attention has not been paid to the effect of team management on accountability: a senior official of the Department of Health and Social Security had to explain to a House of Commons committee that there was no possibility of transferring responsibility for a parliamentary vote to the NHS, as RHA chairmen had requested, because there was no one person who could be held accountable for the expenditure.[25] In an area like Humberside, the problem of accountability in the broader sense is magnified by the sheer difficulty of controlling so many different teams and officers and by the uncertain relationship of area to district officers. The community health councils played a most important role in drawing attention to management failures; but this perhaps does not happen everywhere.

On the other hand, there have undoubtedly been some successes, even if success is, at the time of writing, only partial. After a chaotic interval, resource-management is broadly under control, and it has become possible to look coherently at problems of allocation. This is a direct consequence of reorganisation: the population-based formulae (which will no doubt be further refined) would have been meaningless until health authorities and district teams were made responsible for meeting the needs of defined populations.

The skills of comprehensive planning are still being learnt. But the production of a strategic document has been shown to be possible. Moreover, the cumbersome consultative process has at least been tried, and has produced some unexpected results: for example, the Humberside family practitioner committee, whose relationship to the AHA at one time seemed likely to produce more heat than light, made a substantial contribution to the AHA planning document. On joint planning with local authorities, similarly, some progress has been made with the documentary analysis on which joint plans could be based.

Not everything can be done at once. Three and a half years after the reorganisation, not much had been done about rationalisation (except in plans for the development of hospital buildings), redeployment, or efficiency-monitoring. In spite of the elaborate new structures, surprisingly little had happened in the four services discussed in the last section; and what had happened did not seem to be attributable to the reorganisation.

This leads to two concluding thoughts from the field study. One is that new structures are not enough. They may even prove to be unhelpful: a great deal of energy was consumed in making the 1974 structures work at all, and the DHSS has now admitted that they were in fact too elaborate.[26] But even if some restructuring (like the amalgamation of complementary services under one control) is a necessary condition for better management and planning, it is by no means a sufficient condition. Also to be reckoned with are the attitudes and approaches that people bring into the structure: often these have been acquired in a completely different environment; a very heavy investment in learning may be needed if fundamental change is desired. There is the problem of incentives: why embark on the difficult and politically dangerous minefield of change if there are plenty of easier and more gratifying tasks to be done? Finally, there is a need for tools: the resource-management exercise was impossible until adequate methods of analysing expenditure became available; the failure to tackle genuinely strategic planning, or the more mundane question of redeployment, is associated with the absence of tools, or with the belief that the tools available are not good enough.

The central architects of reorganisation gave a great deal of thought to new structures and processes as a vehicle for change, but not nearly enough to people, inducements and tools. This leads to the second, rather sobering thought. Apart from continuing the necessary administration of services inherited from the old authorities, nearly all the events described in this chapter (the first planning initiatives being a conspicuous exception) were a reaction to pressures from higher authority. The failures were in areas where there was no pressure, or where tools (like the resource-allocation formula) were not supplied. Does this mean that the advances would not have occurred if the pressure had not been applied? Or does it mean that central direction was applied in a way that stifled local initiative? The local people, of course, take the second view. But, to put the question in another way, how realistic is it to expect equal, or greater, innovation from ninety different authorities, many of them much less well endowed than Humberside, in the absence of central pressure? Why was there so little (or so much) innovation in the unreorganised services? And where, on this continuum, do we put the authorities that fail even to carry out tasks that are prescribed in great detail?

NOTES

1   The last of four interim reports was published by the Institute for Health Studies, University of Hull, in September 1975. Its attempt to describe the position at that time is well summarised in the *Hospital and Health Services Review*, Nov. 1975, pp. 377–9; and in both *Lancet*, p. 649, and *British Medical Journal*, p. 53, for 4 October 1975.

2   Under covering letters from the committee chairmen, seventy postal questionnaires were sent to members of one HMC and one health committee each in Hull and Scunthorpe. We received thirty-eight completed questionnaires and interviewed twelve of the respondents.

3   Twelve of the seventeen AHA members replied to this postal questionnaire, but only nineteen out of fifty-one members of the Hull and Scunthorpe community health councils. Ten AHA members and twelve representative CHC members were interviewed.

4   'The approach has been to start with the patient and work up' DHSS, *Management Arrangements for the Reorganised National Health Service*, HMSO, 1972, para. 1.10 *et seq.*)

5   DHSS, *Report of a Working Party on Devolution*, DHSS, 1976; *Report of the Regional Chairmen's Enquiry into the Working of the DHSS in Relation to Regional Health Authorities*, DHSS, 1976.

6   *Review of the Management of the Reorganised NHS*, Association of Chief Administrators of Health Authorities, 1975, as well as contemporary articles and editorials in the relevant professional journals.

7   *Report of a Working Party on the Role of Unit and Sector Administrators in the NHS*, Institute of Health Service Administrators, London, 1976.

8   Stuart Haywood, *Decision-making in the New NHS; Consensus or Constipation?* King Edward's Hospital Fund for London, 1977.

9   Maurice Wright, 'Public Expenditure in Britain: the Crisis of Control', *Public Administration*, London, Summer 1977, pp. 143–69. Perhaps the best account of the effect on the NHS of public expenditure changes during these years is in the series of papers prepared by R. Klein *et al.* on *Social Policy and Public Expenditure* for the Centre for Studies in Social Policy, London, 1974, 1975 and 1976.

10 The annual hospital costing returns were never completed for 1974–5, while the annual digest of *Health and Personal Social Services Statistics for England, 1976* (DHSS, 1977) contains a note that 'during the period immediately following reorgan-isation, it proved extremely difficult to obtain comprehensive and up to date informa-tion . . . . The 1975 figures, however, are believed to be reasonably accurate' (p. 185).

11 DHSS, *Sharing Resources for Health in England: Final Report of the Resource Allocation Working Party*, HMSO, 1976. (Historically, hospital budgets had been based on what had been spent in the previous year, so that inequalities survived from the first budgets in 1948. The reorganisation White Paper promised to deal with this. The formula recommended in an interim report by the working party, which was applied to regions in 1976–7, included an element for caseload; but this was thought to give too much weight to the existing pattern of demand, as distinct from underlying health need, and was left out of the second formula, which was applied for 1977–8. Although the formula was not rigidly applied to areas within regions during these years, Humberside appeared to be under-funded according to the first formula but less so on the second. But at least one of the Humberside districts could claim to be seriously under-funded on both versions. All the national problems of reallocation, therefore, were present within the area.)

12 DHSS, *Management Arrangements for the Reorganised National Health Service, op. cit.* (note 4), ch. 3, describes the essential features of the planning cycle, which was based on the corporate planning procedures then fashionable in industrial conglomer-ates. The complicated consultive procedures were added later, as was the separation of 'strategic' (long-term) from 'operational' (short-term) planning.

13 DHSS, *NHS Planning System*, DHSS, 1975.

14 DHSS, *Priorities for Health and Personal Social Services in England*, HMSO, 1976.

15 DHSS, *The Way Forward*, HMSO, 1977. The regional plans are reviewed briefly in Appendix II. A House of Commons committee also noted the divergences between the consultative document and health authorities' strategic plans and commented that only time would tell if the future pattern 'will be anything more than an aggregation of what each health authority would have done anyway' *(Ninth Report from the Select Committee on Expenditure, 1976–77* (HC 466), HMSO, 1977, para. 5.33).

16 The Health Advisory Service had replaced the Hospital Advisory Service, which was established prior to reorganisation as a discreet form of inspection of long-stay hospitals, where there had been a number of scandals (see chapter 1, note 26). It became concerned with the overall quality of services for the elderly and the mentally ill. A team paid a routine visit to Humberside in 1975.

17 A report by the Central Policy Review Staff on *Relations between Central Government and Local Authorities* (HMSO, 1977), which is generally critical of the fragmented way in which central government departments deal with services in the field, com-mends this experiment as a 'striking and potentially important new development' (see para 7.8 and 13.24).

18 Health Circular HC(77)17.

19 Health Service Reorganisation Circular HRC(74)19.

20 See chapter 7, pp. 128–30.
21 *Sunday Times*, 16 Nov 1975, 'The National Health Sickness'.
22 *Annual Report of the Health Advisory Service for 1976* (HMSO, 1977) comments that 'With the growth of committees since reorganisation the problems of management of geriatric departments have increased . . . Reorganisation has resulted in many geriatricians having less time for patient care' (paras 119, 120).
23 DHSS, *Report of the Committee on Senior Nursing Staff Structure* (HMSO, 1966); National Board for Prices and Incomes, *Pay of Nurses and Midwives in the National Health Service* (Report no. 60), HMSO, 1968; *Report of the Committee on Nursing* (Cmnd. 5115, 1972).
24 On the Solihull case, see *Hospital and Health Services Review*, July 1977, pp. 229–30.
25 *Ninth Report of the Public Accounts Committee for 1976–77* (HC 532), HMSO, 1977.
26 *Ibid.*

III
ANALYSIS

CHAPTER 9

Some Theory

Part II described the process of implementing the 1974 reorganisation of the National Health Service in one English shire county. The two following chapters attempt to draw general lessons from that experience, first about the reorganisation itself and then about the underlying problems of NHS management. To provide a conceptual focus for the analysis, the present chapter summarises some current theories about innovation and change.

There is an extensive literature on administrative and organisational change. But it is sparse in theory that is both comprehensive and relevant to the kind of change described in this book. The managerial literature concentrates on relatively small-scale change at the level of individual or small-group behaviour. There is a reasonable overview in a book by Zaltman and others.[1] Apart from one or two good American studies, the public administration literature tends to be descriptive; analytic works often dismiss the implications of organisational change in a couple of pages.[2] Leemans has reviewed the field in his own contributions to a volume of essays, most of which concern developing countries.[3] There is a brief but useful chapter on 'Change in the Public Service' from the viewpoint of a British civil servant in a book by Keeling.[4] Finally, Schon's Reith lectures contain a seminal perspective on the problems and limitations of large-scale organisational change as a means of influencing behaviour and performance; they offer a useful corrective to the classical centre–periphery model of the diffusion of ideas which was originally implicit in the present study.[5]

Since this is not a textbook, there is no need to give detailed references for every proposition. The newcomer to this field can be referred to the sources mentioned above, while *cognoscenti* will recognise the influence of writers like Downs,[6] Burns and Stalker,[7] Cyert and March,[8] Sofer,[9] Bennis,[10] Hage and Aiken[11] and Kaufman.[12]

169

INITIATION OF CHANGE

The need for a change in structure or behaviour arises from the perception of a 'performance gap' between what an organisation could be doing and what it is actually achieving. The gap may be perceived by participants who are dissatisfied with organisational impediments to their own performance. Even in a stable situation there is some pressure for change since there is a tendency for aspirations to rise slowly and for the resultant gap between aspiration and achievement to be explained in terms of removable obstacles. Changes in the environment create a sharper awareness of the need for change and may be reflected in poor market performance or, in the public sector, by growing evidence of consumer dissatisfaction. Or the performance gap may be seen by those outside the organisation who are aware of unmet needs or downright failures, like the inadequacy of some long-stay hospitals in the NHS.

Ideas for change are more likely to arise in some types of organisational setting than in others. Public bureaucracies tend to be complacent, partly because they are not directly exposed to market forces and partly because their mission is generally directed towards stabilisation and routine rather than towards innovation. In any organisation which is highly structured by formal rules and centralised decision-making there is a built-in inertia and a reluctance to challenge the existing structure. Such challenges are more likely to be made in organisations where authority and decision-making are decentralised, and where there are fewer universal rules and procedures. This applies particularly to complex organisations employing large numbers of professionals. The more actively members of an organisation are enabled to participate in its decision processes, the more opportunities they have for disagreement and thus to initiate proposals for change.

It is therefore tempting to aim to improve the responsiveness of organisations by altering their structure in ways that will encourage the flow of new ideas. As well as changes, such as the introduction of new administrative technologies (consultative and control procedures, new information systems, etc.), which are intended to have a direct influence on performance, possible strategies include instrumental changes in structure (e.g. the introduction of new personnel, professions and task forces) which will eventually lead to more far-reaching effects on performance. This assumes, however, that it is known which structural changes are likely to lead to the desired changes in performance; this is not always the case. Moreover, while it seems to be established that decentralised, participative structures encourage the free flow of ideas, they also reduce the chances that any of them will be implemented. The actual implementation of change may require more centralised, authoritarian structures to fasten on the point of consensus and coordinate the necessary action. A period of centralisation may therefore be needed to create the conditions in which decentralisation can be practised later, perhaps after a period of retraining and resocialisation.

The range of changes that are likely to be initiated within an organisation is limited by the experience, perceptions and occupational interests of those who work within it. More fundamental changes are likely to be initiated from outside. A performance gap may more readily be perceived by independent research workers, committees of inquiry, politicians and champions of causes (both prophets and muck-rakers). The dissatisfaction may have nothing to do with performance but have its origin in wider societal changes, such as changing attitudes to equality, consumer rights, trade unions, and the role of the organisation in society. Wars, crises and select committees all play a part.

A proposal to make changes in a public organisation, therefore, can reflect internal (normally professional) or public discontent with its performance. Or it may be proposed as a means of achieving ends which have nothing to do with the organisation itself, perhaps no more than the desire of a politician to achieve some 'reform' during his term of office. But it is one thing to suggest a change. If the proposal is to be taken seriously it must command a reasonable amount of assent and satisfy at least superficial tests of feasibility. In particular, it has to withstand resistance and opposition.

REACTIONS TO CHANGE

Whoever is in favour of a change, it is likely that others will be opposed to it. Even if there is general agreement that some change is needed, because the current state of affairs appears intolerable, any specific change is likely to arouse opposition. This is partly because a change which some see as to their advantage is likely to be differently perceived by others. In the public sector, changes are often designed to improve central control and coordination of sub-systems which are drifting towards autonomy; such changes are naturally resisted. But it is also because any change can be seen as a threat to established patterns of roles and relationships which are important to the participants. It is not inconceivable that a major change should be opposed by everyone whose support is necessary for its implementation.

A universally valid reason for opposing change is that it involves energy. Somebody, somewhere, is going to have to work harder in order to put it into effect and others will later be required to adapt to it. This is true even if the end-result of the change is to conserve energy and make work easier or more satisfying. The more efficiently an organisation is geared to the pursuit of its current tasks, the more difficult it is to spare energy to effect change. This may be particularly true in public organisations, where the penalties for any breakdown in routine task-performance tend to be high and the rewards for risk-taking tend to be small. A major change is bound to involve long periods of distraction for those at the top and perhaps also for the most able members of the organisation, who can even less easily be spared, while they are engaged in planning, negotiating and coordinating the change process. During this time, they are likely to be drawn into quite minor questions which cannot be routinised because there are no precedents. The ability of an organisation to spare resources to invest in change may impose an absolute limit on its ability to accommodate it. Resources can be increased, by employing consultants or by creating some slack capacity. But, in general, the more efficiently an organisation is functioning (within its own terms of reference, which of course may be the very reason that change is required), the more difficult it is to absorb change without adding to the workload.

Disturbance may be unwelcome for other reasons. Any organisation is a social system, with patterns of interaction that have grown up over time and provide stability and satisfactions for its members. The social system includes implicit theories about what the organisation should be doing and how it should be doing it as well as a structure of roles and relationships which often bear meanings for individuals that go far beyond the formal requirements of their jobs. The organisation is also a political system, with established jurisdictions and pecking orders. Quite minor changes in technology can have major repercussions for the political and social systems, for example by altering reporting systems or by routinising a task in which a worker enjoyed perhaps the illusion of autonomy. Major changes may threaten the relative status and influence of whole occupational groups. The textbooks say that it does not matter whether these threats are real. People attach their own meanings to impending events and if these meanings are shared with others they become entrenched. Change involves uncertainty. Uncertainty promotes anxiety. Anxiety feeds on rumour and can be associated with apparently irrational behaviour. At the extreme, this can lead to downright opposition to a change which to the outsider might appear beneficient. More mildly, it can cause low morale and poor performance until the uncertainty is resolved.

But anxiety, hostility and defensiveness need not be dismissed as irrational. A change which is calculated to increase the power and influence of one group may have foreseen or unforeseen consequences for another. In the health service, more autonomy (or even a better career structure) for nurses alters the political framework by modifying the relative statuses and self-perceptions of doctors and administrators and by raising the aspirations of other professions. Opposition may ensue unless some compensating advantage can be offered. One of the costs of change is the extent to which the pattern of rewards may have to be redistributed or increased to maintain incentives to participate.

Changes differ in their extent, real or perceived. The reactions envisaged in the last two paragraphs will not be evoked if the change is seen as peripheral (perhaps a minor adjustment in relationships with the environment) or consistent with prevailing values, experience and personal needs. But some changes threaten the core activities and structure of the organisation. Changes in administrative technology may raise doubts among senior members about their ability to cope with the new system. Changes in orientation may be deeply resented by those who are proud of their past achievement. Such changes are likely to provoke not just resistance but 'dynamic conservatism'. This means that an immense amount of effort will be devoted to subverting the change and maintaining the status quo.

The first reaction to a challenge to the core system of beliefs and relationships is likely to be 'selective inattention' — a refusal to pay attention to data which suggest a need for fundamental change. If the change becomes imminent, this is followed by a period of active opposition. The opposition may have to be covert: it may take the form of proposing alternative strategies which are alleged to be capable of achieving the same ends within the existing system; or it may take the form of demanding an impossibly high price for cooperation. But if the change becomes inevitable, every effort will be made to contain it and reduce its impact on the existing social and political system. Changes may occur in name only, with the minimum of window-dressing to create an illusion of progress. The following quotation comes from a study of the effect of a change enforced on an American mental hospital:

> Thus when innovation intrudes, the structure responds with various strategies to deal with the threat; it might incorporate the new event and alter it to fit the pre-existing structure so that, in effect, nothing is really

changed. It might deal with it also by active rejection, calling upon all of
its resources to 'starve out' the innovator by insuring a lack of support.

The most subtle defense, however, is to ostensibly accept and encourage the innovator, to publicly proclaim support of innovative goals, and
while doing that to build in various controlling safeguards, such as special
committees, thereby insuring that the work is always accomplished
through power structure channels and thus effecting no real change. . . .
Innovation is thus allowed, and even encouraged, as long as it remains on
the level of conceptual abstractions, and provided that it does not, in
reality, change anything![13]

MOBILISATION OF SUPPORT

The realisation that some change is necessary is accompanied by a search
for alternative means of realising it. Typically this is quite short: only a
limited range of options will be considered. Once a potentially viable option
has been identified, commitment quickly hardens and energy is transferred
to the process of getting it implemented. This involves the mobilisation of
support, including measures to deal with possible opposition.

The larger the proposed scale of change, the more energy is needed to see
it through. Changing the core structure of complex organisations is clearly
more difficult than minor changes in services or technology. This would
suggest the need for careful testing and planning before making a final
commitment. But, in fact, radical changes need to be made fairly quickly if
they are to occur at all. The reason is that they require the personal
involvement of people at the top (including Ministers in the public sector)
who are liable to change. There is therefore a tendency to fix unrealistic
deadlines, and to adopt strategies which *look* like being relatively easy to
accomplish. At the initiation stage, two factors are at work. One is the
desire to win support for the change, and therefore to avoid creating
antagonism by threatening parts of the system which could be left intact: in
an organisation whose existing structure has assimilated a diversity of
competing interests, solutions will be sought within the boundaries set by
earlier compromises. On the other hand, many new problems will be left to
one side to be tackled as they arise. Another factor is the limited stock of
political time and trust. The political agenda is crowded and if ideas of good
currency are not exploited at the right time they will be displaced by others.
Ministers are anxious to be associated with success and with positive
action. They are not likely to support changes which seem unlikely to get
through. On the other hand, it is difficult for them to withdraw from
a firm commitment, even if difficulties emerge later that cast doubt on its

wisdom. Politically, it is easier to modify a policy than to abandon it.

One of the functions of the political system is to filter out changes that would be damaging to established interests. Compromises are therefore inevitable. The proponent of radical change, who seeks to challenge the established power structure, has to build an alternative constituency. Rhetoric plays some part. So does the skill to link the proposal to other political objectives (more participation, efficiency, modernisation, local self-determination, etc.); these need not be mutually consistent. But the most useful constituency will be a coalition of powerful groups who can be brought to see that the change is consistent with their own desire for power, influence and reward.

The change will begin to take off when groups and organisations have begun to coalesce around it and see opportunities for increasing their status and remuneration. By this stage, the centre of action will have moved from the main political arena to the micro-politics of the task force and the working party. These work in different ways. The task force can be used to maintain the impetus of change by harnessing the energy and enthusiasm of 'young Turks' who may either be drawn from within the organisation or be recruited from outside. To be successful they should have a stake in the change and a below-average commitment to the existing structure; but it can be helpful to coopt progressive and influential members of the existing power-structure. The working party is typically an arena for negotiation. Representatives of interest groups meet to explore the implications of the change and to extract such concessions and advantages as they can for their members. If they fail, they can appeal to a higher political court. While political forces at an earlier stage lean towards simplification in order to get the change accepted in principle, the tendency is now towards elaboration, as both negotiators and enthusiasts try to get their pet schemes included in the package.

Since the real function of the working party (or its equivalent under some other name) is to bargain, it will be the scene of conflict and some exaggerated claims. But it may be politic to cloak these claims with the rhetoric of concern for progress and the common good. In any case, the process of negotiation is itself educative and one outcome may be a positive commitment to the change, as distinct from acquiescence in exchange for concessions. It is helpful, for example, if members of a working party can be given a demonstration of what the change would mean in practice.

Both from the working party and the task force a stream of messages is flowing back to other members of the organisation. These can convey reassurance or sound alarms. Unless the change is one that can be introduced autocratically, the support of middling-senior participants is important, since they will have to make the new system work after the task forces have dispersed and senior members of the working parties have retired. The change-activists are therefore likely to try to influence the communication flow by setting up their own channels of announcements, bulletins and training schemes to allay rumours and present the change in a favourable light. It is accepted wisdom that a participative, open system is most likely to win commitment and alleviate unnecessary anxiety. Exercises may therefore be mounted to increase involvement by working through the difficulties. Occasionally, these exercises may be used as positive feedback; but there is usually insufficient time or capacity at the centre to use them in this way. Involvement for its own sake is likely to be helpful only if the participants can see some benefit or reward for their effort. If they feel that they are being asked to consider matters which exceed their competence, authority or field of interest, or that nobody is going to listen to what they have to say, they will rapidly become disillusioned.

For the great majority of participants, the basic need is security. In the public sector, it is relatively easy to offer reassurances about security in the material sense because of the vast opportunities for redeployment. Even when organisations are being broken up, staff can usually be reabsorbed somewhere else, often to do very much the same job. The ease with which central government functions can be shuffled around Whitehall departments bears ample testimony to this. (Even in local government, opposition to change comes from local politicians rather than from the staff.) By definition, such changes are often merely cosmetic. It is more difficult to offer guarantees that the security of an established social and political structure will survive a major reorganisation. Indeed, the long-term consequences may be quite unpredictable. There is therefore a temptation to win support, at some cost to the wider objectives, by promising that most people will not even notice the change.

It may be worth reemphasising that if, as is usually the case, the central authority is seeking to impose change on the periphery it will attempt to control the change process. The more radical the change, the more necessary this will be. But the centre also has a vested interest in uniformity, which enables its own control mechanisms to work. There is, therefore, not much scope for specific concessions to the periphery, unless they can be applied universally. However, a more flexible approach might in some circumstances be more successful in inducing the desired change.

EVALUATION OF CHANGE

It is obvious that the benefits of a change may not exceed the total cost of negotiating and implementing it. The cost will nearly always be greater than expected, because of unforeseen teething troubles and contingencies, including perhaps an under-estimate of the concessions that will have to be made. The benefits may not arise. In the case of instrumental change which is intended to increase organisational flexibility and innovativeness, the new system may end up less flexible than the old one. Keeling makes the point that the true cost of a change is the lost opportunity to make other uses of the resources and energy it consumes.

It is not difficult to draw up a theoretical calculus of costs and benefits. But it is almost impossible to apply one in practice. Organisational change is not a discrete act, but an ongoing social process. The results of instrumental change (or 'meta-change' as it is now fashionable to call it) may take a long time to appear and are almost impossible to measure when they do. The social and political implications of change are equally resistant to identification and quantification. Moreover, the organisation is not a closed system: it is affected by changes in the world around it as well as by those originating within the system. Before-and-after comparisons are, therefore, at best subjective and intuitive and at worst misleading. Moreover, change in the public sector is usually introduced universally, so that there are no controls. (An interesting exception is in local government reform, which took place in London some years ahead of the rest of England, so that it is possible in principle to distribute cost increases between the reorganisation itself and general trends in service standards; but this is still a very limited comparison.[14])

But such evaluations are hardly ever attempted. Even in the early stages of implementation, when a clearer picture begins to emerge of the probable costs and chances of success, there is seldom any opportunity to stop and recalculate the advantages of going ahead or dropping the project. Commitments have been made and the pressure to advance is irresistible. (It should be said that there is a marked difference here between change with a political dimension, like the NHS reorganisation, and changes in administrative technology, like tax collection, which do tend to be carefully tested and are often abandoned after evaluation.) The political and administrative processes which control change are themselves ongoing and it is in their nature that immediate problems take precedence over more fundamental reappraisals. Once the change has been made, attention shifts to new issues (including problems caused by the change) and there is little incentive to evaluate it systemically in retrospect. Moreover, there is no single criterion for evaluation. The central authority might judge the success of a change by the extent to which new processes had been established, while the peripheral agents might judge it by the extent to which these had been absorbed without altering the basic decision-making processes or power structure.

Consequently, there is little learning from experience. Such assessments as are made tend to be crude ('huge increase in administrative costs'), emotional ('a great mistake') or selective rationalisations ('we should have listened to X and not Y'). The success of the change may indeed be judged by the extent to which purely symbolic goals, like the redesignation of posts, have been accomplished in time.

Yet there are important lessons to be learned. For example, how true is it that change has to reach a minimum critical mass if it is to be effective? Is it true that reorganisation requires a massive injection of new resources if it is to amount to anything more than a recombination of existing activities with a thin papering of coordination on top? What are the relative advantages of retraining existing people as against injecting new forces into the political structure? What are the costs and benefits of the centralisation stage in the change process? At the moment, we can approach such questions only by a mixture of historical analysis and informed judgement. But they need to be asked.

It is generally easier to point to costs than to benefits. But there are at least three levels at which the success of a major change can be estimated. First, have the specific intentions of the change been achieved: e.g. have the introduction of new information technologies increased the organisation's learning capacity? Second, has the change contributed to the solution of the problems which put it on the agenda: e.g. has structural reorganisation been followed by the desired change in priorities? Third, is the new system *on balance* causing more satisfaction and less dissatisfaction than the old one; and how far can these differences be attributed to the change?

If these questions seem too simplistic, consider the problem of evaluating the kind of meta-change proposed by Donald Schon, which is not entirely irrelevant to our discussion of the NHS:

If government is to learn to solve new public problems, it must also learn to create the systems for doing so and to discard the structure and mechanisms grown up around old problems. The need is not merely to cope with a particular set of new problems, or to discard the organisation- al vestiges of a particular form of governmental activity which happen at present to be particularly cumbersome. It is to design and bring into being the institutional processes through which new problems can continually be confronted and old structures continually discarded.[15]

SUMMARY AND COMMENT

Most of our detailed knowledge of administrative change processes comes from socio-psychological studies in industry and small groups. The NHS reorganisation itself involved major change, and it was hoped that the new structure would be more change-oriented than the old: 'The structure ought positively to encourage more integrated services and patterns of care'.[16] It is therefore important to review what people have said about change processes.

The first observation is that change on this scale is rare and difficult to achieve. Most people and most organisations survive with the minimum of adaptation necessary for self-preservation. Radical change therefore arises only in unusual circumstances, when influential groups become dissatisfied with some aspects of an organisational performance. Their belief may not be well-based. The problems may not be amenable to the kind of change that is advocated. But the impetus for change comes from a belief that the old system is unsatisfactory. This may come from within: the original impetus for the NHS reorganisation came from doctors who felt that administrative fragmentation was an impediment to effective medical practice. Or it may come from outside, as in the growing dissatisfaction of Ministers with the insensitivity of the old hospital authorities to political pressures. The propensity to change can be encouraged by setting up critical and destabilising forces within the organisation: this was meant to be the role of community physicians in the new set-up.

Once change has been decided upon, it is necessary to establish change-agents. These can be of two sorts: task forces like the joint liaison committees and the DHSS reorganisation unit which have change as their main task and provide some driving power; agencies like the NHS Staff Commission and the working party on collaboration with local government, whose main purpose is to negotiate change with established interest groups. There is substantial overlap: the management study group was concerned both with the mechanics of the new structure and with their acceptability to those represented on the steering committee.

At this point, interesting things begin to happen. The participants begin to interpret the change in terms of their own interests and aspirations. The original objectives can be side-tracked or compromised in negotiations. The pioneering groups can become over-committed to the potential of the change, and pass through alternate periods of enthusiasm and despair. The momentum of change develops to a critical point after which it becomes impossible to turn back. By late 1972, both political parties were committed to the NHS reorganisation, regardless of the consequences.

Unless change can be shown to benefit the participants (in terms of power, incomes, status) it will be resisted. Politically, negotiation is necessary because existing groups have the ability to impede the change process. The side-payments made at this stage may be expensive, but are seldom weighed against the advantages originally sought from the change. At a more personal level, resistance to the change can be reduced by human relations techniques which are aimed at containing anxiety. The underlying philosophy is that participation helps to generate commitment as well as supplying information which prevents the growth of damaging rumours. This was very evident in the human relations exercises associated with the 1974 reorganisation. Nevertheless, major change appears, as in the case of the NHS, to be associated with a period of tight central control because of doubts about the reliability of those at the periphery.

Change is seldom adequately evaluated after the event. This is partly because it is difficult to isolate effects and causes. But it is partly because the change has come to mean different things to its participants, which they are reluctant to expose. Consequently, lessons from one reorganisation are seldom applied systematically to the next. For example, much of what happened in 1974 could have been predicted from a close study of the London government reorganisation in 1965 and the integration of social services departments in 1971. But the social service example was never properly evaluated and there was only a limited amount of reactive learning from the London experience.

NOTES

1   G. Zaltman, R. Duncan and J. Holbek, *Innovations and Organisations*, Wiley, New York, 1973.
2   E.g. C. C. Hood, *The Limits of Administration*, Wiley, London, 1976; only two of the 207 pages deal directly with reorganisation.
3   A. F. Leemans (ed.), *The Management of Change in Government*, Martinus Nijhoff, The Hague, 1976; see 'Overview' and 'A Conceptual Framework for the Study of Reform of Central Government', both by the editor.

4   Desmond Keeling, *Management in Government*, Allen and Unwin, London, 1972, ch. 7.

5   Donald A. Schon, *Beyond the Stable State*, Temple Smith, London, 1971.

6   Anthony Downs, *Inside Bureaucracy*, Little, Brown, Boston, 1966.

7   T. Burns and G. M. Stalker, *The Management of Innovation*, Tavistock, London, 1966.

8   R. M. Cyert and J. G. March, *A Behavioural Theory of the Firm*, Prentice-Hall, Englewood Cliffs, New Jersey, 1963.

9   C. Sofer, *The Organisation from Within*, Tavistock, London, 1961.

10 Warren Bennis, *Changing Organisations*, McGraw-Hill, New York, 1966.

11 J. Hage and M. Aiken, *Social Change in Complex Organisations*, Random House, New York, 1970.

12 H. Kaufman, *The Limits of Organisational Change*, University of Alabama Press, 1971.

13 A. M. Graziano, 'Clinical Innovation and the Mental Health Power Structure: a Social Case History', *American Psychologist*, Jan. 1969.

14 E. Wistrich, *Local Government Reorganisation: the First Years of Camden*, London Borough of Camden, 1972, pp. 126–8.

15 Schon, *op.cit.* (note 5), p. 116.

16 Ministry of Health, *The Administrative Structure of the Medical and Related Services in England and Wales*, HMSO, 1968, para. 16.

CHAPTER 10

Lessons from 1974

The case-study was restricted to one of the ninety new English health areas. Most of the fieldwork was completed about fifteen months after the reorganisation, at a time when the costs were more obvious than the benefits. Even at that time, there was plenty of evidence that the Humberside experience was not unique. This chapter tries to bring together some lessons about the reorganisation process, and about the NHS itself at a time of change. Some of the major organisational problems that are still outstanding will be discussed in the final chapter.

Humberside coped fairly well with the mechanics of the reorganisation. There was no obvious disruption to patient services, except where they had to be realigned with unnecessarily artificial district boundaries. The breakdown in staff consultation did not seem to matter very much. The serious hiatus in administrative services, and the damaging industrial disputes, were the result of decisions (or non-decisions) outside the local sphere of responsibility. So were shortcomings that could be attributed to the new structure itself. Within their terms of reference, the area health authority and community health council members, with their officers, succeeded in establishing a new structure of management and, by and large, getting it accepted. But in general the AHA members and their staff were the agents rather than the architects of change. They had no say (other than through their national professional associations) in the decision to go ahead with reorganisation, or in the shape the new service was to take. Their job was to implement, as efficiently as possible, the strategies determined centrally. The interesting things locally were the enthusiasm and degree of understanding with which the changes were embraced—as well as their realism as seen in the local context.

But even from a local study it is possible to draw some general lessons, first about the way the change was carried out.

MANAGEMENT OF CHANGE IN THE NHS

Pace. The process of reorganisation took longer than had been intended. The Department of Health and Social Security used a technique known as 'project network analysis' to coordinate and concert the various things that had to be done by April 1974. The intention was to advertise new top posts at the beginning of 1973 and to publish staff transfer schemes in October 1973 so that the structural changes could be complete by April 1974. But all this depended partly on the smooth passage of the Reorganisation Bill (which was held up by a political debate on the completely irrelevant issue of family-planning charges) and by the intransigence of the staff associations in negotiating salaries (which were expected to be agreed late in 1972 but were not in fact settled, by unilateral decision of the Secretary of State, until the middle of 1973).[1] It proved impossible to agree other conditions of service until long after the reorganisation date. However, that is not the issue that mainly concerns us here.

The structural reforms were only a means to an end. The real objective was to alter the 'appreciative setting' of large numbers of people engaged in health service management. It was intended to influence their priorities in policy-making and in day-to-day practice. There was therefore a good *a priori* case for getting the whole thing over as quickly as possible, on the principle that old habits would be less likely to survive a severe shock.

In fact, the reorganisation dragged on over several years. Change was introduced piecemeal. The new management processes of planning and monitoring became separated in time from the introduction of the structure that was intended to serve them. Urgent problems in service development had to wait because everyone was preoccupied with nuts and bolts. Many people, still, thought things had been rushed.

Perhaps this was inevitable. The national health service is one of the largest enterprises in the world. It must be among the most complex. There was a vast amount to be done, from negotiations with doctors and nurses about their status in the new scheme of things to the harmonisation of conditions of service for ambulance drivers; from the appointment of health authority members to the collation of information about the merging services; from crash training programmes to finding new offices. All this had to be done on an enormous scale. None of it was easy. Often, painstaking work had to be redone when new difficulties arose. Some parts of the machinery were clearly over-taxed and (even if the work could have been spread more evenly) it is doubtful if the system could have coped with a much faster rate of change.

During the reorganisation, the work of the service had to go on. Disturbance to management processes can be tolerated for quite long periods without serious effects on the basic work of an organisation. But it could not be allowed to affect services to patients. Perhaps, in the NHS, a really traumatic shock was just not on. There is also the question of personal adjustment. Shock treatment may be effective with small groups of full-time managers. But it is hardly appropriate for people whose commitment extends only to an hour or two a week, like many lay members and clinicians who participate in health service management. They certainly needed time to adjust and were probably realistic in guessing that they would need a year or more to run themselves in.

Taking all this into account, it is easy to suggest that in an ideal world the reorganisation would have been handled rather differently:

(a) It would have been introduced in stages, starting with a fairly leisurely pilot demonstration which extended long enough for difficulties to become apparent and solutions found for them before they cropped up on a national scale. On the basis of that experience, task forces would have moved out from the demonstration project, introducing the new systems quickly and completely in an increasing number of areas until the whole country was covered, perhaps over a period of several years. The system could have been adapted to local situations as they were encountered, and a pool of experience accumulated. This method has been used successfully in other NHS innovations, like hospital costing, functional budgeting and the computerised analysis of in-patient statistics. The testing of 'tentative hypotheses' by the management study group in seven putative areas,[2] was no substitute for careful piloting.

(b) There would have been a heavier temporary investment in the actual process of change. In the case of the NHS, there was a tremendous amount of pre-planning at national level, in the management study and various working parties. At area level, however, investment in the change process was limited to the involvement of busy officers in the joint liaison machinery, attendances at training courses (mostly short and rather superficial) and the appointment of authority members and a handful of chief officers a few months before the appointed day. It is not surprising that most of the energy was devoted to structural nuts-and-bolts questions. The missing element was a 'change-agent' (e.g. the task forces mentioned above) working intensively with the local people on retraining and process-management as well as restructuring.

(c) A clearer distinction might have been drawn between those who were going to be responsible for activating the new system, who needed a period of intensive training and freedom from other preoccupations, and those whose main job was to maintain continuity in the provision of services. The training arrangements, in putting most emphasis on the needs of senior officers, did make distinctions of this sort; but they were blurred at the edges. Moreover, it was some time before the key people could be identified in public. The result was that the training courses often missed their target. Overall, there was too little training at the top. The NHS arrangements contrasted markedly with those adopted for restructuring social service departments a few years earlier. There, the first step was to appoint a director who was then sent on a course to find out what his job entailed and returned to construct a supporting structure for the approval of his committee. In the 1974 local government reorganisation, also, the new local authorities were free to adopt their own structures. There is no evidence that these were less successful than those of the NHS.

(d) The opportunity should have been taken to introduce some new blood. There was no guarantee that a radically new approach would take root in a service made up entirely of staff whose experience was of the system it was intended to change. The arrangements for early retirement of senior officers left plenty of room for recruiting outsiders without damaging anybody's legitimate career prospects. In 1974, there were many suitable people available, owing to contraction in industry and the universities. Some of them would certainly have had as much to offer as inexperienced NHS officers who in some cases gained very rapid promotion.

Centralisation. Whether this would have been possible in the NHS is another matter. The service is state-financed, accountable to the Secretary of State, and vulnerable to constraints and timetables not of its choosing. The significance of choosing 1 April as the universal reorganisation day was the political need to synchronise NHS reorganisation with the parallel reorganisation of local government. Moreover, much of what happens at the periphery is determined by central negotiations with professional bodies, staff associations and representatives of local government and other interests. Tight central control was a feature of the reorganisation process. It was the cause of much resentment locally. Since greater delegation was one of the professed objectives of the reorganisation, it was initially believed that the peripheral agencies would be given a good deal of freedom to handle the reorganisation process itself. In fact management structures, detailed role-descriptions for particular jobs and even the arrangements for selection committees were all determined from London. The DHSS also issued detailed 'guidance' about how and when to bring different parts of the new arrangements into operation. There was implicit discouragement to doing anything until the central department had pronounced on how it should be done. This had a numbing effect on the authority we studied.

There is quite a good organisational case for centralised control during a period of reorganisation. Peripheral organisations may not be committed to the change. Even if the ultimate aim is to give them more power, the centre may have to ensure, by temporarily taking over the reins, that the changes at the periphery which are seen as necessary conditions for later delegation do in fact take place. This is especially true when complex changes are being made quickly and universally. It may be more economical to concentrate the thinking in one place. In the NHS example, there was certainly more planning capacity in the DHSS than anywhere else. There was also more knowledge, for example about the number of staff available nationally in a given category—and therefore about the number of posts that could be established. It would have been wasteful as well as unfruitful to leave every peripheral authority to work out its own arrangements.

But much of the central department's involvement arose from the pressure exerted on it by professional and staff associations to restrict, in the interests of their members, the scope for flexibility at the periphery. As such, its contribution was as often a source of weakness as of strength. It was certainly a source of delay. Many aspects of the reorganisation would have been dealt with much more speedily if the peripheral authorities had been left to get on with them (and, of course, had been minded to do so).

They would not necessarily have been more extravagant: Humberside, for example, did not want all the highly-paid posts that they were authorised to fill and indeed left some vacant although in other cases they had to adjust the structure to accommodate the approved establishment. More important, they would have been more realistic. North Humberside would probably not have been divided into two districts.

There would not have been delays while middle-managers went through the unwelcome hurdle of applying for their own jobs through regional machinery. The professional advisory structure, especially on the medical side, would have been much closer to what the local staff wanted and felt able to operate. One of the hazards of centralised negotiations is that national associations will press for, and obtain, complicated concessions which have consequences that are quite unacceptable to their members at the periphery.

On balance, there was too much centralisation. It produced some inappropriate solutions, as well as too many opportunities for scapegoating, and a sea of paper in which few people were able to keep afloat. But the impetus for the change, and its philosophy, had to come from the centre. It is a pity that more attention was not given to making sure that the philosophy got through, instead of controlling matters of detail on which local knowledge was likely to serve as well as centralised wisdom.

One effect of over-centralisation was over-elaboration and rigidity. Quite early on, a distinction had emerged between the area, as the level of authority sharing common boundaries with the matching local government authority, and the district, which would be the natural unit for providing comprehensive health care. In fact, many of the health districts were far from natural: some single-district areas were quite unable to offer comprehensive health services,[3] while other districts were created just as artificially in order to provide arithmetically tidy sub-divisions, of the larger areas.[4] But, once the concepts of area and district had been established, the central authorities felt obliged to offer universal guidance—for example about the way professions should be organised at both levels, and the relationships between them—which in fact created great confusion and complexity. This was seen most clearly in the arrangements for medical representation. But there were traces of the same conceptual rigidity in the attempts to delineate distinctive roles for the (area) health authority and the (district) community health council. It is very hard to find a basis for this in the thirty-four single-district areas. Similarly, reexamination of managerial relationships after the appointed day was hampered by the need to think in terms of 'regions', 'areas' and 'districts' although these terms described quite different situations in the conurbations and in rural parts of the country.

The role of health authority members was defined in terms which seriously overlap those of area and regional authority officers (policy review, performance-monitoring and so forth) while discounting the layman's constituency and watchdog roles.[5] As an example, area health authorities were discouraged from setting up standing committees for fear that these might dilute the collective policy-making role.[6] In practice, lay members have found their managerial roles difficult and unrewarding. In the larger authorities, a committee structure has become essential to allow smaller numbers of members to interact usefully with officers on a limited range of issues, like planning or finance.

Another consequence of over-elaboration at the centre was the elevation of ancillary health professions like nursing, works and finance to equal status with medicine in order to preserve some abstract symmetry, regardless of the calibre and aspirations of people on the ground.

Overcoming resistance to change. It is commonplace in management textbooks that change involves threat and consequently evokes resistance. Considerable resources therefore have to be set aside for winning support for the change, at one level by dispelling misleading rumours and at another by developing a positive commitment. Sometimes opposition may have to be bought out. There was plenty of evidence of this philosophy in the NHS reorganisation. At DHSS level, there was an obvious desire to meet the staff associations all the way. Elaborate arrangements were made to safeguard staff interests. There was a considerable investment in training and in information media. Almost every circular contained the injunction to consult staff locally.

The case-study suggested that this hand was over-played and that the underlying theory deserves reexamination. For the great majority of the staff we talked to, there was no sense of threat, and no question of resistance (except as a possible bargaining counter in national salary negotiations). There was hardly any evidence of the fear of redundancy which impressed the NHS Staff Commission.[7] There was general support for the idea of reorganisation, which did not seem to be much affected, one way or the other, by training courses, information sheets, or the other devices aimed at winning commitment. Nor was there much interest in the details, and much of the disseminated information was thought to be boring and irrelevant. What people did want was specific information about their own jobs. Generalised statements were little help here. It was not a human relations exercise that was needed, but better and more expeditious management of the change process. (It is ironic that so much unnecessary delay and anxiety was caused by the staff associations themselves and by procedures developed by the Staff Commission to make the reorganisation arrangements acceptable.)

There were plenty of specific problems, mainly about conditions of service. But these were management problems, not examples of resistance to change. The general attitude to change was acquiescent. This suggests that the arrangements to protect and involve the majority of staff were unnecessarily elaborate. For most, a simple clearly-written booklet would have met their needs better than all the officialese on the noticeboards.

Acquiescence was not, of course, enough for the handful of top officers who would have to provide leadership in the new service. Unless they were positively committed to it, the reorganisation would be more a matter of form than of substance. There was in fact a good deal of enthusiasm at this level, although not untempered with the cynicism of experience. It arose, however, as much from the roles in which people found themselves as from external attempts to induce it.

Morale-building exercises would be pointless here unless related to the immediate demands of the job. The most successful exercises on Humberside, in fact, were the three weekend conferences at which all the main area and district officers got together to work out solutions to problems which were urgent at the time. The main risk was disillusionment, caused by lack of autonomy, and the loss of a sense of purpose due to the slackening of momentum. Again this called for better management rather than for human relations techniques.

The management of the change process—and especially the pace with which change is implemented—thus emerges as the key to maintaining the commitment and enthusiasm of those who must be won over. This throws us back to the point made earlier about the need to manage a reorganisation so that it can be implemented quickly and completely in any one authority, even if national coverage takes some time to achieve. It also takes us to a point about training, which has been an important part of the attempt to win support for the NHS reorganisation. Much of the training, although pleasant enough for the participants, probably missed its mark because it was insufficiently specific. Again, the colonisation strategy advocated earlier would have permitted training to be based on actual experience in authorities earlier in the chain. Moreover, the training courses would have dealt with topics that had already proved to be difficult (like the concept of 'monitoring') or particularly relevant to people's new jobs (like the techniques of quantitative analysis) instead of issues that were merely thought likely to create difficulties.

DYNAMICS OF CHANGE IN THE NHS

During this massive restructuring, the forces which influence the development of health care became unusually exposed in the various debates and negotiations that went on. It is worth attempting to analyse these in order to understand the influences that are still likely to be at work in the future.

The main contributors to the development of health services are:

(a) central government, where national interests in health are aggregated and related to other aspects of social, governmental and economic policies;

(b) the lay members of authorities, advisory bodies and community health councils, among whom the authority members are technically agents of central government;

(c) the permanent officers who are appointed to assist the lay members in the discharge of their functions;

(d) professional staff who, while providing health care according to the standards of their own professional code, are nevertheless involved in management in the sense that their decisions commit resources and are therefore subject to resource-constraints;

(e) national organisations representing the interests of professional and other groups.

In the last resort, the pattern of health care is determined by the Secretary of State. He (or she) alone has the power to determine the structure of the service, the allocation of resources to particular regions or services and, through selective pricing (e.g. the free family planning service), important aspects of the pattern of demand. The Secretary of State has to take account of pressure groups impinging directly on the central political system, including professional groups, local government associations and cause groups claiming to represent the interests of particular categories of patients, as well as ideological pressures for democratisation, managerial efficiency, and so on. In most respects, central government coopts the national pressure groups into a partnership—albeit a quarrelsome one. But the Secretary of State can over-ride any particular interest group if he has the political will to do so. This may involve him in conflict with his own officials, including the professional members of the DHSS.[8]

The lay members are rooted in their locality. They have a common interest in advocating its special claims and defending them against the 'rationalising' tendencies of higher authorities. Allowing for structural perspectives and the qualities of individuals, there is no basic difference between the approaches of members of community health councils, area health authorities or even regional health authorities. (Even in economy campaigns, CHC members can be just as zealous in seeking out waste and extravagance as those who are formally responsible for efficient management.) There are, however, increasing inhibitions about the advocacy role as one moves upward. Indeed, when there are two levels of authority, as in the old HMC/RHB pattern, role-requirements are likely to force members of the higher level to take a more detached, strategic view. Where there are three, as in the new NHS, the role at the intermediate level is likely to be confused.

This is not to say that lay members cannot be found who will act like a company board of directors within a conglomerate. Selection can ensure that at least some members at each level are more concerned with the rationality of the whole system than with the interests of their particular constituency. It can also try to ensure that specific interests cancel each other out and that each authority, collectively, is concerned with the overall quality of health services within its field. The 'democratisation' of health authorities, however, was designed to increase representativeness (without altering the agency relationship) at the expense of managerialism. It became more difficult to separate the roles of health authority members from those of CHCs.

The full-time administrators play a number of roles. Perhaps the most important in practice is as key points in a series of complex communication networks, linking together different levels in the service and connecting the points of decision with the places of execution. Although the administrators, in their secretarial capacity, are most prominent in this role, the other professional administrators also play a part, as do the part-time authority chairmen, who should therefore be distinguished from the other lay members. As heads of services, the full-time administrators also wield considerable executive authority. Their third role, and the one that is constitutionally most important, is as servants of their authority—filtering its business, advising on action to be taken, and responding to direct instruction.

Textbook analyses of administrative and professional roles depict professionals as pressing for the growth and development of their own specialisms, while administrators are more concerned with overall priorities and value for money. This is partly right. But in the NHS administrators are growth-oriented as well. As servants of the authority which appoints them they identify with the local rather than the national service and are as anxious as the lay members and professional staff to advance its special claims. There is closer identification with the clinical staff than one might expect: in the old hospital service (whose values still predominate in the new integrated service) many administrators found that the best survival strategy lay in a managerial style which consisted of finding out what the doctors wanted and then finding some way of getting it for them. If these wants were not articulated, there was a vacuum which was not entirely filled by policy statements of their own and higher authorities.

The professional staff are, of course, oriented towards expansion, and tend to see even a reduction in the rate of growth in their own spheres as a matter for protest. Doctors will be the last group to be persuaded of the need for retrenchment (except in administration). But those who are not full-time administrators tend to be reluctant participants in management. There is a difference here between the well-established professions, like medicine and dentistry, and those which are still concerned about developing their professional status; activist members of the latter group are anxious to have a hand in things and tend to over-estimate their colleagues' ability to contribute. But the prototype is medicine, whose representatives' insistence at national level on full participation in management is not always matched by their local members' willingness to devote time and energy to it. It has been said that doctors demand to be consulted but are reluctant to give advice. Even within medicine, there is an important difference between those who regard themselves as solely responsible for the care of their own patients and those who accept collective responsibility, with their colleagues, for the provision of a service to the community. There may be a similar dichotomy in other professions, where its effects on attitudes to management would be less obvious.

These five groups were the main actors in the reorganisation story. What parts did they play? There is no need to say more about the role of the Secretary of State. So far as the other actors were concerned, there was a marked contrast between their performance on the local and the national stage. Nationally, the doctors took the lead, occasionally making concessions to other professions to secure the position of influence guaranteed to them under the 'Grey Book' structure.[9] The local authority associations dominated another part of the action, in the working parties set up to examine collaboration between the NHS and local government. They insisted on arrangements that appeared to leave the health service to tackle the problems of socio-medical care with one hand tied behind its back.[10]

But on the local stage the roles were reversed. Neither the clinicians nor the lay members played more than a minor part in applying the structure to local conditions. Lay members were not involved at all in the joint liaison committee. When they did appear on the shadow authority they were more concerned with making the changes acceptable than with influencing their direction; and, on Humberside, the local government nominees did not at that time perform in the politicised style which some observers had feared and others eagerly anticipated. The doctors did not appear on the JLC until very late on. Although they had strong views about one aspect of the reorganisation (the division of North Humberside into two districts) they were unable to influence the outcome. Nor, since the reorganisation, have medical committees played the central role in collegiate management that was envisaged for them. Some clinicians have taken full advantage of medical involvement in the management teams; but we are talking about a handful of highly-motivated individuals rather than of doctors as a body.

In Humberside, the main parts in reorganisation were played by the permanent administrators (again including the AHA chairman, once he had been appointed). The chairman was concerned mainly with the functioning of the authority itself. The professional chiefs concerned themselves with the impact of reorganisation in their own spheres. But the leading parts, both in the preparatory phase and in the overall design of the new machinery and the introduction of new planning processes, were played by the administrators who had been group secretaries, and the community physicians who had been medical officers of health. Even allowing for the mantle of authority they had inherited from their former jobs, we were impressed by the weight of the contribution from these two groups, and the acceptance of their authority by others.

In the new structure, the ability of administrators and senior community physicians to continue to make that contribution appears to be seriously weakened. First, there is the principle of consensus management, which reduces them to the status of equal members of management teams. Second, there is the nominally equal status of district and area officers, which in some respects limits the formal role of the area officers to that of staff advisers to the authority. Both features leave the responsibility for overall coordination with the authority members themselves. The authority's part-time chairman is all that remains of the original intention that each authority should have a chief executive, on the lines of reorganised local government; but even he cannot commit the other members.

In practice, of course, it does not work out like that. Even in the strange leaderless teams that have emerged from the reorganisation, the administrator tends to become the coordinator, which makes him *primus inter pares* except in service planning, which tends to be the domain of the chief medical officer. We have said enough in earlier chapters to indicate that the coordinating role ascribed to the part-time lay members is almost certainly unrealistic. The important linkages from area to region, and from the health service to the local authorities, are handled primarily by the administrators and medical officers. They are still the mainsprings that really make the NHS tick as an organisation. On paper, however, the new structure fails to take this into account. The lack of consonance between formal and requisite structures could be damaging in the future.

Nor does the formal position about accountability reflect the way the NHS actually operates. Each authority appoints its own staff (although there are severe restrictions on its freedom of action—on some appointment panels authority members are in a minority). The line of accountability therefore runs from district and area officers (independently) to the area authority, which is then accountable to the regional authority and thence indirectly to the Secretary of State. The authority members are part-time, many of them appointed indirectly by local government. They do not raise their own finance. Apart from the risk that the non-local authority members may not be reappointed, there is no surcharge liability nor any other sanction to penalise improper or unreasonable decisions about the use of exchequer funds. This seems an improbable vehicle for the 'accountability upward' which was meant to be the accompaniment of 'delegation downward' in the reorganised NHS.

The main lines of effective communication are controlled by the officers, especially the administrators and community physicians, and many questions of management are settled without reference to authority members. The district, area and regional officers are not in a hierarchical relationship, but in a 'monitoring' one, which seems to mean that they operate by persuasion, reporting gross non-cooperation to their own authority. Since this sanction would be a reflection on their own persuasive ability, it is not difficult to guess that it will rarely be applied.

This prompts the thought that a national health service really needs one or more national officer corps to operate it, at least in those fields where there is a need for a continuous chain of executive authority and accountability. There is nothing inevitable about the present system, in which the career structures and loyalties of those on whose shoulders rests nearly the whole administration of an important and vital nationalised service are balkanised among the 100 employing authorities and nearly 300 semi-autonomous units of administration in England alone. The elements of a national career structure are already there, in national organisations, national training arrangements and embryonic national manpower planning. We seem to be near the point where health service administrators and medical officers (and perhaps treasurers, where the accountability problem is even sharper) can be unified into national corps which regulate their internal affairs, exercise self-discipline where necessary, and undertake to meet the needs of health authorities throughout the country, while still retaining a primary corporate loyalty to the service as a whole. This, of course, would involve line relationships between district, area and region. But it is hard to see how effective lines of management and accountability can be sustained without such a relationship.

Such a development might seem incompatible with local democracy: the current arrangements are presumably based on the local government model, and it may be asked how an authority can be held responsible for a service if it cannot select its chief executives. But members of the French prefectural corps act as chief executives of the local authorities in the areas to which they are posted. Even in Britain, the government sees no absurdity in maintaining a unified civil service to serve the proposed Scottish and Welsh assemblies as well as ministers accountable to the Westminster parliament. There are in any case several different possible interpretations of 'local democracy' in a service which is intended to be national rather than federalist and is the ultimate responsibility of a Secretary of State who is accountable to a national constituency.

The recognition of key managerial groups might also seem inconsistent with the trend towards 'participation' in health service management, especially by clinicians. But our evidence is that the desire for participation has been grossly over-stated. Even consultants, while wanting some machinery through which they can influence decisions that affect them, are at the same time prepared to accept a strong administrator who is a visible point of contact. They are impatient with elaborate machinery which appears to give them a say, through layers of representation, in policy-making but cuts them off from direct contact with people who can actually get things done. This may well be true of other professional groups as well. But it is an interesting thought that the pressure for a more authoritative system of health service administration may well come from the medical bodies which prevented its emergence in 1974. It would not be incompatible with the retention of strong medical advisory machinery, nor with existing arrangements for collegiate regulation of clinical matters.

These thoughts about the functional requirements of a national health care system are politically unfashionable. But, since they emerge from an analysis of the dynamics of the system, they are worth pondering.

EVALUATION

The effect of the change in Humberside has been discussed in chapter 8. To recapitulate briefly: the administrative machinery suffered from a long period of confusion and interruption; the morale of a limited number of individuals was affected by personal insecurity; the new structure was cumbersome and expensive to operate. Against these disadvantages, there was a new potential for integrated management, coordination with other services and more rational planning and resource-allocation. But the advances were very slow, and were mostly in response to central pressure. Much of what did happen in the three years after reorganisation would probably have happened anyway. It is necessary to ask whether it was necessary to reorganise at all; and whether the actual and potential benefits resulting directly from the reorganisation were sufficient to justify the costs.

A full balance-sheet would be very difficult to draw up. It would have to show the extent to which the objectives of the reorganisation were realised, with a plus or minus for any unexpected side-effects, set against the short-term and long-term costs of the change. In the course of arguing for another look at London government, a *Times* leader-writer recognised

> the pusillanimous doctrine, coined in the light of recent events in local government and the health service, to the effect that any existing administrative structure, however chaotic, is preferable to any conceivable reorganisation, however rational it may appear in prospect. The upheaval, with its rancour, jobbery, horse-trading and cost, cannot possibly be justified by any system that rancour, jobbery and horse-trading would ever allow to come to pass.[11]

Some of the objectives, including better management and more professional participation in management and planning, have been obstructed by the sheer complexity of the arrangements designed to achieve them. Others, like more comprehensive planning and more critical evaluation of the use of resources, have been impeded by the self-inflicted wounds of the reorganisation itself, including the failure to recruit and retain qualified and experienced staff. (Reorganisation had similar effects on local government.[12]) An unexpected bonus has been the increased accountability of health service managers, through community health councils, to interested members of the publics they serve. Not all CHCs have been successful; but those that are seem to play a larger part than health authority members in making officers account for their performance in public. It might have been possible to set up CHCs without reorganising the

NHS; but there would have been no political impetus to do so, and the work of CHCs does seem to depend on their one-to-one relationships with district management teams and on their right to comment independently in public on district plans and proposals.

The concept of the geographical health district has been helpful here, even if some of the districts are a bit odd. The definition of districts has also made it possible to allocate resources, and to start thinking about priorities, in terms of the needs of a given population. Collaboration with local authorities, whose responsibilities are geographical, is also obviously easier if health authorities are responsible for similar (or relatable) populations. Indeed, the one essential thing that had to be done in 1974 was to make the lower tier of health authorities responsible for meeting all the health needs (so far as they fell within the NHS) of a defined population. Without that, the actual and potential benefits of the reorganisation could not have been achieved.

But it did not follow that these territories had to match those of local government counties and districts. In the shire counties, health authorities deal with a number of local authority district councils on housing and environmental health. It would not be administratively impossible for a number of health authorities to collaborate for liaison with a single county authority, or vice versa, so long as the populations served bore some relationship to one another. If politicians had been less obsessed with the symbolic parallelism, it would have been possible to adopt a much more flexible approach to the definition of health boundaries and avoid the complexity of district–area relationships. A structure of perhaps 120 single-district areas,[13] some larger but most smaller than the matching local authorities, would have achieved the objectives at much less cost. Whatever the merits of the separate arguments for each tier, they are outweighed by the effort involved in making them both viable and operational.

The reorganisation did not stop at geographical realignment. Ambitious ideas about management structure and process were introduced at the same time. Most of them had some merit and deserved a try. But it was unrealistic to introduce them wholesale, under pressure, as an instant solution to status problems arising from the merger (e.g. the relationship between the former medical officer of health and the hospital group secretary) while the formal structure was itself being changed. The attempt to introduce them all at the same time proved too much for the service's digestive capacity.

It also produced some distortions. The pressure to accommodate existing staff was legitimate enough in the context of a redistribution of functions among authorities; but it was incompatible with the need to find people able to operate a demanding new management system. The concept of coterminosity with local authorities was relevant to the desire to promote collaboration; but it was incompatible with the determination of realistic boundaries for the provision of health care—large enough to be self-sufficient but small enough to allow participation by the professions and the community served. The case for a 'managerial' type of health authority was very germane to the development of chains of upward accountability, in which the authority members provided an important link, corporately, between the Secretary of State and the variety of independently account-able chief officers and advisory bodies at each level. But it was impossible to reconcile the managerial criteria for selecting members of such an authority with the political objective of legitimising local autonomy in political terms.

In terms of timing, it was necessary to synchronise the main NHS reorganisation with the reorganisation of local government in April 1974, if only to prevent a double upheaval for the local authority health services. But this could have been achieved by streamlining hospital management committees on a basis of defined catchment areas and attaching local authority staff to them (which is roughly what happened anyway in the 'latching-on' period between the appointed day and the completion of a new management structure). The new structure itself, and the associated professional and consumer machinery, could then have been established later, along with the new management and planning processes it was intended to serve. The establishment of highly-paid new posts could also have waited with advantage until the system was ready for them and *after* existing staff had been redeployed in jobs within their capacities. As it was, the delay in introducing the new planning process meant that there was a period in which nothing activated the new system, and jobs had to be found for the new officers and committees within the traditional pattern of management.

In summary, the health service reorganisation was too ambitious, was in some ways misconceived, and created an undesirable number of side-effects. The benefits will not show until the peripheral authorities are set free (subject to necessary constraints) to modify the over-centralised arrangements by which they still feel stifled. Some of the objectives were realistic and attainable. They are already beginning to appear. This does not, however, provide a justification for the total reorganisation package.

CONCLUSIONS

(a) A major reorganisation is likely to involve heavy costs, in terms of disturbance and delay to ongoing management processes, and uncertainty and adjustment difficulties for staff who are directly involved, spread over a long period of time. Most of these costs are not visible to the public at large and do not appear as figures in the accounts. They are most likely to arise if the same people are expected to manage the reorganisation and manage the service at the same time.

(b) Most of the costs have arisen from structural changes. They would have resulted from any merger of authorities even if no additional changes (e.g. in management process) had been contemplated. If, therefore, structural reform is only a means to an end, every attempt should be made to find a cheaper way. In the NHS case, for example, the real objective was a process one—better information flows, with some incentive to use them as a basis for more rational decisions about the use of scarce resources. If it had been possible to alter the process without altering the structure, the objective would have been achieved more cheaply, more quickly, and almost certainly more effectively. It was not necessary, for example, to set up a separate area tier purely to achieve better liaison with local government.

(c) Structural reorganisation tends to increase the permanent cost of running a service. This is partly because it is difficult to maintain rigorous control of costs and manpower levels at the critical period when the new structure is being established, and it is very difficult later to reverse decisions made at that time. Another reason is that reorganisation provides a happy hunting ground for staff associations, who will naturally seize opportunities to improve their members' pay, career prospects, retirement rights, conditions of service, and so on. Again, concessions made at this time tend to have lasting effects.

(d) The greatest practical difficulties have been caused by the absorption into a national service of relatively small numbers of staff from local government, which lacked uniform conditions of service. The same difficulties have occurred in merging local authorities. It would make reorganisations of this sort much easier in future if there were standard national conditions of service for all staff doing identical jobs throughout the public service.

(e) The process of reorganisation tends to develop its own momentum. At a critical stage, preoccupation with mechanics, and with getting the new system established somehow, may seriously obscure the purpose of the exercise. Even if doubts begin to arise (like the doubts after the February 1974 election about the political acceptability of the managerialism which was intended to be built into the new NHS structure) there is an inclination to brush them aside, perhaps to be dealt with by a further reorganisation later. It is desirable to keep this psychological commitment to the minimum and to retain some flexibility by avoiding (i) excessive prescription of detail, (ii) packages which include elements that are only marginal to the real objectives, and (iii) rigid deadlines, which are always hostages to fortune.

(f) Reorganisation is normally undertaken in a spirit of over-optimism about the net advantages. This is perhaps necessary in order to generate enough enthusiasm to carry it through. Our research, however, should encourage a more sceptical attitude to such claims before a reorganisation becomes inevitable. Any substantial reorganisation should be piloted, not only to identify points that will need special attention when it is introduced on a larger scale, but also so that the case for making any change at all can be reviewed after there is some concrete experience of the costs that will be incurred and of the effect of unavoidable concessions to entrenched interests. Paper planning tends to be over-optimistic, and is no substitute for actual experimentation.

NOTES

1   DHSS, *National Health Service Staff Commission Report (1972–75)*, HMSO, 1975, paras 2.2, 2.3.
2   DHSS, *Management Arrangements in the Reorganised National Health Service*, HMSO, 1972, para. 6.
3   M. J. Buxton and R. Klein, 'Distribution of Hospital Provision: Policy Themes and Resource Variations', *British Medical Journal*, 8 Feb. 1975, pp. 345–9.
4   This applied in some large cities, like Leicester, Leeds and Liverpool, as well as in North Humberside. The first attempt to put the pieces together again was in Liverpool: a decision to scrap its two-district structure was announced in 1977.
5   G. W. Jones, 'The Functions and Organisation of Councillors', *Public Administration*, London, Summer 1973.
6   NHS Reorganisation Circular HRC(73)22, para. 15.
7   *Op. cit.* (note 1), para. 3.1.

8   On this see Richard Crossman, *Diaries of a Cabinet Minister*, Hamish Hamilton and Cape, London, 1977, *passim* (e.g. vol. 3, pp. 410–12, 418, 436, 456, 490).

9   *Op. cit.* (note 2), ch. 4.

10   See chapter 3 above, pp. 48–50.

11   'The GLC's Utility Called in Question', *The Times*, editorial, 25 Sept. 1975.

12   *Report of the Local Government Staff Commission for England*, HMSO, 1977.

13   This arbitrary figure assumes that some of the smaller areas would be combined and most of the larger ones broken up into self-contained district authorities, as recommended in much of the evidence to the Royal Commission on the National Health Service.

CHAPTER 11

The Structure of the NHS

This book has been about the implementation of administrative change. We have not, for example, been concerned with such issues as whether or not there should be a free health service, or whether we should be spending more on it. Our scope has been more limited than that of the Royal Commission: 'to consider . . . the best use and management of the financial and manpower resources of the National Health Service'.

But we have also been describing the machinery for administering a system of health care, and it seems appropriate to end by trying to bring together some of the main administrative considerations bearing on its effectiveness. This chapter therefore touches briefly on the scope and functions of health authorities, on their decision-making processes, and on the roles of the central and regional authorities.

Considered as an organisation, the NHS has four main characteristics. It is very large, and therefore presents all the classic problems of leadership and control in large organisations. Partly because of its size, it has a tiered system of authority, so that it becomes important to get the functions right at each level and to find the right means through which higher tiers can supervise the work of lower ones. Thirdly, it is staffed at the point of delivery by highly-skilled professionals, who are not amenable to bureaucratic patterns of control. Finally, it lies in the public sector which means, on the one hand, that its operations can in principle be coordinated with those of other public services but, on the other hand, that it is affected by considerations which to a medical specialist or nurse might seem irrelevant to the provision of health care.

Any system of administration must reflect these characteristics. Any system will have disadvantages. The lesson of this study is perhaps that it is often better to live with some disadvantages than to incur the costs of major change in order to secure improvements that may themselves turn out to be illusory.

A DECISION-MAKING SYSTEM

Administration is about decision-making, and decisions involve choice. Decision-making patterns can be classified, rather crudely, as incrementalist or rationalist. Incrementalist decision-making amounts to a series of small adjustments to cope with immediate pressures. The aim is to find the most comfortable point of balance among competing pressures. Unless radical new pressures have been taken into account, these decisions will tend to be conservative and to favour established interest groups. A rationalist pattern of decision-making, in contrast, owes more to analysis and the systematic review of alternative methods of achieving defined objectives. Its style is more technical and less political, although political factors may be taken into account: the objectives themselves may be political (winning an election or pacifying the doctors). Rationalist decision-making is more likely to bring radical alternatives into consideration. There is still some bias towards the status quo, because of the cost of change; but it is not so overwhelming as in the incrementalist pattern. All this could be elaborated; but the simple polarity will suffice for our purpose.[1] In practice, the two patterns often occur simultaneously. Most decisions are probably taken incrementally, with rationalist components. It is possible, however, to structure decision-making processes to make them more, or less, rationalist—for example by establishing targets and guidelines, providing an information base, or requiring certain interests to be consulted.

That, in a nutshell, is what the NHS reorganisation was about. Incremental decisions accumulating over a quarter of a century had resulted in an unbalanced health service in which too much priority had been given to high-technology medicine while prevention and whole areas of socio-medical care had been neglected and there was also great geographical inequality. Pressure on resources was emphasising the need for rational choice: the deficiencies could not be remedied if the pace of technological development was maintained. So new structures and processes were introduced to encourage rationality. Health authorities and their senior officers were given a wider span of responsibility than their predecessors, so that they had some incentive to maximise the effective use of resources over the whole field of health care. Certain viewpoints were institutionalised within the structure: community health councils; specialists in community medicine; general practitioner representatives; health education officers; a network of participative and representative machinery. Finally, a planning

204 The Structure of the NHS

system was devised to ensure that all these viewpoints were taken into account when new developments were being considered, while due regard was paid to national and regional objectives and priorities.

The adoption of a rationalist model of decision-making implies wide scanning, explicit choices among objectives and the analysis of alternative means of achieving them. It is therefore necessary to know what the objectives are and to define the field within which they will be pursued. The health authorities are primarily concerned with the provision of medical, dental and related services. Most of these services are concerned with the treatment or alleviation of disease, although some are concerned with its prevention. The Secretary of State for Social Services has a wider span, covering personal social services as well as the NHS and (in what is virtually a separate department) the social security system of cash payments. At DHSS level, health and personal social services are treated together. But the government as a whole is concerned with housing, education, road safety, environmental pollution, conditions of employment, fire precautions, the regulation of drink and tobacco and much else that clearly has a bearing on health. Conversely, the operations of the NHS have implications for employment (both in its own workforce and in restoring others to fitness), social welfare, especially among the elderly and handicapped, and distribution of real incomes: the free health service is part of the 'social wage'.

At this level, it is possible to start thinking of rational choices across a broad spectrum of social policy, if there is appropriate machinery to do it. In his diaries, Crossman writes of his decision, as a social services cabinet minister, to forgo £3 million for the NHS (which in effect came out of raised prescription charges) to pay for improvements in comprehensive schools.[2] (He adds that he got little thanks for it; departmental ministers have little incentive to worry about other ministers' services.) An obvious need for inter-departmental thinking arises from the decline in the birthrate and the increasing number of old people, which implies a shift of resources from education to health and personal social services. On a still broader front, it can be argued that good housing and nutrition contribute more to social welfare (and indeed to good health) than hospitals or doctors. Even in terms of death and disablement, it is probable that measures to improve road safety and to curb alcoholism and cigarette smoking would produce a much higher return on investment than better hospital diagnostic equipment. Health economists are doing some useful work in this field.[3]

In 1975, the Central Policy Review Staff, with support from the DHSS, urged that social service ministers should coordinate their individual services and relate them to broader social objectives.[4] It is known that some such discussions have in fact taken place. Similarly, the Review Staff have suggested that departments which deal with local authorities should adopt a broader, more coherent, approach which is less service-based and allows the local authorities more freedom to trade one service off against another.[5] The scope for trade-offs between the NHS and other services at local level is more limited, because separate authorities are concerned, but the systems of joint planning and joint financing allow some movement at the edges.

The difficulty, however, is deciding on the objectives. One objective for the NHS might be to maximise the availability of medical technology, within a given quantum of resources, to the whole population. But this would result in a very different kind of service from one whose objective was to relieve pain and distress to the maximum extent possible, or to contribute to national efficiency by preventing absences from work due to sickness. All this is fudged in the statutory objective of the NHS, 'to secure improvement in the physical and mental health of the people . . . and in the prevention, diagnosis and treatment of illness'.[6] Broader definitions of social welfare are even more elusive.

Attempts to exercise rational choice over such a broad field are likely to remain difficult and probably inneffective. A service may be shown to be inefficient and wasteful compared to other means of, say, relieving pain and anxiety; but it cannot be abolished overnight, especially if it provides operating territory for a powerful and influential profession. If it is there, it may have to remain there. At best, this kind of analysis can show that there are inconsistencies between different policies. But inconsistencies have their uses: they allow value-conflicts to remain latent and are a hedge against damaging rigidity. One of the problems of rational planning is that it has to be selective: a limited number of indices have to be found which relate to a limited number of objectives. These may drastically oversimplify the real situation. Hence the reluctance of most central NHS policy-makers to make their guidelines binding on lower-tier authorities.

Within the health and personal social services programme, the main current objectives are:

(a) to bring services in the more needy areas and districts up to a target average, measured in financial terms
(b) to give priority to community care instead of care in hospitals

   (c) to improve services for the elderly, mentally ill and mentally handi-
       capped
   (d) to reverse the expansion of hospital maternity services which had
       occurred during a decade of declining birthrates
   (e) to slow the expansion in acute care services and to release resources
       for other developments by seeking economies.[7]

These objectives are controversial and may themselves be inconsistent. But
they reflect a long history of political commitment and rhetoric and will not
be further analysed here. The important point is that none can be achieved
without responsive action at the level of area health authorities; two require
action by local government authorities as well; the major changes in
priorities also necessitate changes in clinical practice. How well is local
NHS administration equipped for the task?

LOCAL ADMINISTRATION

When discretion is delegated to agents, there is some loss of central control.
The compensation should be an increase in robustness—in the sense that
operational decisions have been tested for feasibility and acceptability, in
operating conditions, as well as for consistency with strategic objectives.
The risk is that the local people will not share the objectives and will seek to
evade them.

   A good example is mental illness. Since the days when Powell was in
charge (1962–4), most health ministers have taken a special interest in
mental health and have asked health authorities to improve conditions in
psychiatric hospitals, as well as building up alternative facilities in the
community. There has been measurable progress on both counts. But the
recurrence of hospital black spots indicates massive indifference on the part
of some authorities in spite of injections of cash and visits of inspection. Of
community provision by local authorities, a government White Paper of
1975 said that

> The failure . . . to develop anything approaching adequate social services
> is perhaps the greatest disappointment of the last fifteen years. . . . The
> Government for its part intends to see that over the years the balance of
> health and social services is put right.[8]

The question is whether the new arrangements will make this possible.
   ~ ~ system does, in fact, put considerable pressure on area health
      They receive a good deal of nagging from above and below. The

DHSS and the regional authorities continually stress the priority that should be given to mental health: norms of good provision are published and compared with local statistics; a heavy emphasis on mental illness is expected to be included in area plans. This guidance material is available to community health councils, who also see reports from the Health Advisory Service inspection teams. Most CHCs include representatives of voluntary organisations concerned with the mentally ill, and many have set up working parties or special interest groups to visit psychiatric services, study and report. CHCs have an opportunity to comment on health authority plans, and have adequate means of complaining to RHAs and, through the media, to the local public if they feel that mental illness is being neglected. The system of pressures may not work; mental health is still a low-status Cinderella. But at least there is something there to balance the constant pressure to spend the available money on high-technology medicine.

But the development of a mental health service does not lie entirely with the health authority. Some of the most important elements, including sheltered housing, hostels and social support, are the responsibility of local social service departments. Here there is no equivalent of the community health council and seldom any political pressure to counteract those favouring services for children and the elderly, which come from the same budget. The main pressure group for the mentally ill, in fact, is the area health authority which wants to see local authority services develop in order to relieve its own. But it has little to offer in exchange, and its only weapons are persuasion (on the statutory joint planning machinery) and the power to contribute to the initial cost of relevant local authority projects.

Rather similar considerations apply to the other Cinderella services for the mentally handicapped and to a lesser extent the elderly. All suffer a double handicap because responsibility is divided and both sides have more attractive uses for their money. Many health experts believe that those services will never be planned effectively unless health authorities assume responsibility for social as well as medical care. This would entail a third stage in the removal of health and related services from local to central control (the first being the nationalisation of hospitals in 1948 and the second the absorption of local health authority services in 1974). It would be fiercely resisted on jurisdictional grounds by local authority interest groups. It would also entail dismantling the integrated social service departments which were created in 1971 on the implementation of the Seebohm Report and abandoning the rather dubious philosophy in that report about generic social workers. But that might cause more cheers than tears.

Rather a different problem is presented by the policy objective of altering the balance between primary and secondary care. Here again there has long been a conspicuous gap between policy and performance. In spite of official statements about the importance of primary care and the need to avoid expensive hospitalisation, the load on hospitals has increased and that on general practitioners has declined. Moreover this trend has occurred at a time when the changing age-structure might suggest a greater need for simple domiciliary care. Once a patient has been admitted to the medical care system, either through a general practitioner or through an accident and emergency department, it is the doctors who determine what further demands he will make on the system. Since the ratio of GP consultations to total population seems to be dropping, the costs and queues in the hospital sector appear to be the direct result of medical decisions. What can the health authority do about this, bearing in mind that it is responsible for overall planning but cannot interfere in the executive management of family practitioner services?

It can, of course, try and improve support for primary care by providing health centres and supplying nursing and supportive staff; for example, it could redeploy its physiotherapists to provide a community service. To put it more strongly, it can supply substitute labour for general practitioners and could do this as a deliberate act of policy. But there is not much incentive to do so, given other pressures on its budget. The real issue is not so much the expansion of primary care services as securing the most effective (and humane) balance between care and treatment in hospital and in a doctor's surgery or the patient's own home. This is the kind of thing that doctors are supposed to work out for themselves in the new joint medical committees. The authority can only provide encouragement, in the interests of good-quality care and the effective management of clinical resources. But here again, the English health authorities are at a disadvantage. The main part of the primary care budget (doctors' and dentists' fees and drug costs) is allocated direct to the family practitioner committee by the DHSS. It is impossible to transfer resources from this to the main AHA budget. An AHA that is short of general practitioners or dentists does not get the cash saved to spend on substitutable services. Conversely, the AHA is not directly affected by GPs' prescribing costs and cannot therefore offer the incentive of, say, better diagnostic facilities as a reward for more economical prescribing. Nor, given the separation of budgets, is there much point in considering the most effective way of dividing responsibility for, say, family planning or the dental health of schoolchildren. It would be interesting to know if these matters are considered more comprehensively in Scotland or Northern Ireland, where there are no separate family practitioner committees.

Both in mental illness and in the development of primary care, the ability of a health authority to implement national objectives is restricted by organisational space. What of policy areas that are nominally under its complete control, including the redeployment of resources away from acute care and away from the better-off districts to finance development elsewhere? Area health authorities have the power to make such changes, and a specific duty to look comprehensively at the needs of their areas. Nor is there any lack of evidence that cuts are possible. Comparative hospital running costs suggest frugality at one extreme and (perhaps unconscious) extravagance at the other. Even in clinical treatment, it is now known that many expensive treatments are of little value, while others can often be carried out in less expensive ways at no disadvantage to the patient.[9] Perhaps, as a minimum, procedures that do no good could be abandoned and the money used for something that works. But this brings up the familiar problem of clinical freedom.

Before embarking on that, we have to consider the formidable obstacles to any serious questioning of current practice and standards. There are no pressure groups campaigning for the curtailment of services. On the contrary, every established service has its defenders, from grateful patients to the health service unions. A fundamental review requires considerable confidence and some compensation for the personal and political costs of the inevitable battles. New development makes friends and reputations. Cutting back on inefficient established services makes neither, but consumes a lot of time and energy. In any organisation, it is much easier to focus on the use of any additional money, which can be spent on new services without hurting anyone, than to challenge the ongoing base expenditure. It is not surprising that the health authorities claimed that redeployment without extra resources was well-nigh impossible.[10]

Rational decision-making requires information, the analytical capacity to use it and the incentive to do so. The new planning and consultative processes have greatly increased the flow of information within the local NHS structures—both statistical material about norms, needs and deficiencies, and softer information about objectives and what people want. The capacity to handle all this is less certain: both authority members and officers complain about suffocation by paper and there was not much enthusiasm for the DHSS idea that authorities should use standard forms to compare their current levels of provision with national and regional levels and with target norms; probably most authorities simply lacked the expertise. The problem of incentives is crucial. It is difficult to find anybody at health authority level with any motive for challenging base expenditure on ongoing services. The members are local people, interested mainly in the improvement of local services. The administrators are conditioned to ignore policy statements unless there is new money to go with them. The professionals are committed to their own services. All have some commitment to the inherited pattern and to colleagues whose careers are tied up with it.

Moreover, there are three specific obstacles to change. One is the system by which each authority appoints its own chief officers, whose attachments are thus local rather than national and whose career prospects are hardly likely to be enhanced by quarrels with the consultants.[11] Second is the system of management by consensus teams which, if used skilfully by the participants, can ensure that difficult and contentious issues are never allowed to rock the harmony.[12] Third is the difficult boundary between management responsibility and clinical autonomy.

Medical hegemony is crumbling fast. The doctrine of clinical autonomy is almost indefensible in its present form except as a weapon in the organisational power game: doctors have to testify in a court of law that they have followed good professional practice in treating a patient, and there is no obvious reason why they should not also have to explain to an employing authority that they have followed similar canons in spending the authority's resources. But this would be a break with tradition. However, there is no doubt that the most effective agents of change could be the doctors themselves. Their decisions effectively commit most of a health authority's resources. They have the knowledge to criticise wasteful procedures, and those who work in the under-privileged sectors have, in principle, some incentive to press for economies elsewhere. Several attempts have, in fact, been made to encourage doctors to exercise collegiate control of standards and the use of clinical resources.[13] They have not been particularly successful, at least in terms of the kind of issues we are discussing here. Many doctors are not interested in management. Most are trained to think in terms of the individual patient rather than statistics. Few are willing to criticise colleagues, certainly to a lay management body. Those with the highest prestige tend to be in just those high-technology areas where the results of a cost–benefit exercise would be most revealing. Here again, where is the incentive?

The solution probably hovers around the position of the area medical officer, who knows his stuff, is not himself a clinician, and has some professional interest in rationalisation. But the task of the area medical officer, like all members of the new specialty of community medicine, is an impossibly difficult one.[14] Those who have established themselves with their clinical colleagues have probably done so as much by force of personality as through their formal role. Collectively, their authority in clinical matters is not accepted by other members of the profession. The relationship between management and medicine is thus far from satisfactorily resolved. But the interpretative role of the area chief medical officer looks a better bet than the layers of participative machinery.

To sum up so far, the new structure has perhaps marginally increased the incentive for an agent health authority to implement national policies to develop primary care services and those for the mentally ill; but its ability to do so is severely circumscribed by the independence of the family practitioner committee and the local authority social service departments. Conversely, health authorities have the ability to implement policies about redeploying the resources used by inefficient or less cost-effective services (although there is some doubt about their ability to handle the quantitative data needed to identify such areas); but the structure provides no incentive to do so and in some respects positively militates against such action.

CENTRAL AND REGIONAL ADMINISTRATION

The analysis so far suggests that decision-making should take place at two distinct levels of management. Operational decisions need to be made as close as possible to the level at which tasks are performed. The emphasis here is on realism and feasibility. The people at district and area level are surrounded by pressures and information about needs and deficiencies in existing services, only a small proportion of which can be systematised and transmitted upwards. They know, or should know, what local people want and will accept. They know where there are pressures, where there is slack, and how to get a quart out of a pint pot. But local planners are not living in an ivory tower. Their day-to-day contacts make them more aware of demand (often generated by the service itself) than of unmet need—more sensitive to the pressures on existing services than to the potential of new ones. They work within a web of reciprocal commitments to colleagues, on whose cooperation they rely for smooth operational management and who have a right to expect their own interests to be protected. This is very right and proper. But it is a recipe for incrementalism.

Hence the need for strategic decisions to be made at a higher level, where broad strategies can be worked out in general terms, away from the complex interpersonal relationships at the front line. It is much easier to contemplate radical change in a service if you are not involved in its daily problems nor on close personal terms with those who work in it. The analytical and synthesising aspects of major decision-making can be protected by removing them physically from the incrementalist pressures affecting day-to-day management. At a planning level, too, the pattern of incentives begins to work in favour of rationalism, since success is more likely to be judged by the degree to which it is attained. Moreover, it makes sense to concentrate analytical resources (with which we are not over-endowed) at a small number of centres.

In fact, the NHS does have this kind of basic two-tier structure, although it is considerably confused by the multiplication of tiers and by the fact that they also have executive responsibilities. The distinction is perhaps clearest in Scotland, where two different top-level bodies are superimposed on the area structure. The national Common Services Agency is simply an agent for managing a collection of services which it is more economic to provide on an all-Scotland basis. But the Scottish Planning Council, which works closely with the Scottish Home and Health Department, concerns itself with strategic issues; its structure accommodates representative and consultative procedures as well as technical analysis.[15] In England, the position is complicated first by the existence of a regional tier, whose functions overlap those of the central DHSS, and second by the fact that some of the larger multi-district area authorities feel sufficiently detached from frontline operations to carry out a planning role.

A regional tier of some sort is almost indispensable for NHS administration in England: administration from London would be too remote. But there are a number of possible permutations. The 1974 structure, in which regional health authorities look like area authorities on a larger scale, fails to recognise the essential differences in function: it is hard to see an effective role for RHA members or for chief nursing officers matching those at the operational level. An earlier proposal, that the regional authorities should be made up of representatives of the areas with general advisory functions, may be sound as a basis for common services but fails to give enough bite to the planning role. A stronger alternative is that regional planning should be the responsibility of regional officers of the DHSS, thus avoiding some duplication and tension. The DHSS has a substantial analytical capacity; but civil servants are the immediate agents of the

Secretary of State and as such are not immune from political pressures of a different sort from those affecting field administrators, but equally damaging to rational analysis of health needs. Hence the attraction of a national NHS Board, with regional officers, to carry out top-level administration and planning under the general directions of the Secretary of State. (But this would create its own difficulties: similar arrangements have not worked conspicuously well in the nationalised industries.[16]) Yet again, it would be possible to have a technocratic regional office (accountable either to the DHSS or to a central board) with some sort of advisory council as a sounding board.

The actual details may not matter a great deal. There is much to be said for avoiding a wholesale restructuring. What does matter is that the need for two levels of decision-making should be recognised, that these should be accommodated in the structure with the minimum of confusion and duplication and that the strategic tier should be superordinate to the operational one.

The reason for this last stipulation is that weak planning structures tend to be ineffective against incrementalism. Strategic decisions serve a variety of functions: some aim only to broaden the framework of reference within which the operational decision-makers work—to provide an indication of what the strategists would like before the tacticians become committed to something totally different.[17] The document setting out DHSS priorities for the NHS described itself as 'consultative'. But the history of both hospital and local authority services since 1948 suggests how little effect general admonitions are likely to have. The first round of the new planning cycle in 1976–7 differed from previous efforts to reverse the trend of development in that the guidelines were comprehensive and attempted to set targets in an order of priority within the context of available resources. The elaborate arrangements for consultation and feedback in the form of area and regional strategic plans amounted to a massive educational exercise. But the feedback itself contained more statements of good intention than positive proposals. It suggested that, once peripheral authorities realise that the guidelines have no bite, they will be safely ignored and things will go on much as before.

One of the strands in this discussion has been an emerging distinction between managerial and strategic decisions, with the implication that managerial decisions should be taken as close to the ground as possible, while strategic decisions cannot be. The danger is that strategic intentions will, as in the past, be compromised by a succession of *ad hoc* incrementalist managerial decisions at the periphery. This is not easy to avoid. Even those members of a health authority who are quite clear about the way they would like their services to develop are seldom equipped to detect contrary tendencies in the lists of capital works, staff appointments and equipment purchases that are submitted to them for approval. A strategic authority needs the ability to detect such tendencies and the power to intervene and correct them.

The fashionable term for this activity is 'monitoring'. But nobody is very clear what the word means: if it means that the higher authority should maintain a continuous watch over the activities of lower tiers, the obvious risk is that both levels will try to protect themselves by excessive consultation, thus sapping management vitality at the periphery and hampering the detachment which is needed at the centre. Except in crisis conditions, the higher authority should probably be content with routine information about what is going on, concentrating its intervention on key points of control. The most important areas of control concern decisions which would affect the development of the service for a long time to come. They include major new building, new medical appointments and some say in the allocation of budgets, which would include earmarking. The list is familiar enough and all controls have imperfections. (If, for example, part of the budget is earmarked for mental health development, and is liable to be surrendered if it is not spent on that service, a disproportionate amount of effort is likely to be spent in redefining expenditure so that it counts and in using up the allocation somehow.) But perhaps the case has sufficiently been made that some controls of this sort are needed to ensure that strategic thinking is geared into operational decisions.

DECENTRALISATION AND PARTICIPATION

In this discussion, the assumption has perhaps too easily been made that central direction of the NHS is feasible and desirable. In fact all that is claimed is that complete decentralisation is unlikely to secure the implementation of national policies, which is hardly an original observation. But there is a bit more to it than that.

The underlying philosophy of the new NHS structure is that progress is best made by a continuous dialogue, in which all the participants are engaged in a mutual learning process. This is most clearly seen in the planning system, which not only tries to involve all the peripheral authorities in the articulation of coherent *national* strategies but also invites views and opinions from every staff, professional or consumer interest institutionalised in the local consultative system. As an occasional exercise in participation this has its attractions. It also serves an educational purpose. But as a method of running the national health service it seems to be misconceived.

In the first place, it is difficult to reconcile continuous dialogue with effective management. Some industrial analysts draw a distinction between decisions on policy, in which all participants are entitled to have a say, and decisions taken in the course of implementing the policy, which are best entrusted to a responsible and accountable executive. The distinction is perhaps too facile (and skates over the possible conflict between industrial democracy and democratic political control in a public organisation); but it does recognise the advantages of a firm structure of authority for getting things done. This tends to be lacking in the NHS, both in terms of vertical command and in terms of day-to-day management within the districts. If everything is open for discussion, there can be no certainty. Many of the criticisms made in evidence to the Royal Commission relate to the absence of firm leadership and decision rather than to the arbitrariness of decisions made. (One comment was that the NHS structure impedes planning by vastly increasing the number of groups who can veto any development.[18])

Second, there seems to have been an over-estimation of what people can or will contribute, given their knowledge base and other demands on their energies. It has been argued earlier that analytical skills are scarce and are best concentrated in a few strategic centres. *Per contra*, it is both uneconomic and unrealistic to expect more than a handful of doctors, CHC members, trade unionists and others to involve themselves deeply in demographic analysis, health statistics and public expenditure planning in order to contribute to national strategies. They have better (and perhaps more important) things to do. In practice, the consultations on the first round of plans were often rushed and superficial, and it is hard to see much hope of change. The benefits of consultation have to be set against its cost to the participants, and even the intrinsic value of participation for its own sake has to be measured against the anxieties and false hopes which it can engender. There is certainly no evidence that (either in the NHS or in local government) there is a vast pool of creative talent just waiting to be tapped.

A participative and decentralised style of administration is currently fashionable, in rhetoric if not always in reality. This seems to be linked with changing attitudes to authority and more specifically with a reaction to 'over-government'.[19] But at least three strands need to be separated.

Authority can be shared, by decentralisation and participation, in the hope that better decisions will result from the application of local and sectional perspectives. Purely from a managerial point of view, however, decentralisation usually takes place for negative reasons: the central authority cannot cope with the mass of detail, or lacks local knowledge. Decentralisation is the lesser of evils. The price, as we have said, is some loss of uniformity and control. A bonus might be more involvement and satisfaction for those at the periphery, and more flexibility. (In the public sector, these are not necessarily virtues.[20]) The test here is whether decentralisation does in fact increase efficiency and whether it can be reconciled with accountability to the controlling authority.

Authority can be shared because of a political belief that it is desirable to do so. Ministers may wish to avoid responsibility for detailed administration, and put a local authority or *ad hoc* body in the firing line. Or it may be believed that 'local democracy' is good in itself because services administered locally are more responsive to the needs of those they serve. This argument has certainly been over-stated. Local authorities can be remarkably insensitive to local opinion: opinion surveys suggest that local government is if anything less popular than central government.[21] Often the kind of local involvement that seems to be desired is of the 'consumer defence society' sort (and then only when emotions are aroused by some bureaucratic blunder) rather than the decentralisation of executive authority. Tests here are more elusive; but they have something to do with public satisfaction and participation indices.

There also seems to be an assumption that participation will somehow produce consensus, as if people only have to see the light to want to follow it. Consensus will emerge, like Venus, from the sea of consultation. But this is all very dubious. People have different interests—rooted in their localities, occupations and affiliations—and evidence about the NHS suggests more conflict than consensus except at the most abstract 'welfare of the patient' level.[22]

Finally, authority may be shared because there is no alternative. The cooperation of people at the periphery may have to be bought by involving them in decisions and granting them a measure of autonomy. This is implicit in the arrangements for involving clinicians in management teams—although it may have come as a surprise to the doctors that other health professions and staff groups, including the health service unions, have also demanded their share of the power cake. It is also part of the implicit bargain with voluntary members of health authorities—power in exchange for supervisory and public services. The test here is whether the loss of power is compensated by the increase in commitment.

The amount and kind of decentralisation in the NHS should therefore be related to these tests—both organisational and political. Organisationally, the case for decentralisation of day-to-day management is very strong. This must include the involvement of doctors in the management of clinical resources. But decentralisation of responsibility for strategic planning is another matter, consuming far too much energy at the periphery and likely to be counter-productive. The political arguments for decentralisation do not stand up to inspection: if anything they tend to favour tighter central control in the interests of territorial justice and there is certainly no justification here for a return of the NHS to local government, or for the greater involvement of busy local councillors in local health administration; their record on community health councils is not impressive.

The power game argument is more subtle. The cost of coopting potential dissidents into the power structure can be very high and can be more of an impediment than an aid to progress.[23] At local level, some of the professional and staff groups have not been organised to seize their new opportunities, and it may be that national bodies have exaggerated their local members' desire for consultation. Britain is a highly centralised country, and professional organisations and other interest groups often operate most successfully at national level. Here again, it is perhaps necessary to draw a distinction between the participative structures appropriate to day-to-day management and those relevant to the formulation of strategic policy. Local NHS administration appears to be overloaded with structures which would be more relevant at the strategic level.

CONCLUSIONS

After all the restructuring of 1974, we are left with a national health service which, although dauntingly complex, still seems unable to cope with some of its basic problems. We have not yet, for example, found machinery through which health objectives can be related to wider social objectives; and perhaps indeed this is too complex a task.

Within the NHS, however, an attempt has been made to determine desirable lines of development within the available resources. The need for painful choices has been made explicit at national level. The problem is whether the structure of authority and decision-making will enable these priorities to be adequately reflected in local decision-making.

At first sight, the local decision-making process has been designed to create a balance of pressures within each authority which roughly mirrors the national pressure-group system. But in practice it is unlikely to produce the same kind of synthesis, because of unequal access to information and ability to handle it. It has been suggested that the NHS planning process had to be invented to make its complex administrative arrangements work.[24] These are certainly too elaborate for day-to-day administration. But they appear to be unsuitable for strategic planning also. Strategic planning requires a capacity for analysis and a detachment from ongoing pressures which is not possible at local level. Unrealistically high returns have been expected from giving everyone a chance to influence the planning process. The political need for participation has also been exaggerated. If it were accepted that the essential local tasks are management and programming, rather than strategic planning, the local decision-making process could be considerably simplified and streamlined. The main problem identified in this chapter has been the relationship between central strategies and actual operations. National and local perspectives may not coincide; and there is a risk that national objectives will continue to be eroded by a succession of incrementalist local decisions. On the assumption that the national strategy has some value, it is necessary to ensure that there are controls and checks on local operations by some superordinate body. The two essential levels are operational (area/district) and strategic (region/national). These need to be kept separate; but this does not exclude the possibility of finding better answers than in 1974 to the structural needs at each level.

When we come to the actual scope for action that is open to a well-intentioned health authority, we find a number of weaknesses. Some are internal to the NHS: the most important is the persistent failure to find an adequate conceptualisation of the relationship of clinicians to management. Another internal weakness is the independent budget (in England) for family practitioner services. But the most serious impediment to the rational development of priority services is the division of responsibility for them between health and local social service authorities.

It is probably impossible to deal adequately with the socio-medical care problem without a further adjustment to the boundaries of the NHS. Other improvements could be made without major structural change. It is desirable that this should be so, and that in administrative change as in the provision of health care 'low-cost options' should be pursued wherever possible.

NOTES

1 For a fuller discussion, see R. G. S. Brown, *The Management of Welfare*, Fontana and Martin Robertson, London, 1975, pp. 44–7 and 174–91; or *The Administrative Process as Incrementalism*, Open University Press, Milton Keynes, 1974.
2 Richard Crossman, *The Diaries of a Cabinet Minister*, vol. 3, 'Secretary of State for Social Services'. Hamish Hamilton and Cape, London, 1977, pp. 304, 309, 475–6, 483, 489, 496.
3 E.g. A. J. Culyer, *Need and the National Health Service*, Martin Robertson, London, 1976, ch. 5.
4 Central Policy Review Staff, *A Joint Framework for Social Policies*, HMSO, 1975.
5 Central Policy Review Staff, *Relations between Central Government and Local Authorities*, HMSO, 1977.
6 *National Health Service Act, 1977*, section 1(1).
7 DHSS, *Priorities for Health and Personal Social Services in England*, HMSO, 1976.
8 DHSS, *Better Services for the Mentally Ill*, HMSO, Cmnd. 6233, 1976, para. 2.8.
9 See note 7, p. 206, above.
10 DHSS, *The Way Forward*, HMSO, 1977, appendix II.
11 See chapter 10, pp. 191–2.
12 See chapter 2, pp. 30–2.
13 See chapter 1, pp. 16–18.
14 David Towell, 'Making Reorganisation Work: Challenges and Dilemmas in the Development of Community Medicine', in K. Barnard and K. Lee (eds.), *Conflicts in the National Health Service*, Croom Helm, London, 1977.
15 Scottish Home and Health Department, *Scottish Health Service Planning Council; Report for 1974*, HMSO, Edinburgh, 1975.
16 National Economic Development Office, *A Study of United Kingdom Nationalised Industries*, HMSO, 1976.
17 Bernard Taylor, 'New Dimensions in Corporate Planning', *Long Range Planning*, London, Dec. 1976.
18 R. Klein, evidence to the Royal Commission on the National Health Service, 1976 (unpublished).
19 L. J. Sharpe, 'Instrumental Participation and Urban Government', in J. A. G. Griffith (ed.), *From Policy to Administration: Essays in Honour of William A. Robson*, Allen and Unwin, London, 1976. See also Bernard Crick, 'Participation and the Future of Government' in the same volume.
20 For a critical discussion of this whole issue, see Peter Self, 'Rational Decentralisation', in Griffith (ed.), above.
21 Commission on the Constitution, *Research Papers 7*, 'Devolution and Other Aspects of Government: an Attitudes Survey', HMSO, 1973.
22 K. Barnard and K. Lee (eds.), *Conflicts in the National Health Service*, Croom Helm, London, 1977.
23 Philip Selznick, *TVA and the Grass Roots*, California University Press, Berkeley, 1949.
24 Neil Thomas and Bryan Stoten, 'The NHS and Local Government: Cooperation or Conflict?', in K. Jones (ed.), *The Year Book of Social Policy in Britain 1973*, Routledge, London, 1974.

APPENDIX A

Health Service Reorganisation Circulars Issued by DHSS

1972

June	HRC(72)1	'Reorganisation Circulars'
	HRC(72)2	'Boundaries outside London'
	HRC(72)3	'Joint Liaison Committees'
Aug.	HRC(72)4	'Command Paper, National Health Service Reorganisation: England' (a copy of the document was enclosed)
Sept.	HRC(72)5	'Accommodation for Area Health Authorities'
Nov.	HRC(72)6	'Working Party on Financial Administration'
Dec.	HRC(72)7	'Joint Liaison Committees, Preparation of Area Profile'
	HRC(72)8	'Filling of Vacancies by Existing Authorities before April 1974'
	HRC(72)9	'Issue of Guidance by the Department—Community Health Services'

1973

Jan.	HRC(73)1	'National Health Service Reorganisation: Staff Appointment and Transfer Arrangements'
	HRC(73)2	'General Guidance to Area JLCs'
	HRC(73)3	'Management Arrangements for the Reorganised NHS'
Feb.	HRC(73)4	'Management Arrangements for the Reorganised NHS: Defining Districts'
	HRC(73)5	'National Health Service Reorganisation: Joint Liaison Committees. Supply Matters'
Mar.	HRC(73)6	'Transfer of Health Building Schemes from Local Authorities to Health Authorities: Transitional Arrangements'
	HRC(73)7	'Joint Liaison Committees: Membership'
Apr.	HRC(73)8	'Development of Planning in the Reorganised National Health Service'
	HRC(73)9	'Training for National Health Service Reorganisation'
	HRC(73)10	'Ambulance Services (excluding the London Ambulance Service)'
	HRC(73)11	'Consultation between Joint Liaison Committees and Staff Organisations'

221

	HRC(73)12	'Reorganisation of the National Health Service: General Medical Services. Splitting and Merging of Executive Council Registers'
	HRC(73)13	'Accommodation for the New Health Authorities'
June	HRC(73)14	'NHS Reorganisation: Transfer of Local Health Authority Property. Transfer of Local Education Authority Property Held for School Health Purposes'
	HRC(73)15	'Transfer of Local Health Authority Trust Property'
July	HRC(73)16	'Stationery for the Family Practitioner Services'
	HRC(73)17	'Working Party on Collaboration—Report on its Activities to the End of 1972'
	HRC(73)18	'NHS Reorganisation Act 1973: outlines the arrangements for bringing the Act into operation and describes the timetable for subordinate legislation'
	HRC(73)19	'Management Arrangements in 2-District Areas'
	HRC(73)20	'Regional Health Authorities. Determination of Boundaries and Constitution'
Aug.	HRC(73)23	'Transitional Arrangements: Coding of Health Authorities and Health Institutions'
	HRC(73)24	'Area Health Authorities. Determination of Boundaries and Constitution'
	HRC(73)25	'Transfer of Staff'
Sept.	HRC(73)21	'Transitional Arrangements: Staffing Support for Regional and Area Health Authorities'
	HRC(73)22	'Membership and Procedure of Regional and Area Health Authorities'
	HRC(73)26	'Statutory Provisions: Framework of National Health Service after Reorganisation'
	HRC(73)27	'Transitional Arrangements: Statistics of Health Service Activities. Summary of Arrangements for Securing Continuity in 1974'
	HRC(73)28	'Operation and Development of Services: Organisation of Pharmaceutical Services'
	HRC(73)29	'Transitional Arrangements: Transfer of Hospital Trust Property'
	HRC(73)30	'Transitional Arrangements: Transfer of Hospital Trust Property: Appointment and Functions of Special Trustees'
	HRC(73)31	'Finance: Advice and Checklist. Interim Financial Arrangements'
Oct.	HRC(73)32	'Establishing Family Practitioner Committees'
	HRC(73)33	'Working Party on Collaboration. Report on its Activities from January to July, 1973'
	HRC(73)34	'Transitional Arrangements and Organisation and Development of Services. Control of Notifiable Diseases and Food Poisoning'
Nov.	HRC(73)35	'Transitional Arrangements: Implementation of NHS Reorganisation by Health Authorities'
	HRC(73)36	'Transitional Arrangements: Interim Management Arrangements for Health Authorities'
	HRC(73)37	'Operation and Development of Services: Organisation for Personnel Management'

	HRC(73)38	'Organisation and Development of Services: Coding of Health Districts and Health Institutions'
	HRC(73)39	'Personnel: Appointments Procedure for Posts in Community Medicine'
Dec.	HRC(73)40	'Membership and Procedure Regulations for Family Practitioner Committees'

1974

Jan.	HRC(74)1	'Transfer of Staff: Superannuation Options for Transferred Officers'
	HRC(74)2	'National Health Service Reorganisation. Protection of Salary and Other Terms and Conditions of Service'
	HRC(74)3	'Notification and Registration of Births and Deaths'
	HRC(74)4	'Community Health Councils'
	HRC(74)5	'Operation and Development of Services: Child Health Services (including School Health Services)'
	HRC(74)6	'Operation and Development of Services: Welfare Food Service'
	HRC(74)7	'Patients Liable to be Detained under Mental Health Act 1956—Discharge by the Managers of Hospitals'
	HRC(74)8	'The NHS (Staff Transfer Schemes) Order 1974: SI 1974 No. 35'
Feb.	HRC(74)9	'Local Advisory Committees'
	HRC(74)10	'Transitional Arrangements. Charities Connected with Hospital Purposes—Amendment of Trust Instruments'
	HRC(74)11	'Organisation of Nurse, Midwife and Health Visitor Training and Education'
	HRC(74)12	'Arrangements to Permit Certain Senior Officers Employed by Health Authorities in England to Retire'
	HRC(74)13	'Transitional Arrangements and Organisation and Development of Services: Environmental Health'
	HRC(74)14	'The Work of Family Practitioner Committees'
	HRC(74)15	'Transitional Arrangements: Transfer of Departmental Circulars and Other Documents to Health Authorities'
	HRC(74)16	'Statutory Provisions: Charges under Section 2(2) of National Health Service Reorganisation Act 1973'
	HRC(74)17	'Arrangements for Vaccination and Immunisation against Infectious Disease'
Mar.	HRC(74)18	'Statutory Provisions: Functions of Regional and Area Health Authorities'
	HRC(74)19	'Collaboration between Health and Local Authorities. Reports of Working Party; Establishment of Joint Consultative Committees'
	HRC(74)20	'General Practice Pharmacy Services: Arrangements from 1st April 1974 for Pharmaceutical Services under Part IV of the National Health Service Act 1946'
	HRC(74)21	'Health Centres'
	HRC(74)22	'Transfer of Health Service Social Workers to New Local Social Service Authorities'
	HRC(74)23	'Management Arrangements: Health Districts'

	HRC(74)24	'Personnel: Appointment of Administrative Dental Officers'
	HRC(74)25	'Statutory Provisions: The NHS (Transferred Local Authority Property) Order 1974: SI 1974 No. 330'
	HRC(74)26	'National Health Service Reorganisation Act 1973 —Section 16. Transferred Assets and Liabilities, General Financial Arrangements'
	HRC(74)27	'Reorganisation of National Health Service and of Local Government. Organisation and Development of Services. Health Education'
	HRC(74)28	'Transitional Arrangements: The Winding Up of the Affairs of Abolished Authorities, Provision for Continuity and the Enforcement of Rights and Liabilities'
Apr.	HRC(74)29	'Management Arrangements: Consolidation of Interim Arrangements: Preparation of Substantive Schemes: Filling of Posts'
	HRC(74)30	'Management Arrangements: Administrative Management Structures and Preparation of Substantive Schemes'
	HRC(74)31	'Management Arrangements: Nursing and Midwifery Management Structures'
	HRC(74)32	'Management Arrangements: Agency Arrangements and extra Territorial Management'
	HRC(74)33	'Reorganisation of National Health Service and of Local Government: Operation and Development of Services: Chiropody'
	HRC(74)34	'Management Arrangements: Financial Management Structures and Preparation of Substantive Schemes'
June	HRC(74)35	'Management Arrangements: Community Medicine and Dentistry: Schemes of Management and Approval of Posts'
July	HRC(74)36	'Statutory Provisions: National Health Service Reorganisation: Subordinate Legislation'
Oct.	HRC(74)37	'Management Arrangements: Works Staff Organisation and Preparation of Substantive Schemes'
Dec.	HRC(74)38	'NHS Reorganisation: Management Arrangements'.

APPENDIX B

List of Organisations Consulted about Composition of Health Authorities

(These are reproduced from HRC(73)24.)

Local Bodies
Regional Hospital Boards
Executive Councils
Hospital Management Committees
Boards of Governors of Teaching Hospitals
University Hospital Management Committees
The specified University for nomination

National Bodies
Age Concern
The Association of Independent Hospitals
Association of Nurse Administrators
British Council for the Rehabilitation of the Disabled
British Dental Association
British Hospitals Contributory Schemes Association
British Medical Association
British Red Cross Society
Central Council for the Disabled
Confederation of British Industry
The Faculty of Anaesthetists of The Royal College of Surgeons
The Faculty of Community Medicine, c/o Royal College of Physicians
Faculty of Dental Surgery, Royal College of Surgeons of England
Health Visitors Association
Joint Committee of Ophthalmic Opticians
National Association for Mental Health
National Association for the Welfare of Children in Hospitl
National Corporation for the Care of Old People
Guild of British Dispensing Opticians
National Joint Committee of Working Women's Organisations
National Association of Leagues of Hospital Friends
National Society for Mentally Handicapped Children

Royal College of Midwives
Royal College of Nursing
Royal College of Obstetricians and Gynaecologists
Royal College of Pathologists
Royal College of Physicians
Royal College of General Practitioners
Royal College of Psychiatrists
Royal College of Surgeons of England
Society of Chief Nursing Officers (Public Health)
Society of Chief and Principal Nursing Officers
The Society of Community Medicine
The Faculty of Radiologists at the Royal College of Surgeons of England
St. John Ambulance Association
Trades Union Congress
Women's Royal Voluntary Service
The Pharmaceutical Society of Great Britain

APPENDIX C

Government Publications

For convenience, the main Stationery Office publications dealing with the National Health Service reorganisation in England are listed together below. References to non-governmental sources, as well as to more peripheral official documents, are given in the notes at the end of each chapter.

ACTS OF PARLIAMENT

National Health Service Reorganisation Act, 1973.

National Health Service Act, 1977.

CENTRAL POLICY REVIEW STAFF

A Joint Framework for Social Policies, 1975.

Relations between Central Government and Local Authorities, 1977.

COMMAND PAPERS

Report of the Committee into the Cost of the National Health Service (Guillebaud), Cmnd. 9663, 1956.

A Hospital Plan for England and Wales, Cmnd. 1604, 1962.

The Development of Community Care, Cmnd. 1973, 1963.

Report of the Royal Commission on Medical Education, 1965–68 (Todd), Cmnd. 3659, 1968.

Report of the Committee on Local Authority and Allied Personal Social Services (Seebohm), Cmnd. 3703, 1968.

Report of the Royal Commission on Local Government in England, 1966–69 (Redcliffe-Maud), Cmnd. 4040, 1969.

Reform of Local Government in England, Cmnd. 4276, 1970.

Local Government in England: Government Proposals for Reorganisation, Cmnd. 4584, 1971.

National Health Service Reorganisation: England, Cmnd. 5055, 1972.

Report of the Committee on Nursing (Briggs), Cmnd. 5115, 1972.

DEPARTMENT OF HEALTH AND SOCIAL SECURITY

The Future Structure of the National Health Service (Green Paper), 1970.

Second Report of the Joint Working Party on the Organisation of Medical Work in Hospitals (Cogwheel), 1972.

Report of the Working Party on Medical Administrators (Hunter), 1972.

Management Arrangements in the Reorganised National Health Service (Grey Book), 1972.

Reports from the Working Party on Collaboration between the NHS and Local Government on its Activities: (a) *to the End of 1972,* 1973; (b) *from January to July 1973,* 1973; (c) *from July 1973 to April 1974,* 1974.

Social Work for the Health Service (Otton), 1974.

Third Report of the Joint Working Party on the Organisation of Medical Work in Hospitals (Cogwheel), 1974.
Democracy in the National Health Service: Membership of Health Authorities, 1974.
National Health Service Staff Commission Report, 1972–75, 1975.
Priorities for Health and Personal Social Services in England, 1976.
Sharing Resources for Health in England: Final Report of the Resource Allocation Working Party, 1976.
The Way Forward, 1977.
MINISTRY OF HEALTH
Report of the Committee of Inquiry into the Recruitment, Training and Promotion of Administrative and Clerical Staff in the Hospital Service (Lycett Green), 1963.
Report of the Committee on Senior Nursing Staff Structure (Salmon), 1966.
First Report of the Joint Working Party on the Organisation of Medical Work in Hospitals (Cogwheel), 1967.
The Administrative Structure of the Medical and Related Services in England and Wales (Green Paper), 1968.
PARLIAMENTARY PAPERS
Ninth Report from the Select Committee on Expenditure, 1976–77, 'Spending on the Health and Personal Social Services', HC 466–V, 1977.
Ninth Report from the Public Accounts Committee, 1976–77, HC 532, 1977.

Index